DATE			

Treasures of Independence

The Friends of Independence National Historical Park
has sponsored and assisted the publication of *Treasures of Independence*.

Treasures of Independence
Independence National Historical Park and Its Collections

Edited by John C. Milley

With essays by Lynne A. Leopold-Sharp, Robert Lewis Giannini, III, Jane Bentley Kolter, Charles G. Dorman, and John C. Milley

Photography by George J. Fistrovich

A Main Street Press Book
Mayflower Books, New York

Library of Congress Catalog Card Number 79-55756

ISBN 8317-8593-4

Published by Mayflower Books, Inc., U.S.A.
575 Lexington Avenue, New York City 10022

Produced by The Main Street Press, Inc.
William Case House, Pittstown, New Jersey 08867

Designed by Carl Berkowitz

Printed in the United States of America

Contents

Foreword

Treasures of Independence is a title which refers to the most important historical site in the United States and to the contemporary urban role of Independence National Historical Park, a role which combines historical precision, accurate restoration, and adaptive use for the benefit of visitor and native Philadelphian alike.

A generation has passed since the establishment of the Park in 1948 and the commencement of its active administration by the National Park Service in 1951. During that time the trees have grown along Dock Creek; two free associations—The Carpenters' Company of Philadelphia and The American Philosophical Society—have pursued their goals first defined in the 18th century; neighboring Quaker, Roman Catholic, Methodist, and Episcopalian congregations have worshipped in churches designated as historic sites. A few business and insurance firms founded in the 18th century have carried on modern transactions nearby. Botanical and arboreal growth has re-established a not inconsiderable part of Philadelphia's green city blocks. But most of all, the Park has managed to create for visitor and resident alike vistas of startling conviction: the Old State House (Independence Hall) and garden from the west; Franklin Court and the Second Bank of the United States from the north; City Tavern and the Merchants Exchange from the east; the homes of Bishop William White and John Todd from the south.

That these inward and outward prospects succeed to convince the viewer is no accident. To the architectural fabric has been added a host of objects which were sought out with archaeological precision and historical documentation. Although this publication is the first to call attention to the variety and quality of these collections, their nucleus has a history as long as that of the buildings themselves. The narrative commences with objects like the Old State House bell, the silver inkstand used at the signing of the Declaration of Independence, and the chair occupied by George Washington as presiding officer of the Constitutional Convention. But this is only the beginning. By 1802 and the opening of his museum on the upper floor of the State House, Charles Willson Peale demonstrated a clear conception of how an historical collection might contribute to the creation of an American national identity as well as express the country's political independence. His galleries impressed visitors with the richness of American fauna, the variety of the nation's natural history, the promise of its prehistoric archaeology, and the all-surmounting vigor and strength of its political and military leadership as expressed in the portraits—in short, the artistic, political, and scientific independence of the United States.

Peale's death in 1827 and the failure of the United States Congress or the Pennsylvania Legislature and the Philadelphia City Council to purchase Peale's collections led to their dispersal. The move of the Pennsylvania capital to Lancaster and then to Harrisburg and the growth of Philadelphia's municipal bureaucracy forced the extensive remodeling of the former State House, but preserved it for future purposes closer to the ideals of Peale. In 1855 the city opened a Museum of historical relics in the Assembly Chamber. Objects like the State House bell had by then entered the stream of American historical consciousness as symbols of liberty. Many more objects associated with the building and its patriotic events were added to the museum throughout the 19th century. The growth of the collections since the establishment of the Park, comprising seventeen buildings, has been phenomenal. This publication, necessarily selective, demonstrates how well the past thirty years have been spent. One hopes that *Treasures of Independence* will stimulate, as well, scholarship and public interest in the balance of the Independence National Historical Park collections.

Anthony N. B. Garvan
Department of American Civilization
The University of Pennsylvania

Preface

This work presents a selection of historic and symbolic objects from the museum collections of Independence National Historical Park, the area in Philadelphia where our nation was born. Visitors to the Park are often visibly moved when they are reminded that the great 18th-century debates centering around the Declaration of Independence, the Constitution, and, later, the Bill of Rights took place there. It is only natural, then, that the Park collections have become inextricably associated with the attainment of political, religious, and personal liberties. Independence Hall and the Liberty Bell are foremost in the minds of the world's citizens as symbols of these liberties, but there are thousands of other treasures less known. All together they make Independence Park far different from other historical areas, and this difference is the reason that the Friends of Independence National Historical Park has undertaken to sponsor the publication of *Treasures of Independence*. In fact, this is the first book to deal exclusively with these collections.

Established by an act of Congress in 1948 and administered by the National Park Service, the Park is located in the heart of Philadelphia's oldest residential district. The restoration of the area became one of the most extensive projects ever undertaken in the United States. The building of the collections of artifacts in the decorative or fine arts made between 1740 and 1840 also was a monumental project. The objects are exhibited in fifty-four historic room restorations and forty-five separate exhibit areas throughout the Park's buildings. Over the course of the years it became apparent that in order to develop "the most historic square mile in America" and its furnishings to their full potential, funds from the private sector were required to supplement government appropriations.

The Friends of Independence National Historical Park was founded in 1972 to meet this purpose. In the eight years of its existence some 1,600 individual and corporate members have helped conserve, develop, and interpret the Park for almost four million visitors a year. The organization has funded, either directly or through collaborative grants from private foundations, almost $400,000 in acquisitions of antique objects and exhibits of a permanent nature. Among them are the John Penn chairs pictured on the jacket of this book. The Friends group has helped to make the Park a place where people fully enjoy history. A tea garden operated in the summer, historical street dramas, receptions for special exhibits, commemorative events, and, most recently, a week-long annual event termed "Philadelphia Open House" are some of these activities. Interpretative and educational programs relevant to the Revolutionary period are central to the purpose of the organization. These include lectures, tours, symposia, concerts, and publications. The cooperation between the Park and the Friends is a dynamic example of what government and its citizens can accomplish together. The end result is that the Park and its unique collections are interpreted more fully and are better preserved as a symbol of freedom for everyone.

Any publication of the quality and scope of this book demands the cooperation and assistance of many persons and institutions to make it a creditable accomplishment. On behalf of the Friends and the authors of this book, I am indeed grateful to have this opportunity to acknowledge the help received from numerous persons.

Assistance of a supportive nature came from Hobart G. Cawood, Superintendent, and Bernard Goodman, Assistant Superintendent of Independence National Historical Park. Their aid is central to every Friends' undertaking. A major contribution was made by William S. Ayres, board member of the Friends, who exercised a combination of skills to coordinate this project. Martin I. Yoelson, Chief Park Historian, aided John C. Milley, general editor, in preparation of the manuscript. Typed revisions of the manuscript were prepared by Gloria J. McLean, Secretary of the Division of Museums, INHP. Beverly Orlove was employed to help compile data for the catalogue section of the book. Margaret C. Brown, a member of the Friends, researched the names and working dates of Philadelphia craftsmen. Central to the preparation of the objects and their settings for photography were the services of Preston A. James, Museum Specialist; J. Michael Jenkins, Museum Technician; and Daniel J. Sharp, former Museum Intern. The photographic work was supervised by Jane B. Kolter.

Much of the development of this book can be credited to those who are neither associated formally with the Park nor who are members of the Friends. The cooperation among museums, libraries, and institutions of higher learning in the Delaware Valley has been exemplary, and something for which the Park has always been grateful. Resources at institutions outside of this area were utilized as well. Specifically, the authors gratefully acknowledge the assistance of the following institutions and individuals:

American Philosophical Society: Stephen Catlett, Manuscripts Librarian, and Roy E. Goodman, Reference Librarian; Colonial Williamsburg Foundation: John D. Davis, Curator of Metal Work and Assistant to the Director; The Historical Society of Pennsylvania: Peter J. Parker, Chief of Manuscripts; The Library Company of Philadelphia: Kenneth Finkel, Curator of Prints, and Marie E. Korey, Curator of Printed Books; the National Park Service, Mid-Atlantic Regional Office: David G. Orr, Regional Archaeologist; Longfellow Homestead National Historical Site: Kathleen M. Catalano, Curator; Pennsylvania Historical and Museum Commission: Nancy Kolb, Administrator of Pennsbury Manor; The Philadelphia Historical Commission: Barbara Liggett, Consulting Archaeologist; Philadelphia Museum of Art: Beatrice B. Garvan, Associate Curator of American Art; The Smithsonian Institution: Richard K. Doud, National Survey Coordinator, Catalogue of Portraits, National Portrait Gallery, and Susan Myers, Associate Curator, Division of Ceramics and Glass, Museum of History and Technology; The University of Pennsylvania: Anthony N. B. Garvan, Professor, Department of American Civilization; the Henry Francis du Pont Winterthur Museum: Donald L. Fenimore, Assistant Curator, Benno Forman, Research Fellow and Teaching Associate, Arlene Palmer Schwing, former Associate Curator of Ceramics and Glass, Beatrice K. Taylor, Librarian, and the staff of the Joseph Downs Manuscripts and Microfilm Collection.

Mary C. Carroll
Chairman, Friends of Independence National Historical Park

Introduction

Both George Washington and James Madison claimed that the outcome of the proceedings, debates, and compromises that produced a Constitution for the United States in 1789 was nothing less than a miracle—a miracle that took place in Philadelphia.[1] It may be said with equal conviction that a comparable miracle occurred in Philadelphia in 1776, when delegates from thirteen disparate colonies declared themselves united and independent of their mother country, Great Britain. The break was permanent, but certainly not one that was unanimously entertained. While a vast expanse of ocean and different natural environments separated the two countries, ideologically they shared a culture of common origin, and it was only many years later that other forces would give them identities of sharper contrast. John Adams understood the reasons for the separation to be much more profound than either political or mercantile expedience. An attitudinal change had occurred in "the minds of the people," of which the contest on the battlefields of the American continent was but the physical manifestation. And to understand so profound a change it is necessary to consult the documents of each of the thirteen colonies.

Since World War II historians have turned in increasing numbers to documents as source material for their postulations, with results that give us a less jaundiced picture of the American Revolution, its causes and effects, than was possible some years before. "What was essentially involved in the American Revolution," Bernard Bailyn found after having analyzed the contents of pamphlets printed in America between 1763 and 1776, "was not the disruption of society with all the fear, despair, and hatred that entails, but the realization, the comprehension and fulfillment, of the inheritance of liberty and of what was taken to be America's destiny in the context of world history."[2]

What we have come to learn through the advances of historical and intellectual enquiry, and what the study of the collections of antiquities at Independence National Historical Park has come to be concerned with, is that all objects are documents, symbolic of their time and place of origin, and that they may be in some ways more reliable as a form of historical evidence than the written word. When we study these objects, when we look at them individually and collectively (an opportunity which this book provides), we come a bit closer to understanding both the conditions that existed in colonial America and the intellectual and cultural environment in which changes of so profound a nature could have taken place. While we attempt to divest ourselves of opinionated thinking concerning the aesthetic quality of objects to ascertain their credibility as documents, their meaning, or intrinsic beauty, just as often escapes us as it reveals itself through study. These objects are at the same time "treasures" constituting a part of America's material culture, and *objects d'art* that can be fully appreciated. "The decorative arts," wrote John Sweeney, "are not only decorative; they are often functional. Historical examples represent choices, and, as such, they reflect not only aesthetic preferences but also economic and social factors."[3] This is as true of the things produced locally, in the Delaware Valley, as it is of those made in other regions, where the commingling of peoples of different national origins manifested itself in material forms that carry a distinctive character.

This distinctive character is a sign that was either intentionally or subconsciously imparted to the object by its maker. First recognized by art historians as key to the classification of objects by style, such evidence has been utilized by scholars from other disciplines to broaden our knowledge of past cultures considerably. Obviously, many objects made in one region of colonial America differ markedly in their material form from those of the same kind made in another. Taken collectively, such signs and objects become symbols insofar as they tell us something other than what we grasp visually, a "something other" that requires explanation and interpretation to be understood.[4]

With its energies and vast natural resources turned more to the purposes of internal growth and development in every endeavor that sovereignty would permit, be its reason a premature sense of self-sufficiency or a subconscious fear of its own immaturity, America for thirty years after 1776 made extraordinary efforts to exist independently and, in the process, to proclaim itself a destiny of herculean magnitude. The maturation period—politically, economically, sociologically, and culturally—was one of successes and failures, a complex admixture of forces to which there seemed no pattern. The telling of this story in historical buildings, in the events which happened in and about these structures, and in the collections of antiquities related to them, is a saga that has and will engross the minds of countless persons for some time to come. Simple enough in its telling for popular consumption, the implications and the deeper meanings of this story have not yet been probed to their fullest potential. Why and how were these objects made? What did their manufacture and use have to do with forces that shaped people's lives? These questions, and many more like them, are relatively new to the antiquarian or to the historian who has turned his attention to the object.[5] These are the kinds of questions that were asked of the authors of this book. Their answers, although restricted to specific classes of objects—i.e., furniture, metals, ceramics and glass—tell of how great was the concern of the Philadelphia community with the manufacture of material things and the cultivation of commerce for the importation of those needs not met at home. Pride of craftsmanship, perpetuated through the system of apprenticeship, and a highly developed sensitivity to the physical beauty of the things with which they lived and worked out their social and political problems are also evident in the things they made and imported.

How were these objects conceived, and how did some of them come to convey or to take on meanings of a symbolic nature, meanings other than those intended by either their makers or their users in some instances? Lynne Leopold-Sharp has found such questioning to reveal in maps and political cartoons the emergence of an American identity. She expresses it quite well: "For some, their design and production were visible symbols of the emerging identity; for others, their design and production initiated that emergence. As the idea of 'things American' began to gain cognizance, the work of individual colonists received increasing recognition, and residents began to look closer to home for both decorative and utilitarian objects."

Answers like that need to be put in the context of our political and social histories, a challenge that is much beyond the scope of this publication. They may give balance to past conceptions concerning the causes for such happenings as the American Revolution or help to explain more fully the beginnings of our cultural and economic institutions. This approach of historical questioning is less appreciated than new, perhaps. Erwin Panofsky expressed it succinctly as early as 1939: "As we could supplement and correct our practical experience by inquiry into the manner in which, under varying historical conditions, objects and events were expressed by forms . . . just so can we supplement and correct our knowledge of literary sources by inquiry into the manner in which, under varying historical conditions, specific themes or concepts were expressed by objects and events. . . ."[6]

Unlike Hector St. Jean de Crèvecoeur who, in the early nineteenth century, saw Americans as a distinctly different breed of man, we find today more that ties us in with the heritage of the Western world than anything which might say we are different. This is not to deny that differences did exist, and still exist, between the cultures of America and its principal benefactor, Great Britain, for the differences are there in tangible form for us to see, as well as the similarities, both of which call for some rational explanation. A former curator of the Museum of Fine Arts in Boston recognized that need when he admonished his colleagues: "Let us tell them what these works of art are about and not merely tell them things about these works of art."[7] Thus, in what may be a unique way to introduce the collections of a museum, or the Park, to the general public, the essays in this book look for meanings beyond the recitation of facts about them.

Endlessly fascinating are the accounts we read of how man has unconsciously said something about himself and his culture through signage, signs which then or later came to symbolize something, and even later, perhaps, became part of a tradition. In a recent publication, Michael Kammen examined the growth of a tradition, or the lack of one, in the United States and how "under varying historical conditions" some objects or signs were transformed in meaning. Basic to the establishment of a tradition is the need of a historical event to rally around. To Kammen it is the "basic referent" of a nation in times of crisis or stress, and for Americans that elixir became the American Revolution. Associated with the event are material things, sites, buildings, and objects which became more important to the populace as symbols of the event or its meaning to them than they do as things of interest in their own right.[8] For the most part, Independence Hall (the old State House of Pennsylvania) was preserved as a historic shrine for this very reason.

Kammen further observed a curious divergence in content between the major exhibitions of Anglo-American decorative arts and their respective catalogues produced during the Bicentennial. The exhibitions seemed to say one thing, and the catalogues quite another. "Several of the authors," he noted, "assert that pictures and artifacts are historic documents in themselves, which is true enough. Nevertheless, their texts do not consistently analyze the objects as cultural symbols that really do have a story to tell us . . . some of the most critical relationships remain inert because our attention is not called to them, and so their interconnectedness remains unexplored."[9]

The interconnectedness in meaning of historical events, buildings, and objects, is cen-

1. This coat of arms of the State of Pennsylvania, painted by George Rutter, c. 1785, still rests within its original frame, carved by Martin Jugiez. It was made for a location over the judges' bench in the Pennsylvania Supreme Court Chamber in the old State House. There it replaced the coat of arms of George III that was ripped from the wall and burned following the first public reading of the Declaration of Independence on July 8, 1776.

tral to the Park's collections and to their exhibit, with many of the objects having histories that well illustrate the points made by Kammen. The chair made by John Folwell in 1779 (pl. IV) is a singularly interesting example of the metamorphosis which an object might undergo in changing times and the changing needs of a given culture or country. Made to serve as the Speaker's chair in the Pennsylvania Assembly, the "rising sun" chair, as it came to be known, was conceived to convey something of a symbolic nature. Benjamin Franklin interpreted that to be the ascendancy of a new nation upon the successful conclusion of the Constitutional Convention in 1787. The liberty cap and rising sun carved into its crest rail were probably more than just decorative embellishments common to the design vocabulary of the day. With the successive relocations of the State's capital, Folwell's chair was taken to Lancaster in 1799, and then to Harrisburg in 1812, where it was used by the Speaker of the House of Representatives. It served a practical purpose until some time after 1824, when the chair was erroneously labeled the seat occupied by John Hancock at the signing of the Declaration of Independence. With the advent of the Centennial of 1876, the "rising sun" chair was returned to Independence Hall, where it was exhibited as a "relic" associated with the building and the events of the American Revolution. It had become a symbol of liberty; what is more, it had entered the stream of public consciousness as integral to a tradition.

Today we know a good deal more about the design and uses of the "rising sun" chair than was possible under the circumstances of its history. Folwell's chair tells us that the craftsman was conversant with all of the influences that made up the style of furniture we have come to call Chippendale—namely, things of classical, Gothic, rococo, and oriental origins. To combine all of these elements into one chair was nothing less than a naïve bit of braggadocio, a theme of boastfulness that in the early nineteenth century whetted the tongues of the "barkers of an American culture" (as Russell Lynes is wont to call them), a culture that was fully formed and perfect.[10] In effect, the design of the chair belies a cultural independence; rather, its inspiration is English. The chair was indeed used by George Washington as the presiding officer of the Constitutional Convention, which might have been reason enough for its reverence as a relic. It was the distortion of the chair's history, however, that caused its appropriation as a distinctly American symbol, which we now recognize as attributable to a burst of nationalism that swept the country with the return visit of the Marquis de Lafayette to America in 1824-25.

The original purpose of the Liberty Bell, another utilitarian object, was only to announce meetings and events of importance to the populace through its tolling. After cracking, reputedly in 1835, the bell itself began to take on the status of a symbol of liberty. In 1847 George Lippard, a popular novelist of Philadelphia, fabricated the myth of the old bell-ringer, a hypothetical gentleman who waited breathlessly to ring in the adoption of the Declaration of Independence. The story was perpetuated by well-known historians throughout the nineteenth century.[11] The prophetic inscription cast into the bell, "Proclaim Liberty Throughout All The Land, Unto All The Inhabitants Thereof," lent itself admirably to the purposes of an impresa, a motto that could be assigned multiple meanings. During the pre-Civil War period the bell symbolized anti-slavery; during the Vietnam War it symbolized protest both for and against foreign involvement. David H. Bishop, a former student of mine in American Studies at Temple University, wrote a history of the Liberty Bell's *Assent to Significance* as a senior thesis. His summary of research findings is particularly relevant here:

> The nature of the educational process in the nineteenth century, an expanding sense of nationality and historical past, and a struggle to preserve the union, all added to the setting in which a symbol was reared. . . . The Centennial accelerated a process by which the symbolic literary content of the Liberty Bell was transferred to the actual physical form of the bell. . . . Not only was it now the symbol of an indefinable liberty, it had become the metaphysical representation of an entire nation, its history and progress . . . the bell was the object of national celebration, the focal point of an effort to link an historical past with a fervently optimistic view of the future. Fantastic celebration accompanied the bell throughout the country on its many railroad excursions to expositions where unprecedented numbers of people saw it on display, clamored to touch it, and nearly destroyed it with patriotic zeal. . . . [12]

The postscript to Bishop's paper is that the attempt by the National Park Service to remove the Liberty Bell from a physical proximity to Independence Hall, to safeguard both the bell and the building from abusive treatment during the Bicentennial, was met with open hostility across the country. The object-symbol had become irrevocably wed to the building, and to the event, the "basic referent" of a nation.

Neither the "rising sun" chair nor the Liberty Bell would have been elevated to the status of symbol without their association with a building that figured prominently in the nation's history. For better than a century and a quarter now, Independence Hall has been venerated by Americans as the birthplace of their nation. But it took many years after the signing of the Declaration of Independence and the adoption of the Constitution of the United States—both in the Assembly Room of Independence Hall—before such veneration was bestowed upon the building. The old State House has symbolized many things to Americans, the most important of which is the exercise of human liberties freely expressed within the strictures enumerated by the Constitution of the United States. It is impossible to fathom the depth of meaning that the building represents because it can and has changed significantly in the course of national events.

Nationalism followed by sectionalism in the second quarter of the nineteenth century worked as forces to stimulate interest in Independence Hall as a historic structure, where prior to 1824 the State House was looked upon as little more than a public building that was fast becoming obsolete. Elaborate preparations were made in that year for the visit of Lafayette, with the State House serving as focal point for the fête. "Across Chestnut Street, in front of the building was erected a huge arch 'constructed of frame work covered with canvas, and painted in perfect imitation of stone.' The old Assembly Room, called for the first time 'Hall of Independence,' was completely redecorated." Printed descriptions tell of the room's festive appearance at this time, with its walls and ceiling painted a stone color and the windows hung with star-studded scarlet and blue draperies. For the occasion, a beautiful second-hand glass chandelier was purchased, under which was placed William Rush's statue of George Washington. Portraits of Revolutionary heroes were borrowed from the museum of Charles Willson Peale (located on the second floor of the building) and filled virtually all of the available wall space. Mahogany furniture was "tastefully and appropriately disposed" throughout the room.[13]

That was the auspicious beginning of the evolution of Independence Hall as a national shrine and also of the acquisition of objects related to the founding of the United States to place on exhibit in the building. A short-lived, ill-conceived attempt to restore the Assembly Room to its 1776 appearance followed immediately upon the fanfare of 1824. A quest generated in City Council to locate the furniture used by the "Sages of 76" was either half-hearted or nonproductive. A full-length portrait of Lafayette was commissioned by the city from the artist Thomas Sully and placed in the Assembly Room in 1827. In 1831 the city purchased Rush's life-sized statue of George Washington. Next, in 1832, Robert Vaux and Thomas I. Wharton, a committee of two, deposited a full-length idealized portrait of William Penn, painted by Henry Inman, to commemorate the

1. *Opposite:* The Liberty Bell needs little by way of introduction to the majority of Americans, and to millions of foreign peoples as well. It is first and foremost a symbol representing freedom of speech, religion, and the press. The prophetic inscription from the Book of Leviticus that was cast into the bell reads: "Proclaim Liberty throughout all the land unto all the inhabitants thereof." Initially, however, it was the tolling of the bell, not the bell itself, that carried a message. The term, "The Liberty Bell," was first used as the title to an anti-slavery booklet published in Boston in 1839. It was also the first time that the Liberty Bell was graphically portrayed.

A bell for the tower of the old Pennsylvania State House was first cast at the Whitechapel Bell Foundry of London, England, in 1751. It cracked while being tested for tone, before being raised into the steeple. John Pass and John Stow, two Philadelphia brass founders, were commissioned to recast the bell. The original bell was broken up and melted down, with the addition of American copper. The tone proved unsatisfactory, and a second attempt, now known as the Liberty Bell, was made. Confident of their success, these ingenious craftsmen insured their own lasting acclaim by casting into the bell "Pass and Stow, Philad[a] MDCCLIII." This "signature" is here seen against a wood engraving by David Scattergood showing how the Liberty Bell was exhibited during the period of the Centennial.

II. *Interior View of Independence Hall,* lithograph by Max Rosentnal, 1856. A view of the Assembly Room in the old Pennsylvania State House (Independence Hall) as it appeared when first opened to the public as a shrine on the eve of Washington's birthday in 1855. The woodwork paneling was installed in 1831 by the architect John Haviland in what was the first but erroneous attempt to restore the room to its 1776 appearance. Almost all the objects shown are still a part of the collections of the Park, from the Liberty Bell surmounted by Peale's eagle, and the portraits by Charles Willson Peale and others, to the "liberty and equality" chair in the right foreground. Designed in 1838 by John Fanning Watson, the latter is a curious improvisation upon the "rising sun" chair (*see* pl. IV).

III. Coat of Arms, or Seal of the City of Philadelphia, oil on canvas by John A. Woodside, c. 1816. Probably painted for the Common Council Chamber of the Old City Hall at 5th and Chestnut Streets, this monumental painting was found rolled up in the basement of Congress Hall in 1951. It was virtually unrecognizable before restoration, during which the signature of Woodside was uncovered. Here the figure of Justice holds a plan of the grid-patterned streets of Philadelphia, while the figure of Plenty holds a cornucopia symbolizing the abundance of Pennsylvania's agriculture and commerce.

IV. "Rising sun" chair, by John Folwell, Philadelphia, 1779. Made for the Speaker of the Pennsylvania Assembly, this carved mahogany armchair was used by George Washington as the presiding officer of the Constitutional Convention of 1787. It was Benjamin Franklin who first implied a significance to the carving in the crest rail by referring to it as a "rising sun" symbolic of the new nation under the Constitution.

V. *Bishop White's Study,* oil on canvas by John Sartain, 1836. From 1787 until his death in 1836, Bishop William White occupied the house on Philadelphia's Walnut Street in which this room is located. The painting was commissioned by his immediate family. Where the Rosenthal lithograph of the Assembly Room (pl. II) records the appearance of a room that had been altered and adapted to a purpose other than that for which it was intended, Sartain's painting records the exact milieu in which a person lived. Many of the objects shown in the painting, like the Windsor armchair made by John Letchworth, in the left foreground, have been returned to the restored house. Even a portion of the Bishop's library has been returned, making the Bishop White House one of the best documented restorations in the country. Substantial documentation of either a pictorial or textual nature has served to guide the development of the collections at Independence National Historical Park.

VI. *The Second Bank of the United States,* watercolor on paper by William Henry Bartlett, c. 1836-39. Designed by William Strickland, and constructed between 1819 and 1824, the Second Bank of the United States is recognized as one of the best examples of the Greek Revival style in American architecture. Obviously derived from the design of a Greek temple, particularly that of the Parthenon of Athens, the building and its style symbolized the strength and solidity of the new American republic. Chartered for a twenty-year period in 1816, in what was the second attempt to regulate the nation's economy, the bank and its concentration of power became the platform issue of the 1832 presidential elections. Although the building ceased to operate as a national bank in 1836, and as a state bank in 1841, it continued in use as a customs house. In 1974 it was adapted to serve as a gallery to house the Park's incomparable collection of portraits of Americans of the Revolutionary era.

2. American bald eagle. The eagle holds a premier position among the symbols of America. It was not the American bald eagle, but the German imperial eagle, however, that was incorporated into the U.S. Seal when it was adopted in 1782. The imperial eagle was heraldic and of ancient origin, signifying power and self-sufficiency. Artistic license taken with renditions of this eagle in all media of the visual arts soon effected the substitution of the bald eagle, but it was not until 1904 that the present U.S. Seal was made official. The eagle shown here was in the Philadelphia Museum of Charles Willson Peale, at first caged, and, following its death in 1805, mounted as a natural history specimen in the Long Gallery of Independence Hall, where Peale's Museum was located from 1802 to 1828. Peale's eagle has served as a model for renditions of the American eagle on coins and on regimental flags from as early as 1806.

founding of Pennsylvania. The donors expressed a wish that with their donation a beginning be made of a collection of portraits of distinguished Pennsylvanians for the Assembly Room.[14] There appears to have been no clear-cut idea of how best the Assembly Room might serve or be apportioned to express its historic importance.

Sectionalism more than nationalism was the order of the day in the second quarter of the nineteenth century. Aside from the establishment of the Smithsonian Institution (with an initial grant from a citizen of England), there was virtually no public sympathy with ideas that entertained a national museum, as Charles Willson Peale learned to his utter consternation. Aside from a handful of persons who were looked upon as eccentric, there was virtually no interest in collecting Americana for other than its importance locally. Sectionalism did more to foster the creation of a plethora of state historical societies than it did museums that were national in purpose and ownership. The nationalism awakened by a successful conclusion to the War of 1812, and the triumphal return of Lafayette, did not eradicate a widely-held argument that the Constitution of the United States made no provision for federal subsidy of museum-like institutions. Independence Hall was a building of totally local concern.[15]

The precedent of unity exemplified by the American Revolution revived interest in Independence Hall in the decade preceding the Civil War. In 1854, at the sale of paintings from the museum of Charles Willson Peale, the city purchased more than 100 portraits of persons of Revolutionary and early Republican fame for placement in the Assembly Room. A remarkable view of the room as it appeared when opened to the public as a national shrine on the eve of Washington's birthday in 1855 is preserved in the lithograph by Max Rosenthal (pl. II). Almost all of the objects illustrated in the lithograph are still a part of the collections of the Park. What is of particular interest, however, is the nature of the original collection, how it was exhibited, and what was considered to be of historic relevance. Rosenthal's print reveals that, by mid-century, objects like the Liberty Bell had already come to take on importance as symbols. If the two large upholstered armchairs seen against the rear wall in the lithograph are those said to have been used by John Hancock and Charles Thomson during the proceedings of the Continental Congress, any questions concerning their style, authenticity, or history of ownership were considered either academic or irrelevant. They were "relics," and any such questions as to why or how they acquired or deserved such recognition were seldom, if ever, asked. The intention was purposeful, although a long way removed from the kind of rational thinking that governed the formation of museums in the seventeenth and eighteenth centuries.[16]

The rationale behind the exhibits in Independence Hall at this time is contained in passages from a delightful history of the building published by D.W. Belisle in 1859:

> How impressive are the associations that cluster around this sacred
> Temple of our national freedom. . . . The venerable appearance of the
> Hall itself has an awe-inspiring sanctity about it that makes us realize
> we are treading hallowed ground—while the carefully arranged relics
> and mementoes excite our enquiry and deeply interest our thoughts.
> . . .[17]

The last part of the excerpt deserves more than a passing reference, for in it, Belisle hints of a growing interest in, and the development of a spirit of inquiry into, the "relics and mementoes" of our past. What did they all mean? The interest in collecting, and the questions centering around its meaning, accelerated during the last half of the century, however much it may have been bound up with the teaching of morals and in counteracting the perceived evils of industrialism. "Such critical introspection has usually accompanied a resurgence of nationalism," Lillian B. Miller observes in *Patrons and Patriotism*, "when as a result of internal or external pressures, Americans have felt the need to reassert the value of their institutions and national ideals."[18]

From the mid-nineteenth century to the mid-twentieth century—a hundred-year period in which the historic preservation movement gained momentum and took shape, a period in which most of the major museums in the United States were founded, a period in which our universities introduced such disciplines of study as art history, and a period in which the country came near dismemberment politically—the collections at Independence Hall were swelled by the addition of hundreds of objects of both great importance and of little significance at all. The most intense years of activity were those immediately preceding and following the Centennial, an extravaganza that catapulted Independence Hall to the premier position among historic buildings in the United States.

Donations of objects were encouraged, "however trivial," as an "offering upon the altar of patriotism." Those are the words of one Col. Frank M. Etting, an unheralded and indefatigable antiquarian who in the years just before the Centennial of 1876 headed up the "Committee on Restoration of Independence Hall." His success at ferreting out objects became a source of some embarrassment to him, and to city officials, in the sheer number of things collected. Exhibit cases in the Assembly Room were filled "with relics and memorials of distinguished men of the period from 1682 to 1787 . . . with pamphlets, wearing apparel, newspapers, and everything illustrative of the daily life in America during the same period . . . appropriate platforms [were] reserved to display furniture once in use by the patriots of that day."[19] Etting was overly zealous on another score. The time and the occasion called for patriotic zeal, and Etting could no more ap-

3. Silver inkstand and tray, by Philip Syng, Jr., Philadelphia, 1752. It is not known how the Syng inkstand was sequestered during the British occupation of the Pennsylvania State House in 1777, but as an object of precious metal its safety was assured. Made by the Philadelphia silversmith Philip Syng, Jr., for the speaker's table of the Pennsylvania Assembly, at a cost of £25 6s., it is believed to be the instrument that was used for the signing of the Declaration of Independence. As property of the State of Pennsylvania, the inkstand continued in use by the speaker of the House of Representatives long after the capital was removed to Harrisburg. Sometime prior to the Centennial of 1876, it was returned to Independence Hall as an object of veneration. Next to the Liberty Bell, and Independence Hall itself, the Syng inkstand has been so profusely illustrated and reproduced that it too has become a symbol of liberty and independence.

proach "relics" with objective questions about their authenticity or meaning than we can divest ourselves of them. To him may be attributed the misnomer "Signer's chairs" for the seating furniture made by Thomas Affleck in 1790 and 1793 for Congress Hall. But to him must be credited the preservation of that furniture and the return to Independence Hall from the State House in Harrisburg of such great treasures as the Syng inkstand (fig. 3) and the "rising sun" chair (pl. IV).[20]

The collections spread throughout Independence Hall and spilled over into the sister buildings on Independence Square: Congress Hall, which was the capitol of the United States in the decade 1790-1800; and Old City Hall, which was the seat of the United States Supreme Court in the same decade. So vast had the collections become—approximately 4000 objects in all—that, by 1873, Etting proclaimed the Independence Hall complex "the National Museum" without the justification of any Congressional enactment whatsoever. There is in the minutes of the Select Council, however, note of the receipt in 1872 of a resolution from the United States House of Representatives, accompanied by a letter from the House Committee on Public Buildings, which inquired into the possibility of purchase by the federal government. The city declined to entertain the overture, obviously anticipating a windfall of benefits through ownership of the buildings during the Centennial.[21]

Patriotic enthusiasm waned with the passing of its catalyst, the Centennial, although the ensuing years witnessed historical events that served to increase public concern over the preservation of Independence Hall and its related buildings. While the neighborhood in which these structures stand was allowed to degenerate "into a most unsightly area," extraordinary advances were made in all fields of professional endeavor related to the preservation and interpretation of our material heritage. From the end of the nineteenth century, to the establishment of Independence National Historical Park by an act of Congress in 1948, organized groups of private citizens (especially the National Society of the Daughters of the American Revolution and the American Institute of Architects) gave of their resources and talents to assist the city of Philadelphia in its increasingly burdensome responsibility to preserve the Independence Hall complex. Municipal resources were inadequate to the undertaking of an extensive restoration project, which is not to demean the city's accomplishment in staying deterioration of the buildings through erosive treatment by both man and nature. The nation-wide movement for the conservation of cultural resources during World War II became particularly active in Philadelphia.[22]

The Congressional act of 1948 transferred custody of the buildings on Independence Square, and the collections of antiquities they contained, to the National Park Service. As established, the Park encompassed four city blocks in the heart of Philadelphia's oldest residential area and buildings within that area which figured prominently in America's attainment of nationhood. Included were the First and Second Banks of the United States; the home of Bishop William White, chaplain to the Continental Congress and the rector of Christ Church and St. Peter's; the home of John and Dolley Todd (later Dolley Madison); the Merchant's Exchange; and the sites of City Tavern and the home of Benjamin Franklin. Supplemental acts of Congress added other historic buildings and sites either adjacent to or outside of the Park, such as the Germantown residence of George Washington (the Deshler-Morris House), the site of the Graff House in which Jefferson drafted the Declaration of Independence, and the Philadelphia residence of Thaddeus Kosciuszko.

All of these buildings, and those that were reconstructed to re-establish a semblance of the physical environment in which historical events occurred, called for antique objects with which to refurnish them. The need far exceeded what became available through the transfer of properties in the establishment of the Park. Collecting was guided by the documentation provided through research, compiled and analyzed in the form of furnishings plans. As governing documents, these reports proved invaluable. They provided reliable information on the furnishings used in specific buildings at specific times in their histories, and they have served as indispensable resource material for the Park's interpreters. Further, they served to guard against indiscriminate collecting, giving definition to the collection assembled.

To date, the Park has acquired approximately 13,000 antique objects. In the process of restoration work supplemental collections were formed, consisting of artifacts retrieved from archaeological excavations conducted within the Park and architectural elements salvaged from the Park's buildings and other structures in its vicinity. The materials in these collections provided documentary evidence in three-dimensional form that was also utilized for the purposes of refurnishing and for special exhibitions on related subjects.

Neither an "offering upon the altar of patriotism," nor the rarity of an object has been allowed to influence the Park's acquisitions policy. Antique objects have been collected for their interpretive value first and foremost, for their aesthetic quality only secondarily. As a result, the collection has a unique character, obviously regional. What is offered through the essays in this book is the essence of that flavor: what the collections as a whole reveal about the greater Philadelphia region and its peoples of the Revolutionary and early Republican periods. In the objects of native manufacture, particularly, is revealed the acculturation of peoples predominantly English and German, and

4. Life-sized statue of George Washington, by William Rush, c. 1814. Carved in pine and painted to simulate marble, this work by Rush, "the father of American sculpture," has a prominent place in the history of the collections of the Park. Only infrequently has it been exhibited elsewhere than in Independence Hall or in adjacent buildings. It was conceived as much as a symbol of the "father of the country" as it was a piece of commemorative statuary. Rush insisted that the statue be placed upon a cubic base measuring exactly three and a half feet in each direction, and that it be viewed from a distance of twenty-five feet, details which tell of his artistic intentions and of his indebtedness to statuary of classical origin. Very few pieces of American sculpture of this date compare favorably to the masterful handling of this work, the grandeur that is conveyed through the broadness of the overall conception, and the interest that is sustained in the painstaking detail.

predominantly Quaker in their religious beliefs.

The startling contrast in the furnishing of public buildings from Colonial to Republican times is also instructive. The unpretentious surrounds of the Continental Congress in the Assembly Room of the old State House would never have done for the patriarchal body of Senators that convened in Congress Hall following the founding of a new nation—even though both legislative bodies contained several of the same persons. The sophistication of the furniture made for the Senate Chamber in Congress Hall is considerably less "showy," however, than the elegant furniture made in the same decade for the State Senate Chambers in both Annapolis, Maryland, and Hartford, Connecticut. That may say more about the differences between States than it does about a Quaker influence upon Philadelphia-made furniture, but the point is made: with the publication of this book a beginning has been made by the Park in the analysis of its collections.

Intellectually speaking, the beginning may be no less auspicious than the Lafayette reception of 1824. The "interconnectedness" between objects and ideas that Kammen found lacking in so many of the Bicentennial exhibits presents a challenge for us to come up against. Although early historians did not approach the study of objects as seminal to the understanding of our culture and history, let us hope in the process of correcting that oversight that we do not lose something of the spirit and enthusiasm Etting brought to his approach to the meaning of these same objects. A poignant observation made by George A. Kubler, a noted professor of history at Yale University, is a particularly appropriate conclusion here: "The moment just past is extinguished forever, save for the things made during it."

1. The Emergence of American Identity: Words and Images on Paper
by LYNNE A. LEOPOLD-SHARP

Printed and engraved works—books, sermons, almanacs, scenic views, political cartoons, maps, and a plethora of similar creations—were produced in increasing quantity in Europe during the seventeenth and eighteenth centuries. They depicted, and sometimes influenced, the societies which made and used them. The engraved pieces, in particular, included both the straightforward recording of persons, events, and places, and the representation of beliefs and ideas using standardized symbolism.

Europeans brought printed and engraved works with them when they emigrated to America and continued to import them in large numbers in the years which followed. Domestic production of these objects was slow to begin, its scope reflecting the guiding principle of most early American manufactures: simplicity and, even more importantly, practicality. Functional pieces—blank legal forms, maps, almanacs, and engravings of well-known personages—highlighted the output of the early American presses. Until the post-Revolutionary period, when symbolism was employed with increasing frequency and sophistication, most engravings were realistic portrayals of people and events.

The development of an American society was dependent upon communication within and among settlements, and the arrival of the first printing press in Cambridge in 1638 was an important advancement. The Reverend Jose Glover, a dissenting English clergyman of some means, funded the project, seemingly as a commercial venture. He died during the transatlantic crossing, but his widow and Stephen Daye, a locksmith with whom he had contracted to operate the press, carried out his plans. Nearly twenty years passed before a second press arrived, that belonging to the English corporation charged with propagating the gospel among the Indians, but by 1693 there were presses operating in Cambridge, Boston, St. Mary's City (Maryland), Philadelphia, and New York.

Early American publications were eminently practical. An important part of each

Opposite page: L'Amerique Indépendante (detail), 1778. *See* fig. 24.

printer's work was the production of those blank forms most suited to the needs of his community, and these jobs, in addition to government printing, formed the staple business. The realization of the convenience of blank forms, readily available, was encouragement enough for an increase in the number of presses. The *Freeman's Oath,* printed in Cambridge in 1638 or early 1639, was just such a form, and the first known product of the American press. It was followed by an almanac in 1639 and the nation's first book, *The Psalms in Metre, Faithfully translated for the Use, Edification, and Comfort of the Saints in Publick and Private, especially in New England,* a year later.

Although the presses were few in number, early American colonists did not feel especially deprived of printing facilities since such service was as available in North America as in England during the latter part of the seventeenth century. Restrictive legislation, passed decades earlier in England, limited printing in that nation to London, York, and the universities from 1586 until 1693, while presses began to appear throughout the colonies during these years.[1] Colonial leaders probably considered their self-imposed licensing and monitoring activities mild by comparison.

Officials in Massachusetts, in an effort to prevent the publication of radical religious literature, appointed licensers of the press in the mid-seventeenth century to avoid "irregularyties [sic] and abuse." The question of content was a particularly sensitive one in the Bay Colony, and every effort was made to reinforce the tenets of the faith in printed materials. Philadelphia Quakers were equally zealous in this regard, and William Bradford, the city's first and only printer, was arrested in 1692 for printing "seditious" material. Bradford, supporting the position of George Keith, a controversial Quaker who was employed as superintendent of the Friends' schools in Philadelphia, printed the writings of members of Keith's faction. The opposing group, in the majority, included important governmental and judicial officials. Keith was condemned at city meetings but appealed to a general meeting of the Philadelphia Quakers and wrote an address, which Bradford printed, to explain his case prior to the gathering. This was the final insult to the ruling body, and Bradford and a number of others were imprisoned. He was eventually released, but left Philadelphia, where he had been resident for nearly a decade, for New York, where he was appointed the government printer.[2]

More than three decades passed after the printing of the first document before a visual representation of the colonists or their new land was created in the Bay Colony. John Foster's 1670 woodcut, the first in the colonies, portrayed Richard Mather—Massachusett's spiritual leader. Foster's inclusion of a woodcut map of New England in his 1677 publication of William Hubbard's book *The Present State of New-England, being a Narrative of the Troubles with the Indians* satisfied the curiosity of Europeans who wished to know more about the settlement of New England and created, for the first time, a realistic, although somewhat imperfect, map of the area.[3]

Although the convenience of printed materials was quickly realized, the widespread production of a substantial number of forms, pamphlets, and books, as well as prints and maps, was hampered by the relative paucity of equipment and supplies in the colonies. Before the Revolution virtually all presses were imported from England, and, although printers occasionally fabricated individual letters, most of the type fonts in use before the war also came from England or Holland.[4] The first paper mill in the colonies was opened by Wilhelm Rittenhouse on a tributary of Wissahickon Creek, near Germantown, in 1690, but it was the only one in the colonies until the late 1720s. Even with increased production, the supply of paper lagged behind demand, and three generations of Americans relied on imported English and European paper.[5]

The volume of printed materials increased with the growth of the population, while the production of engraved works proceeded at a somewhat slower pace. By the 1720s

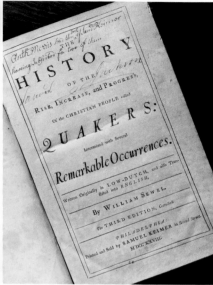

5. *Above (left):* William Wollaston, *The Religion of Nature Delineated,* London, 1725. Benjamin Franklin traveled to London personally to purchase his first set of type in 1725. While there, he found temporary employment in the shop of Samuel Palmer, a respected printer, and worked as a compositor on this volume, the third edition of Wollaston's book.

6. *Above (right):* William Sewel, *The History . . . of the Christian People Called Quakers . . .,* Philadelphia, 1728. Benjamin Franklin and Hugh Meredith were contracted to print the remaining pages of this book after a long delay in Samuel Keimer's shop which he attributed to a dearth of local paper. They tackled their first job enthusiastically, and Franklin related that "I compos'd of it a Sheet a Day, and Meredith work'd it off at Press. It was often 11 at Night and sometimes later, before I had finish'd my Distribution for the next days Work. . . ."

newspapers had begun to appear in cities throughout the colonies and the first copperplate prints drawn and engraved in America had been published. Printmaking was frequently a sideline for artisans in the eighteenth century, and those skilled in silver engraving often advanced to the engraving of prints on copper. Many early prints were unrefined, with confused spatial relationships and inaccurate renderings of perspective, but they were nonetheless a factual portrayal of people and places in the American colonies.

A great number of these early prints, just as Foster's woodcut map of New England, were designed for inclusion in printed volumes. The first copperplate portrait engraving executed in America, of Increase Mather, appeared in three of his works in 1701 and 1702. Prints of American cities first appeared in the late 1720s, the work of William Burgis, an English immigrant. His view of New York, shown from the south, was sent to London for engraving and distribution, but he personally engraved his rendering of the Boston lighthouse.[6] These three prints were important visual representations of the new land and its people, and Burgis's publication of the Boston view in the colony suggests sufficient pride among the citizens to make his work profitable.

Despite limited local production, there was a distinct market for prints and maps for use as decoration in colonial homes and meeting rooms by the 1720s. In Philadelphia John Copson advertised that he had ". . . Useful and Cheap Ornaments for Room's being 6 New Beautifull Mapp's each on two large Sheets of Royal Paper," and Bostonians enthusiastically subscribed for Peter Pelham's 1728 mezzotint portrait of the late Cotton Mather, the first mezzotint in the colonies.[7] In its meeting room the Library Company of

Philadelphia proudly framed and hung its only print, a rendering of an orrery sent as a gift from a close associate in London.[8] Some American-made prints were sent abroad to family, friends, and business associates, while Americans with sufficient interest and income sought out prints from England and Europe, thereby supporting a lively import trade.[9]

The growing population created a market for increased services, but this fact was not always acknowledged by those already in business. Benjamin Franklin and Hugh Meredith found this to be the case in 1728, when they opened their own printing shop in Philadelphia: ". . . the general Opinion was that it must fail, there being already two Printers in the Place . . . ," but they quickly proved their worth. Their first job was the completion of a book which had been in progress for three years, and they eventually assumed responsibility for the failing *Pennsylvania Gazette* and developed it into an influential publication. The printers' pride in their work, and their savvy appraisal of the political climate in the province, soon procured the most valued printing contract for their shop—the public documents. In Franklin's words:

> He [Bradford] had printed an Address of the House to the Governor in a coarse blundering manner; We reprinted it elegantly and correctly, and sent one to every Member. They were sensible of the Difference, it strengthen'd the Hands of our Friends in the House, and they voted us their Printers for the Year ensuing.[10]

Within a few years, Franklin's financial success, as well as his interest in the growth of the colonies and the potential for future income, prompted him to help his former journeymen establish themselves as printers in Philadelphia and other cities.[11]

Pragmatism overshadowed the colonies' early printed works, and books were ranked far down the scale from forms, government documents, and even almanacs. Neither local nor imported volumes were plentiful in America, so colonists formed associations to purchase additional volumes jointly. The first subscription library in the colonies, the Library Company of Philadelphia, was founded under Franklin's direction in 1731, with its membership representing a broad cross-section of vocational and professional interests. The company's books, once in hand, were treated with great care and borrowed according to strict procedures, and only occasionally was the length of the borrowing period extended for someone living a distance outside the city.

Procuring books in the early eighteenth century in colonial America was, in its own right, a difficult task. Since printers in Philadelphia and New York sold only paper, almanacs, ballads, and a few common school books, Franklin lamented that when he came to Philadelphia there was not a good bookseller's shop south of Boston: "Those who lov'd Reading," he said, "were oblig'd to send for their Books from England."[12] Even Boston booksellers were not always well stocked. After difficulties with its first book purchase from London, the Library Company wrote to a Boston merchant only to learn that he did not have the volumes in which they were interested. The group finally resolved its dilemma with the help of Peter Collinson, an influential Quaker merchant, who acted as their agent in London.[13]

Despite its broad-based membership, the Library Company limited its number of subscribers, meaning that most colonists had little or no contact with the kinds of books it owned. Locally published almanacs, on the other hand, were in evidence everywhere. The first volumes published in Cambridge and Philadelphia were both almanacs (William Peirce's *Almanack for the Year 1639,* Cambridge, and Samuel Atkin's *Kalendarium Pennsilvaniense or American Messinger,* Philadelphia, 1686), and the public's enthusiasm for them often made almanacs more widely read than the early newspapers.[14] Franklin's *Poor Richard's Almanack,* first published in 1732, was the most successful of all. As he later recorded:

> . . . [it] came to be in such Demand that I reap'd considerable Profit from it, vending annually near ten Thousand. And observing that it was generally read, scarce any Neighborhood in the Province being without it, I consider'd it as a proper Vehicle for conveying Instruction among the common People, who bought scarce any other Books.[15]

Unlike the colonists, who were interested in the growth and development of their land and its ability to nurture new communities, English interest in North America was focused more narrowly on the concerns of political control and the potential for reaping economic gain from the land's vast natural resources. The British were particularly conscious of the tremendous expansion of the colonies in the early years of the eighteenth century, and, as these lands were improved and became more desirable, officials became increasingly anxious about the establishment of clear-cut territorial claims. Their concern fostered increased interest in, and execution of, cartographic work.

The first British map to depict the interior of the colonies was Henry Popple's 1733 *Map of the British Empire in America with the French and Spanish Settlements adjacent thereto.* Sanctioned by the Lords Commissioners of Trade and Plantations, Popple's renditions included inset enlargements of the harbors of Boston, Providence, New York, Annapolis, and Charleston, providing the first accurately detailed views of these areas. Several extant French maps showed the interior lands, but geographical inaccuracies and French claims which conflicted with British records made these renderings unacceptable in England.

The standardized European iconographic representations of the American continent were carefully portrayed in the cartouche of Popple's map. There were scantily-clad Indian men and women, surrounded by the customary alligators, as well as monkeys, palm trees, and exotic birds. The head of a European, pierced by an arrow, illustrated the natives' savageness.[16] Potential for economic gain from America's resources was portrayed by materials being loaded onto ships under the watchful eye of European merchants.

Popple's map received mixed reviews upon publication. In many respects it was more accurate than earlier English coastal renderings which were less extensive in scope, but the British were angered by Popple's reliance on the French interior maps; his completed map seemingly supported French territorial claims. The map's credibility and consistency were sometimes further diminished by unscrupulous mapsellers who, to suit themselves, added color and arbitrarily changed boundary lines. Although the Lords Commissioners may not have fully approved of Popple's geography, however, they did request funds to distribute a copy to each governor in America in 1733.[17]

By the 1740s the colonists were becoming increasingly attentive to the geography of their continent, an interest which encouraged local map production. Lewis Evans, an accomplished surveyor and geographer, published a map of Pennsylvania, New York, and New Jersey in 1749, measuring longitude from the city of Philadelphia. It was engraved by Lawrence Herbert, a Philadelphian, and published locally, enabling Evans to seek the expertise of local mathematicians, make revisions, and check the plate just prior to printing. An advertisement for Evans's work, alluding to American frustration with the inaccuracies of earlier European maps of the area, gave potential purchasers good "Reason to expect the Geography of these Parts of *America* will be render'd sufficiently exact."[18] The map was published by subscription, as were many maps and prints in the colonies and later in the young republic; purchasers often paid one-half the price at the time of subscription and the other half upon receipt of the piece.

Many colonists extended their business efforts beyond their immediate geographic area by this time, and the scope of Evans's map prompted him to advertise the first edition as far south as Maryland. When publishing a revised edition in 1752, he advertised to customers in New York, as well as Philadelphia purchasers, that "In Justice to the Buyers of the former Impression, their colour'd Maps, tho' torn or defaced will be exchanged for the new Edition at Five Shillings, and their plain Ones at two Shillings and Six-pence."[19] The culmination of Evans's regional mapmaking was his 1755 *General Map of the Middle British Colonies in America,* accompanied by an explanatory essay printed by Franklin and Hall.

The first comprehensive map of Virginia and its adjoining colonies, Joshua Fry and Peter Jefferson's . . . *Map of the most Inhabited part of Virginia containing the whole Province of Maryland with Part of Pensilvania, New Jersey and North Carolina,* was published under different circumstances. The project was ordered executed by the Lords Commissioners for Trade and Plantations, and Fry and Jefferson worked in the capacity of employees. They surveyed the boundary line between Virginia and North Carolina in 1749, and completed work on their map of Virginia by the summer of 1751, but the main portion of their work ended there; the final appearance of the map passed beyond their control when it was sent to the Commissioners in London and then published by Thomas Jefferys, geographer to the Prince of Wales. The result was an American map with distinctly English ornamentation: the cartouche, designed by Francis Hayman, a popular historical painter, was a stylized English view of colonial life.

Additional information became available after the 1753 publication of the map, and a new edition appeared in early 1755. This, and subsequent versions, included extensive data gathered in western areas by Christopher Gist, a respected cartographer, and a table of distances between three principal Virginia towns (Williamsburg, Fredericksburg, and Alexandria) and other settlements. Most of these were in Virginia, but John Dalrymple, the table's compiler, also included the mileage to Fort Necessity and Fort Duquesne in western Pennsylvania. The inclusion of these distances acknowledged the proximity of the various colonies, and evidenced, in the accurate data gathered and organized by these four men, increasing American specialization and technical competence in surveying and cartography.[20]

Accurate maps of individual colonies and regional areas played an important role in the colonists' recognition of the American land: they reinforced the fact that the colonies were but one part of the larger North American continent. They could also be useful in the resolution of colonial boundary disputes and as advertisements for available land. In the day-to-day life of the colonists, however, maps illustrating smaller areas in greater detail were much more useful. Charts of coastal regions were particularly necessary.

Navigation features of the Delaware Bay and River, for example, may have first been shown on Augustine Herrman's *Virginia and Maryland,* published in London in 1673, but this and subsequent maps, as well as successive editions of the principal coastal navigation guide, *The English Pilot,* all lacked sufficient detail to be followed in navigating these waters. It was not until the mid-eighteenth century that Joshua Fisher, a Quaker merchant, produced a detailed navigation chart for the area from Cape Henlopen to just north of Philadelphia. It was so useful that it was published in ten editions in Philadelphia, London and Paris between 1756 and 1800. Even this document was not detailed enough for large vessels navigating the narrow waters, however, and local pilots were still necessary.[21]

The practicality of maps insured their production in the colonies: they were

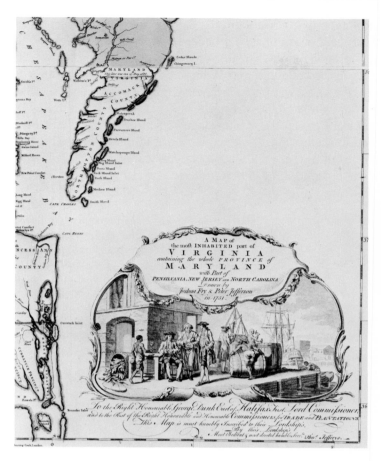

7. Joshua Fry and Peter Jefferson, surveyors, *A Map of the most Inhabited part of Virginia . . .,* engraved by Thomas Jefferys, hand-colored engraving, London, 1768. Fry and Jefferson's map was the first printed state to show the area beyond the tidewaters, and, with the wagon routes added by Christopher Gist, proved particularly valuable in the westward expansion of settlements.

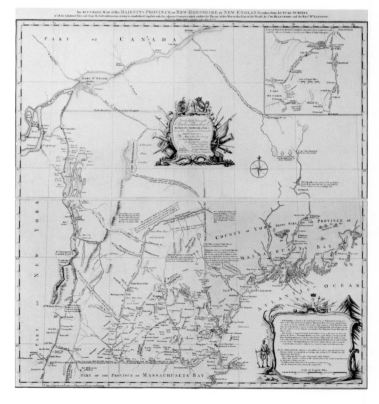

8. Colonel Joseph Blanchard and the Reverend Samuel Langdon, cartographers, *An Accurate Map . . . of New Hampshire . . .,* engraved by Thomas Jefferys, hand-colored engraving, London, 1761. Both Blanchard and Langdon speculated in the land market in New Hampshire, and this map may have been published to give potential settlers and/or purchasers an idea of the look of the land.

decorative, functional, and interesting at one and the same time. The production of prints, on the other hand, proceeded more slowly because they generally lacked the practical applications of cartographic works. The first engraved Philadelphia "view" did not appear until nearly a quarter of a century after William Burgis's late 1720s views of New York and Boston, and even then it was part of a larger work: George Heap's rendering of the northern facade of the State House was used as ornamentation on the 1752 map of Philadelphia and environs executed by himself and Nicholas Scull. The British, who were more accustomed to architectural prints, saw merit in the view itself, however, and, within three months of the map's Philadelphia publication, the State House elevation was reprinted alone in London's *Gentleman's Magazine*.[22]

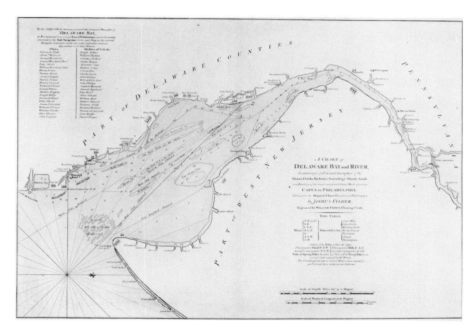

9. Joshua Fisher, cartographer, *A Chart of Delaware Bay and River*, engraved by William Faden, hand-colored engraving, London, 1776. Fisher's initial publication of the chart, in 1756, was apparently limited because it encountered governmental disapproval—officials feared that a copy might reach French enemy hands. An improved second edition, published in the early 1770s, corrected some details but still placed Cape Henlopen too far south, thus extending the Penn family's territorial claims.

Thomas Penn, proprietor of Pennsylvania, wished to show his London friends his bustling new world colony and so sought to have an engraving made of Philadelphia from the east. He corresponded with his provincial agent who attempted to dissuade him from the project (Lewis Evans had already been unable to find a good eastern vantage point); after considerable prodding the agent engaged one, and later a second, local artist. The attempts of each were unsuccessful. George Heap, knowing of the circumstances, undertook the task on his own in 1754: he intended to have his drawing engraved and to sell the prints as a commercial venture. His completed drawing was exhibited to encourage the sale of subscriptions for the print, which was to be seven feet four inches in length, engraved in England, and printed there on high quality white paper.

Heap's untimely death prevented the expeditious completion of the project. The drawing was eventually shipped to London by Nicholas Scull, the provincial surveyor general and Heap's collaborator on the earlier Philadelphia map, to Thomas Penn, and he oversaw its engraving and printing. Penn retained fifty copies of the *East Prospect of the City of Philadelphia* for himself and sent 450 copies back to Philadelphia. There had been substantial colonial enthusiasm for the undertaking, and Scull, acting as distributor, advertised in November, 1754, that ". . . it being doubtful whether there be a Sufficient Number for all who have subscrib'd, they who apply first, will be first serv'd." Copies of a later, corrected state were also sent to America.[23]

The engraving and publication of prints in the colonies gradually expanded to serve as a medium for news reporting and the chronicling of historical events. European artists had long been involved in the quick publication of prints to report current events, and by the middle of the eighteenth century American artists began to do the same. One of the first such prints was *A Prospective Plan of the Battle fought near Lake George . . . ,* drawn by an American supplier, Samuel Blodget, and engraved by another American, Thomas Johnston. It was advertised in November, 1755, two months after the battle, and available for sale slightly more than a month later; its publication a mere three months after the battle predated the report of the fighting in many distant newspapers by more than a month. The print was equally valued as a record of British participation in the battle, and Thomas Jefferys published a version of Blodget's print in London less than three months after the American publication.[24]

As printmaking increased in the colonies, residents eagerly anticipated the publication of renderings to commemorate local events, institutions, and personages. Even though Philadelphia was a prominent city it was not until 1761, however, that prints were first issued to honor one of its local institutions. In that year two competing views of Pennsylvania Hospital were published: one sponsored by the hospital's managers, engraved by Henry Dawkins and available from Robert Kennedy, a prominent print-seller, and the other drawn and engraved by James Claypoole, Jr., another local artist. Both seemed to have sold well, as Kennedy's later appeared in a second state, and their production encouraged the publication of other Philadelphia views, including one of the German Lutheran Schoolhouse in 1763 and one of the House of Employment and Almshouse about 1767.[25]

Prints were an important decorative element in colonial homes, although their cost was not low enough to enable everyone to purchase them. In many households where they could be afforded, however, they appeared in great numbers. New England inventories from the mid-eighteenth century included listings of small groups of prints, and others of much larger collections:

> One Picture by Hogarth coloured &
>   gilt frame
> 7 Copper plate Pictures
> 38 pictures on ye stair Case
> On the Stair Case . . . 33 Great & small Glass
>   pictures . . . 51 Great & small pictures
> 16 Metzitinto Pictures fram'd & Glaz'd
> 20 Pictures Lachered Frames.[26]

Prints in the home were equally popular in Philadelphia: Kennedy's bill of sale to John Cadwalader, a prominent civic leader, listed the titles of three-dozen prints which he purchased to decorate his new home.[27]

A variety of prints, both locally produced and imported, were available to decorate homes and public buildings. Robert Kennedy advertised on his trade card that he could supply the public with prints and maps ". . . on much lower terms than they can be Imported; of equal Quality." Prints were available in subjects to suit any interest. Kennedy advertised pictures in the contemporary English taste, including: ". . . scriptural, historical, humorous and miscellaneous designs . . . elegant gardens, landscapes and American Views . . . battles by sea and land; horse-racing and hunting . . . Royal and Illustrious personages, ladies of quality and celebrated Beauties . . . ." Portrait engravings, more commonly called "heads," were always available. Prints were often published in series to hang in a hall or ascending a flight of stairs; popular subjects for such series included the seasons, the months, and the arts and sciences. Views of European cities and Roman antiquities were favored, as were prints where the moral message illustrated the triumph of good over evil.[28]

Prints were available "plain and coloured," without frames or "neatly framed and glazed." Glass was available from printsellers or from glaziers who stocked glass for clocks, samplers, pictures, street lamps, and other purposes; frames were also available from printsellers or from carvers and gilders who advertised that a gentleman could have ". . . any Sort of Prints framed and glazed . . . in the neatest and best Manner." Merchants often advertised different kinds of frames and glazing as well as other methods of exhibiting prints, and occasionally complete sets were sold ready for installation; one mid-eighteenth-century advertisement, for example, called attention to "several setts of black and white prints glaz'd, with black and gilt frames."[29] Maps were often treated somewhat differently than prints: they were pasted to a linen backing and varnished to protect their surface. Special types of prints were noted in advertisements, including mezzotints, those printed with grey-green ink, and perspective views. The last group was used with a perspective glass, a viewing instrument with a lens and moveable mirror set on an angle. The prints, seen through the glass, took on a three-dimensional quality.

The domestic production of engraved and printed works was inextricably linked to the emergence of a national identity. For some, they were visible symbols of the emerging identity; for others, their message initiated that emergence. As the idea of "things American" began to take hold, the work of individual colonists received increasing recognition and residents began to look closer to home for both decorative and utilitarian objects. In some cases local governing bodies actively encouraged the publication of works.

A map of the built-up areas of Philadelphia, for example, begun by Nicholas Scull before his death, was completed in 1762 by Mary Biddle, his daughter, and Matthew Clarkson, a local merchant involved in the copperplate printing business, with the assistance of the city's Common Council. Clarkson solicited municipal support:

> . . . having presented to the Board a Ground Plot of the City of Philadelphia, which he designs to publish, with a Dedication to this Corporation; the Board, on Consideration thereof, do agree to give the said Mathew [sic] Clarkson the sum of Ten pistoles/toward defraying the expenses of the plate; on Condition, nevertheless, that the publick Squares laid down in the original Plan of the City, be so described that the claim of the Inhabitants to said City thereto may not be prejudiced . . . .

And, having secured it, he advertised his proposal to publish the map by subscription. A few months later the completed piece was available. Two respected city plans, Thomas Holme's original 1683 grid layout and a more realistic grid executed by Benjamin Eastburn, provincial surveyor general from 1733 to 1741, were added as inset illustrations to meet the criteria established by the Council.[30]

In other cases local governing bodies were more interested in being identified with specific groups of objects. The elected members of the Pennsylvania Assembly, for example, directed their efforts toward the development of their library. These volumes served an important reference function, and their possession was an indication of the

VII. Henry Popple, cartographer, *A Map of the British Empire in America...*, engraved by William H. Toms and R.W. Seale, hand-colored engraving, London, 1733. Benjamin Franklin ordered two copies of the map for the Pennsylvania Assembly in 1746—one bound and one with its twenty sheets loose to be mounted. To hang opposite the mounted copy he sought a companion rendering: "...there must be some other large Map of the whole World, or of Asia, or Africa, or Europe, of equal Size with Popple's to match it... if none can be had of equal Size, send some Prospects of Principal Cities, or the like, to be pasted on the Sides, to make up the Bigness."

VIII. Leonard Cushee, globe maker, *A New Celestial Globe...* and *A New Globe of the Earth...*, hand-colored engraving over cardboard and wood globe frame, mahogany stand, London, c. 1750. Pairs of celestial and terrestrial globes complemented other scientific apparatus in the eighteenth century, and their attractiveness and usefulness make their popularity easily comprehended. Thomas Penn sent pairs of globes to a member of the Governor's Council in 1766 to give to two Pennsylvania academic institutions, and it is possible that he also sent a pair for the Council's own use; in later years a pair of globes was counted among its most important possessions.

38

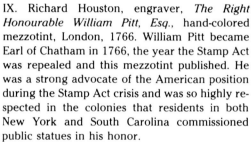

IX. Richard Houston, engraver, *The Right Honourable William Pitt, Esq.*, hand-colored mezzotint, London, 1766. William Pitt became Earl of Chatham in 1766, the year the Stamp Act was repealed and this mezzotint published. He was a strong advocate of the American position during the Stamp Act crisis and was so highly respected in the colonies that residents in both New York and South Carolina commissioned public statues in his honor.

X. Valentine Green, engraver, *A Youth Rescued from a Shark . . .*, hand-colored mezzotint after a painting by John Singleton Copley, London, 1779. Engravings of "current" events were popular even when they appeared years later. This depiction of Brook Watson's 1749 mishap in Havana harbor, in which he lost a foot, was not recorded on canvas until decades afterwards, but the engraving was published in the year following the painting's exhibition.

THE COUNTRY CLUB.

XI. William Dickinson, engraver, *The Country Club*, hand-colored stipple engraving after a drawing by Henry William Bunbury, London, 1788. Eighteenth-century taverns often had small rooms which could be reserved for private club gatherings. The scene depicts just such an occasion: friends meeting for jovial conversation and sumptuous dining, well lubricated with generous quantities of spirits.

XII. Hand-colored engraving and etching, probably European, c. 1780. The English caricature *A Picturesque View of the State of the Nation for February 1778*, published anonymously, was the first showing this scene. In it an American saws off the horns of English commerce, while a Dutchman milks the cow dry, a Spaniard and a Frenchman gleefully await their share of the spoils, and an Englishman beats his chest in despair. In this untitled copy, perhaps of French or Dutch origin, the Dutchman's bucket is inscribed "B. FRANK. . . ."

XIII. Attributed to the Sussel-Washington Master, fraktur of an equestrian George Washington, watercolor and ink on paper, Pennsylvania, 1780-90. The equestrian George Washington, accompanied by a poem which speaks of German delicacies, seems to be an invitation to a party of some sort. Imaginative speculation suggests that the gathering might have been in celebration of the General's birthday; Congress voted the day a holiday in 1800, a few short weeks after his death.

XIV. William and Thomas Birch, artists and engravers, *Second Street North from Market Street . . .*, hand-colored engraving, Philadelphia, 1799. The character of Philadelphia was vividly recorded in William and Thomas Birch's twenty-eight views, published in 1799 and 1800. Here the Court House and Christ Church, prominently illustrated, served as backdrops for the bustling activity of the city's citizens.

Drawn & Engraved by W. Birch & Son.

Published by R. Campbell & Co. Nº 30 Chesnut Street Philadª V.

SECOND STREET. North from Market Sᵗ wᵗʰ CHRIST CHURCH.

PHILADELPHIA.

members' pride in their political position: "*Ordered,* That the Clerk do cause a fair Catalogue to be made out of all the Books belonging to the Assembly Library, and order the said Books to be stamped with the Words *Assembly of Pennsylvania* in gilt Letters, on the outside of the Cover of each Book."[31] The Penn family often recognized the role and status of provincial bodies through gifts, including scientific apparatus and cartographic delights, such as globes, which were more readily available in London than in provincial Pennsylvania.

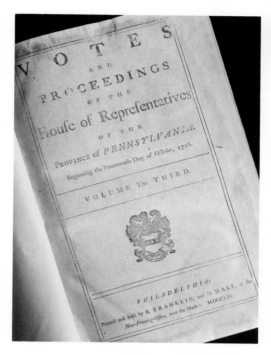

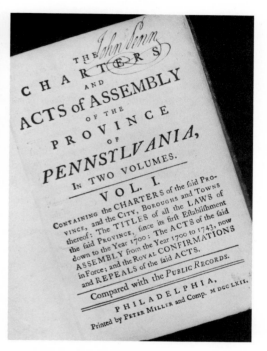

10. Votes and Proceedings of the House of Representatives of the Province of Pennsylvania . . ., printed by Benjamin Franklin and David Hall, Philadelphia, 1754. The cover of this volume bears the gilt inscription "ASSEMBLY OF PENNSYLVANIA" ordered placed on all books in the Assembly Library in 1767. The book was the third and final volume of Franklin and Hall's reprints of provincial votes, 1682-1744; the fourth volume in the set was completed by another printer.

11. *The Charters and Acts of Assembly of the Province of Pennsylvania . . .,* printed by Peter Miller, Philadelphia, 1762. The State House was home to another library as well, that of the Provincial Council. John Penn, grandson of the colony's founder and Deputy Governor, inscribed the fly leaf of this volume: "John Penn 1765/For the Use of The Council Board," in addition to signing his name here on the title page.

Much as the Penn family might be interested in the intellectual development of their provincial residents, they were more concerned, however, about the resources and power deeded them with their large tract of land. Ongoing boundary disputes with the Baltimores punctuated the years, with specific disagreements about the proper location of Cape Henlopen, the boundaries of Delaware, and the southern and western boundaries of Pennsylvania, and it took nearly eighty years to resolve these difficulties. Maps of Pennsylvania, as well as larger regional maps, added to the debate: precise locations of geographic positions and man-made structures often varied with a particular publication's sponsors. William Scull's 1770 *Map of the Province of Pennsylvania,* an expansion of the work of his grandfather, Nicholas Scull, finally delineated the boundaries. The map was considerably more detailed than anything else published at that time and was particularly valuable in representing the area west of the Susquehanna River.[32]

By the mid-eighteenth century colonial loyalties felt strong pull from both the English Constitution and the American homeland. The colonists still thought of themselves as British subjects, distant from London but ruled by the English monarch and governed by English laws, and yet those born in the colonies, without memories of the Old World, often felt closer to their immediate families, friends, and homes—in America. As early as the 1740s colonial troops no longer called themselves "provincials"; they insisted on the appellation "Americans."[33]

Britain's actions in the 1760s, during the French and Indian War, spelled out most clearly for the Americans her real interest in the colonies, and in 1764 a plan to increase colonial revenues was quickly put into effect. It included enforcement of the Writs of Assurance and passage and implementation of the Sugar Act. These developments upset many colonists, but their impact was not universal. News of the passage of the Stamp Act in 1765, however, met with angry words and angry mobs throughout the colonies. It had many opponents in England as well, and this legislation prompted a new method of publicizing American affairs in England—the publication of hundreds of satirical caricatures, in the best English tradition, commenting on the American position. Nearly all appeared to be pro-American, although at heart they were, perhaps, more indicative of dissatisfaction with English politicians and their policies, and later with the war itself.[34]

The satires were issued for the sizable English market, and some eventually found their way to America where they were reengraved, sometimes with modifications, and published.[35] American engravers rarely published original political satires, not because the colonists were disinterested or because the engravers were unqualified, but because such prints were too expensive to produce and sell on a small scale. Unlike London, where the metropolis constituted a substantial market, the American colonies were by and large rural, with their population widely dispersed. Inexpensive printed pamphlets served best to publicize political concerns and viewpoints in America.[36]

When Americans did design and engrave original political prints, the artists frequently chose to illustrate specific events. The confrontation between Bostonians and British soldiers on March 6, 1770 (the "Boston Massacre") was recorded in Paul Revere's print *The Bloody Massacre,* which he published at the end of March. It was based on a drawing by Henry Pelham, a local painter and engraver, and had been taken "impolitely"; Pelham's own print was published a week after Revere's. The event so stunned the populace that prints were in great demand, and Revere's print was eventually copied by a Newburyport clock and watch maker.[37]

The arrival of British troops in Boston two years earlier had enraged the citizenry and prompted Christian Remick, an observer, to record the event in a sketch. Revere used this drawing as the basis for the frontispiece of a 1770 almanac and published a variation of the frontispiece as a separate engraving, *A View of Part of the Town of Boston in New-England British Ships of War: Landing Their Troops! 1768,* while anti-British sentiment was still running high in the spring of 1770. The view was published again in January, 1774, in the first issue of the *Royal American Magazine,* a short-lived Boston periodical which included political essays, poetry, love stories, songs, and prints. Although printed for little more than a year, its fifteen issues included twenty-two engravings, primarily copies of British satires, most of which were done by Revere.[38]

Although fueled by actions like the British intervention in internal affairs in Boston, identification of the geographically diverse colonists as a separate American people emerged only gradually. In 1774 Patrick Henry claimed that "The distinctions between

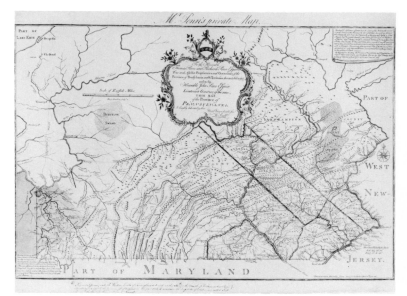

12. William Scull, cartographer, *Map of the Province of Pennsylvania,* hand-colored engraving, Philadelphia, 1770. Inscribed "Mr Penn's private Map," this copy is thought to be the personal reference copy used by John Penn. A handwritten notation across the bottom margin explains the controversy over the western border and the earlier survey work of the region done by Joshua Fry and Peter Jefferson for their map of Virginia.

13. *The Repeal. Or the Funeral Procession, of Miss Americ-Stamp,* unidentified engraver, engraving after Benjamin Wilson, probably England, c. 1766. One of the most popular satires of the Revolution, this print appeared just days after the act's repeal. In May, two months after its London publication, a Philadelphia newspaper advertised the imminent availability of a local edition: ". . . The Repeal, or, The Funeral of the Stamp Act; such as is shown in an engraving which was first designed and made in London and is here reproduced. . . ."

Virginians, Pennsylvanians, New Yorkers, and New Englanders, are no more. I am not a Virginian, but an American."[39] But ties to English culture were not severed. Imported engravings remained popular, and prints made from the paintings of Americans Benjamin West and John Singleton Copley, resident in London, began to join the products of Englishmen and Europeans in the westward trade. Even in Philadelphia, where merchants carried on a successful boycott of English goods, London taste remained the accepted standard. In 1772, when a number of the city's most prominent citizens joined together to build The City Tavern ". . . without any view of profit, but merely for the convenience and credit of the city," its first manager advertised that he went to great expense to purchase ". . . every article of the first quality perfectly in the style of a London Tavern . . . ."[40] London remained an especially important city to American merchants and sea captains because marine insurance was written there and because most of the important maps and charts, so necessary for navigation, were published there.[41]

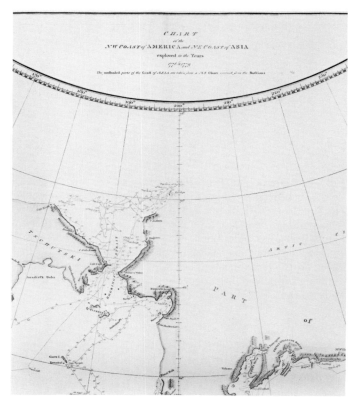

14. *Above (left):* Valentine Green, engraver, *The Golden Age,* hand-colored aquatint after a painting by Benjamin West, London, 1777. The tranquility of family life is depicted by this rendering which includes members of three generations. Such allegorical symbolism was popular among print purchasers on both sides of the Atlantic.

15. *Above:* Don Juan de la Cruz Cano y Olmedilla, cartographer, *A Chart of the Straits of Magellen,* hand-colored engraving, London, 1775. The Straits provided the crucial sea connection between the Atlantic and Pacific, and their treacherous waters were unavoidable for those seeking to round South America. This chart, the most accurate available in 1775, was based on a Spanish rendering and included improvements made possible by more recent surveys by English and French navigators.

16. *Left:* James Cook, navigator, *Chart of the N W Coast of America . . .,* engraved by T. Harmar, hand-colored engraving, London, 1784. Lucrative trade with Asia prompted continued searches for a passage through or above the North American continent to connect the Atlantic and Pacific Oceans. The survey work accomplished by James Cook's voyages, combined with materials received from Russian traders, is shown here; it accurately depicted the shape and outline of the land, but failed to establish whether the coastline was part of an island or the mainland.

American resistance to British intervention mounted with the passage of each new restrictive act. In September, 1774, representatives from every colony except Georgia convened at the First Continental Congress in Philadelphia. The delegates represented both conservative and radical points of view, but when their work was completed those most resentful toward Britain had prevailed. Their grievances unredressed, Congress reconvened the following May, and in the intervening months the fighting at Lexington,

Concord, and in northern New York had widened the rift between England and the colonies. The Second Continental Congress debated about the situation for more than a year, and by spring of 1776 the mood in Congress was shifting toward a break with England.

Delegates from North Carolina were the first in the Congress empowered to vote for independence. The Virginia House of Burgesses passed a resolution of independence and sent Richard Henry Lee back to Philadelphia to propose the resolution to the Congress in June of 1776. Debate of the issue was tabled temporarily, but a committee was appointed to prepare a draft for a declaration of independence.

Thomas Jefferson's manuscript, slightly revised by members of the committee and reworked more extensively by the Congress, remained a masterpiece of style and composition and was finally adopted on July 4, 1776. The ideas were not new, nor should they have been; his task was ". . . to act as advocate of his country's cause before the bar of world opinion." His declaration embodied those ideas, concepts, and phrases from their tradition which became a fundamental statement of purpose for the American people.[42]

No colony had ever before declared its independence in such a fashion. Congress was concerned about the official announcement and

> *Ordered*, That the declaration be authenticated and printed.
> That the committee appointed to prepare the declaration, superintend and correct the press.
> That copies of the declaration be sent to the several assemblies, conventions and committees, or councils of safety, and to the several commanding officers of the continental troops; that it be proclaimed in each of the United States, and at the head of the army.[43]

Late on July 4th, the committee took the handwritten copy to John Dunlap, whose printing shop on Market Street was nearby, and he and his assistants set to work immediately. They may well have worked through much of the night; John Hancock,

17. Edward Savage, engraver, [*Congress Voting Independence*], unfinished stipple engraving after a painting by Robert Edge Pine and/or Edward Savage, Philadelphia, late-eighteenth century (plate); Massachusetts, post-1859 (print). The grouping of figures is most surely conjectural since the painting which served as the original artwork for this engraving was begun years after the adoption of the Declaration of Independence, but the architectural rendering of Independence Hall's Assembly Room is shown in accurate detail. This image corroborated written descriptions of the room and extant architectural evidence, and was an aid in its restoration.

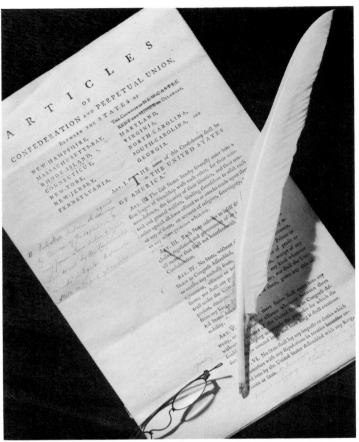

18. John Dunlap, printer, Declaration of Independence broadside, laid watermarked paper, Philadelphia, July 4-5, 1776. The text of the declaration was first available publicly in this broadside edition: copies, as directed by the Congress, were sent to the various state assemblies, councils and troop commanders. This copy descended in the family of Colonel John Nixon and may have been the one from which he read aloud in the State House Yard on July 8, 1776.

19. *Articles of Confederation and Perpetual Union . . .*, Philadelphia, 1776. Elbridge Gerry, a delegate from Massachusetts, owned this copy of the second draft. His detailed notations of changes in the text, made during the debates, provide a valuable glimpse into the difficult process of developing a new frame of government for the states.

president of the Congress, began sending copies to the various state conventions and military commanders on July 5th.[44]

When independence had first been proposed by Lee in June, Congress established a committee to ". . . prepare and digest the form of a confederation to be entered into between these colonies."[45] The committee was chaired by John Dickinson of Pennsylvania and included one member from each of the other colonies. The group's initial draft of the Articles of Confederation was presented to Congress on July 12th, shortly after independence had been declared, and the delegates resolved to have exactly eighty copies printed. They were to be completed under strictest secrecy, with the printer to agree under oath to deliver all copies to the secretary and to remain silent about their content. Revision continued throughout July and August, and, after presentation of a second draft on August 20th, Congress resolved to have eighty copies of the Articles printed under the same tight security. There was considerable debate over the Articles, but the document was finally completed and sent to state assemblies for ratification in November, 1777. Implementation of the Articles required ratification by all thirteen states, however, and that did not occur until March of 1781.

With the eruption of full-scale fighting, the Americans quickly realized that they would have to learn to operate without ready access to London goods, especially maps. There were some extant copies of maps published in America and in England, but many were out of date, and even more covered too large an area to be of much assistance in planning troop movements. Congress, conscious of its need to follow troop movements, began its own collection of maps; as John Adams wrote to his wife: "America is our Country, and therefore a minute Knowledge of its Geography, is most important to Us and our Children. The Board of War are making a Collection of all the Maps of America, and of every Part of it, which are extant, to be hung up in the War Office."[46]

Information about the fighting, available to Congress through dispatches, was also of interest to the citizenry. At least one Philadelphia engraver, John Norman, took advantage of this market, as well as of the American troops' need for accurate cartographic information, and published a number of maps of the "present seat of the war." His publication of a map of all the states, including roads marked with distances between principal places, stressed that

> This map is engraved from a very late copy done in England on a new and accurate plan, calculated for the use of the officers in the British army. The American publisher therefore apprehends that the utility of this map will be equally self evident to all the officers of the Continental army, and the inhabitants of the Thirteen United States in America.[47]

Military action proved a popular topic for engravings. The spring encounters at Lexington and Concord were painted shortly afterward by Ralph Earl, with engraver Amos Doolittle posing as a model. Doolittle spent the fall transferring the scenes to a series of four engravings which were available in December, 1775.[48] The fighting at Bunker Hill, although less successful for the American forces, was also the subject of several contemporary engravings; a view published in *The Pennsylvania Magazine* and another print issued separately were both available in September, 1775, a mere three months after the battle. Subsequent engagements were illustrated in both American and English engravings, and prints of respected military and political figures, like Washington and Hancock, as well as war heroes like General Richard Montgomery, also began to appear during the war.

The British Army also needed maps, in both large and small scale, to plan major campaigns and maneuvers for individual engagements. British publishers quickly met this need, choosing reliable, if somewhat outdated, maps to reproduce. William Faden, geographer to the king, reissued Joshua Fisher's *Chart of Delaware Bay and River* in 1776, twenty years after the original engraving; its overall navigational accuracy was still undisputed. Fisher's popular work was reissued by two other London publishers in 1776 and one of them, Andrew Dury, also used it to replace the insets of Holme's and Eastburn's city grid plans when he reissued the Clarkson-Biddle map of philadelphia in 1776. This publication was popular, and it was also printed in France and Germany during the Revolution. London publishers printed earlier British maps of the colonies during the war, including John Montresor's mid-1760s survey of New York City. As was often the case, Dury merely changed the date on the title cartouche and reissued the Montresor work without revision.[49]

During the actual fighting, the British Corps of Engineers executed detailed plans of action which were returned to England for publication. The first major staged battle, that at Bunker Hill, was carefully recorded by an aide de camp to Major General Howe during the engagement. Although his was the most detailed record of the action, and

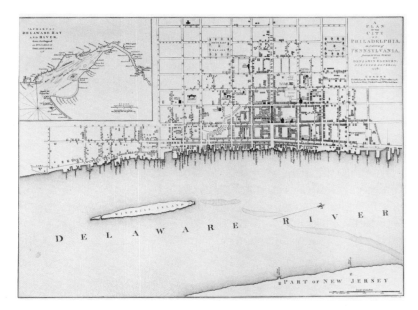

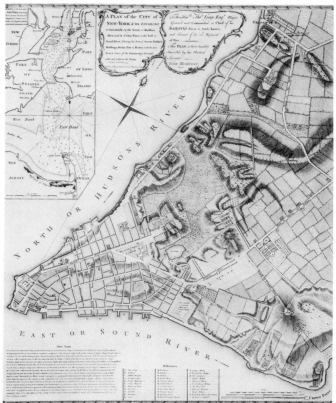

20. *Above:* Nicholas Scull, surveyor, *A Plan of the City of Philadelphia . . .,* engraving, London, 1776. Andrew Dury, the publisher, mistakenly identified Benjamin Eastburn as the surveyor on this engraving; the map was actually the work of Nicholas Scull, Eastburn's successor as Surveyor General of Pennsylvania, and had been published posthumously in 1762 by his daughter and a local Philadelphia printer. The rendering was a precise reference tool when executed by Scull, but the 1776 edition was somewhat less useful: Dury reprinted the map without changes, even though the city's population had nearly doubled in the intervening decade and a half.

21. *Above (right):* John Montresor, surveyor, *A Plan of the City of New York & its Environs . . .,* engraving, London, 1775. John Montresor prepared this plan for military purposes under strict secrecy during the Stamp Act riots, the probable explanation for a number of inaccuracies and omissions. Despite these obvious disadvantages, British needs prompted its reissue.

22. *Right:* Lieutenant Page, engineer, *A Plan of the Action at Bunkers Hill,* hand-colored engraving drawn on a survey by Captain Montresor, London, 1775. Page's work was truly a plan of the battle's action: an overlay labeled "№ 1" showed the initial British attack which was repulsed, and the main map, in the same area but labeled "№ 2," showed the offensive which was eventually successful.

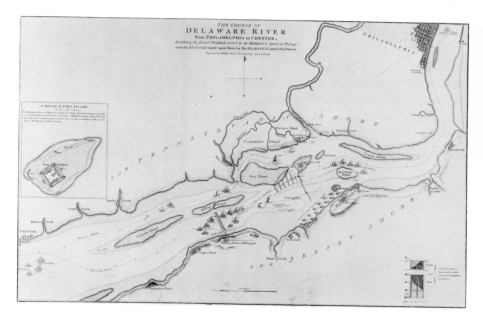

23. *The Course of Delaware River from Philadelphia to Chester . . .*, engraved by William Faden, hand-colored engraving, London, 1778. The Pennsylvania State Navy mounted a substantial defense on the Delaware River to protect Philadelphia and other points inland, including the implantation of chevaux de frise underwater to damage British ships as they progressed upstream. It was only after the British army had occupied the city by land, from the southwest, that the river defenses were finally broken.

although he used an earlier survey of the area made by Montresor, the portrayal included several major geographical errors.[50] The publication of a plan of the British and American Delaware River defenses, in April, 1778, was so swiftly executed that a surveyor must have sent it home just as soon as the British won control of the waterway in November, 1777.

The publication of a wide variety of prints, caricatures, and maps related to the war and its political implications continued in Britain and America and spread to Europe as well. Many English and European prints portrayed events and political developments utilizing an accepted allegorical vocabulary, generally representing America by an Indian accompanied by an alligator. Mythological figures were popular, as were contemporary symbols, particularly the liberty pole and liberty cap. Prints designed by Americans were generally less symbolic, concerned, rather, with the portrayal of historical events. Pragmatism, so long a part of American sensibilities, continued to exert its influence over wartime creations. The popularity of prints which depicted the political and military situation was widespread, however, and the same basic image was often reengraved on the Continent or in America following its publication in London.

Pride in American achievements and in the new American nation swelled following the conclusion of fighting and the formal recognition of America's independence by Britain. Merchants advertised their latest "American publications" as well as colored and mezzotint engravings "emblematical of the return of Peace to America." Engraved portraits of General and Martha Washington and of other popular figures were advertised frequently. Likenesses of Washington, Franklin, and the American eagle were even produced by members of such tightly-knit ethnic groups as the Pennsylvania Germans, who were far removed from the mainstream of Anglo-American culture. Historical accounts of the fighting appeared as early as May, 1783, when Philadelphians could purchase "An Impartial History of the War in America . . . In Two Volumes large Octavo—Adorned with Twelve beautiful Engravings of American Patriots and Generals, with the View of the Battle of Bunker's Hill, and the burning of the Town of Falmouth by Capt. Mowat."[51]

The popularity of engraved portraits or "heads" prompted Charles Willson Peale to plan the first series of engravings of prominent Americans in 1787:

> I have begun 1 other great work, the making of Mezzotinto prints from my collection of Illustrious Personages. This undertaking will cost me much labour as I am obliged to take the plates from the rough and doing the whole business myself, even the impressing. I have just finished 1 of Doct^r Franklin which I am giving out as a specimen of the size & manner I intend this series of Prints . . . .[52]

Peale's project was not a financial success, however, and he eventually returned to his portraiture in oils. The public, it would seem, was still too involved with other concerns to become interested in the creation of an entire series which served no purpose other than to honor its fellow citizens.

24. J. C. le Vasseur, engraver, *L'Amerique Independante,* engraving after a drawing by Antoine Borel, France, 1778. A toga-clad Benjamin Franklin protects the newly-freed America from the surrounding turmoil, as she clings to Liberty's skirts in this allegorical print. Franklin agreed to pose for the engraving, but asked not to have it dedicated to him.

25. John Ogborn, engraver, *The Birth of American Liberty,* colored mezzotint, after a painting by Sylvester Harding, London, 1784. America appears here as a Matron Queen, with the infant Liberty on her lap. The ever-popular liberty cap and pole are borne aloft by a cherub, dubbed "Freedom's Genius" in the accompanying poem.

Identification with America was further strengthened by the publication of engravings which depicted the nation's growth. One of the most popular was Amos Doolittle's *Display of the United States of America,* first issued in 1778, an engraving which honored the president and each of the individual states. His symbolic linking of the state seals and the Great Seal represented the newly confirmed federal union, while the detailed information included in the rings—population statistics and numbers of representatives and senators—satisfied the Americans' interest in practical details. This was one of the first pieces to combine symbolic representations, familiar to Americans but up until this time rarely included in prints which they designed, with standard straightforward facts. Doolittle published six editions of the print during George Washington's presidency, updating the statistics in each succeeding edition, and continued to publish

26. Amos Doolittle, engraver, *Display of the United States of America,* stipple and line engraving, New Haven, Connecticut, c. 1790. Symbolism in American engravings evolved using a realistic, rather than an allegorical, representational framework. This linked chain of states was particularly popular: it also appeared as the central motif in a half-dollar bill printed in Philadelphia in 1776 and in the carpet designed by William Peter Sprague for the United States Senate's Chamber in Congress Hall, Philadelphia.

it in slightly altered form, showing Washington's successors, during the terms of Adams and Jefferson.[53]

American artist John Trumbull, who had resided in England for a number of years, chose to publish a series of engravings copied from his historical paintings of the American Revolution in the late 1780s. He was encouraged in the undertaking by Benjamin West because many artists made more money from the sale of prints of their paintings than from the paintings themselves. Trumbull completed the first two paintings in the series, *The Battle at Bunker's Hill* and *The Death of General Montgomery,* and arranged to have them engraved, but progress toward a completed pair of prints was slow. He journeyed to America in 1789 to solicit subscriptions for the series, but, without a finished product, subscriptions met only three-quarters of his expenses; lacking the motivation of financial gain the project was never completed.[54] Trumbull had portrayed the historic scenes with artistic license, while many of his potential subscribers expected a realistic rendering of the action, and his failure to recognize this aspect of the national personality was, no doubt, partly responsible for the commercial failure of his undertaking.[55]

Other American engravers, more sensitive to the tastes of the people, issued prints which portrayed historical events in a straightforward manner, and these prints were oftentimes humorous as well. A confrontation between two members of the House of Representatives was quickly illustrated in two such views: *Cudgeling as by late Act in Congress, USA,* which portrayed the House of Representatives Chamber in Congress

27. John Trumbull, *The Death of General Montgomery . . .,* engraved by Johan Frederik Clemens, London, 1798. Trumbull presented copies of this engraving and its companion piece, *The Battle at Bunker's Hill,* to the United States House of Representatives and Senate late in 1799 to hang in their chambers in Congress Hall.

28. *Congressional Pugilists,* unidentified engraver, engraving, Philadelphia, after 1798. Such behavior, an uncommon sight on the floor of the House Chamber, erupted after a heated exchange of insults between Matthew Lyon of Vermont (*l.*) and Roger Griswold of Connecticut (*r.*).

Hall fairly accurately but showed Representative Matthew Lyon of New Hampshire with a lion's head and mane, and the *Congressional Pugilists* which portrayed the chamber and representatives in a farcical manner. John Bower's *View of the Bombardment of Fort McHenry,* printed years later, shared the same blend of fact and creativity.

The concept of American nationality and the nation itself were best illustrated, however, in the work of transplanted Britons William and Thomas Birch. They were enthusiastic about their adopted nation, and its capital city in particular, and were most enthusiastic about the people and their achievements. Their series of Philadelphia views illustrated the contemporary scene—new and even unfinished buildings, as well as the most important older structures—and people everywhere. They were looking ahead to a new century:

PHILADELPHIA

The ground on which it stands, was less than a century ago, in a state of wild nature; covered with wood, and inhabited by Indians. It has in this short time, been raised, as it were, by magic power, to the eminence of an opulent city, famous for its trade and commerce, crouded in its port, with vessels of its own producing, and visited by others from all parts of the world . . . This Work will stand as a memorial of its progress for the first century . . . .[56]

29. John Bower, engraver, *A View of the Bombardment of Fort McHenry . . .,* aquatint, Philadelphia, c. 1814-19. The carefully-curved trajectories of the shells, and the people and animals shown amid the battle scene, lend personal touches to this print. The details of the naval siege of Baltimore are rendered so precisely that it is likely that the engraver was an eyewitness to the action.

30. William and Thomas Birch, artists and engravers, *Back of the State House, Philadelphia,* hand-colored engraving, Philadelphia, 1799. The State House remained a scene of considerable activity at the end of the century, and in this view well-dressed Philadelphians, young boys with their dog, and visiting Indians all shared the adjoining garden.

2. Ceramics and Glass from Home and Abroad
by ROBERT LEWIS GIANNINI, III

> The Land containeth diver Sorts of Earth, as sand yellow and Black, Poor and Rich: also gravel both Loomy and Dusty; and in Some places a fast fat Earth, like to our best vales in England, especially by Ireland-Brooks and Rivers . . . . The Back Lands being generally three to one Richer than those that lie by Navigable Waters. We have much of another soyl, and that is a black Hasel-Mauld, upon a Stony or Rocky bottom . . . .[1]

This passage is from a description of Philadelphia and the surrounding countryside in an account which William Penn delivered in 1683 to the Committee of the Free Society of Traders of Pennsylvania in London to encourage immigration. The description of the "soyls" indicates the way in which his hopes for the establishment of glass and ceramic industries in the new colony were promoted. Penn's description of the various types of soils would have been meaningful to the potters and glass blowers of England and the Continent, who would have easily recognized the "fast fat Earth" as clay for ceramics, and the "sand yellow and Black, Poor and Rich" as important for the production of glass.

Industries were soon established in Penn's colony. Potters, their names generally unknown today, produced redware and stoneware steadily and abundantly. In fact, Philadelphia pottery eventually acquired something of a reputation in the other colonies. Sporadic attempts were made, with less success, to produce porcelains of both hard and soft pastes. The output of local glassmakers was mostly window glass and bottles.

At the same time, England's policy of mercantilism, implemented by a series of parliamentary acts that began in 1651 and gradually tightened through the eighteenth century, acted to discourage the production of finer wares. These acts forbade all manufacturing in the colonies and stipulated that only English ships could carry goods to or from North America. Further, all the main colonial products could be exported only to England, and only foreign products that had been brought to England could be imported by the colonies. Dutch wares, for example, had to be shipped from Holland to England and then shipped to Philadelphia on English vessels. The system naturally raised profits for English merchants and prices for American colonists. The authorities, however, paid scant attention to the Philadelphia glass and ceramics industries producing common wares because they provided little competition to England's factories.

Philadelphia eventually became an important manufacturing city in the eighteenth century but, as a fledgling city, it remained dependent on imports for the finer products of glass and ceramics. Imports of china and glass were plentiful in the years before the Revolution. After 1781, Oriental wares poured into Philadelphia on American ships, and English ceramics, especially pearl ware and creamware, assumed a special popularity. From the earliest days, however, local potters and glassmakers were helping to supply the common wares essential to everyday needs. By examining information from archaeological excavations, contemporary newspaper advertisements, and household inventories, it is possible to piece together the history of the growth of the local industries and the tangled story of imports.

These combined sources of information suggest at least four chronological periods between the dates of 1682 to 1800 that place the making of glass and ceramics in Philadelphia into historical perspective. Even these four periods are somewhat arbitrary since they apply more to the imports of finer wares, which are distinguishable by style and materials, than they do to the locally-produced common wares which were much less influenced by such changes. Business, social, and political factors figure just as prominently in this division of periods, variously dictating or ignoring what was made and/or imported. From 1682 through the 1720s, craftsmen recruited from England and the Continent applied their acquired skills to lay the groundwork for domestic production. From the 1720s to about 1760, local merchants came to play an important role in the importation of fine wares from England, even though mercantile regulations officially discouraged American craftsmen. Philadelphia potters of common wares flourished with the support of an increasingly prosperous economy. From 1760 to the end of the Revolution the glassmaking industry grew; local potters continued to service the city's populace with common wares, and America's first porcelain factory, Bonnin and Morris, was established. From then to the end of the century prosperous Philadelphians imported an extraordinary amount of pottery and porcelain from the Orient and from England, while American ships joined those from Great Britain in bringing furnishings from around the world to the city. During this last period, the local ceramics industry tended to relocate in more rural areas than in the heavily residential older part of the city.

Early Philadelphia potters began with the essentials of living: bricks, clay pipes, household redwares, and stonewares. Glassmakers began with windows and bottles. Both groups produced a variety of forms. For lighting there were candlesticks and fat lamps. Flower pots and bulb jars were available for the gardener. Inkwells came in both glass and clay. Locally-made insect traps, bird feeders, storage jars, pitchers, colanders, plates, cups, bowls, cake and jelly molds were also products of the local craftsman.[2]

The first craftsmen brought to Philadelphia skills learned in their respective homelands. Often their talents were put to the practices of another trade, either to supplement their income or to provide the services needed in a growing community. They were of various nationalities—French Huguenots, who had made their way to England and thence to Pennsylvania; the Welsh and the English; the Dutch; and the Scotch-Irish. German immigrants began settling in Germantown, just north of the city, in 1683, and by 1750 comprised forty percent of Pennsylvania's population.[3]

XV. A set of Bristol tin-glazed earthenware plates, c. 1750, is representative of one of the more popular types of dinnerware available in early Philadelphia before the establishment of the great English factories and the exportation of their wares.

XVI. *Above:* Probably made in Derby, England, c. 1815, this colorful and rich porcelain service reveals the influence of Japanese Imari design. Interest in Oriental decorative motifs in tableware remained strong in America from the mid-eighteenth century to the 1850s.

XVII. *Left:* Three dinner plates, in porcelain, creamware, and pearl ware, illustrate important aspects of late-eighteenth-century English ceramic production. The center plate is attributed to the factory of Josiah Wedgwood and is flanked by China-trade ware in the Fitzhugh pattern and the popular scalloped feather-edge of Liverpool.

59

XVIII. *Above:* Common potters of English and German origin found a steady market throughout the eighteenth century in Philadelphia for colorful decorative redwares such as those illustrated.

XIX. *Left:* Asia, America, and Africa are portrayed with bountiful agricultural attributes and stand with Europa portrayed as a queen with attributes of the arts and sciences. This group succinctly exhibits the eighteenth-century mercantilist theory of colonial dependence upon the mother country and personifies the Euro-English view of non-European cultures. Made in England about 1780, probably at Derby, the group's rarity is in the survival of four separate figures as a set through the vicissitudes of time in virtually mint condition.

XX. A group of Staffordshire polychrome earthenware biblical figurines, "Elijah," "St. Philip," and "Nicodemus" surrounding "The Widow and Her Children." Religious or moral representations such as these were popular forms of mantel decoration throughout the late eighteenth and early nineteenth centuries.

31. Slip-decorated red earthenware chamber pot, English, *c.* 1710. Identified generically as of the "Metropolitan slip-ware type," this is one of the earliest of ceramics excavated at Franklin Court. It provides but a clue to what the first generation of Philadelphians brought with them from England and to what the local production of redwares looked to as a prototype.

32. Probably made in Philadelphia, this slip-decorated red earthenware pie plate was excavated at Franklin Court in the physical context of shards that date it to *c.* 1730-60. Decorated with splashes of green slip and a spirited rendition of a gaming hen, it was a very fanciful utilitarian object when made.

Vast quantities of redware shards of various glazes, colors, and designs have been excavated from potters' dumps, wells, and outdoor privies at Franklin Court, Independence Square, and from other sites throughout the Park, attesting to the productivity of early Philadelphia potters. "The hundreds of locally-made vessels," reports one scholar, "provide, from dated levels, a measure of a good part of the potters' range. Their skill in imitative technology, form and decoration, clearly English in origin, show visible evidence of kinship to Staffordshire."[4]

German potters brought to Philadelphia a traditional redware production which emphasized bold and full decoration applied to basically standardized shapes. They transposed their decorative motifs, including distinctive calligraphy and stylized animals, birds, and flowers, onto English forms and thus established a hybrid American tradition in ceramics. Unfortunately, these earliest of potters and their wares, until recently, have been almost forgotten because few of their products are identifiable, being neither signed by their maker nor dated.

Historical records provide brief glimpses of these early potters. One of them was Joshua Tittery, also a glassmaker. The minutes of the Free Society of Traders of November 27, 1698, show that Dennis Rocheford (Ratchford) was apprenticed to Tittery until he was twenty-one years old. Tittery agreed to teach Rocheford the trade of potting and to instruct him in reading, writing, and arithmetic. On May 20, 1717, Rocheford was admitted as a potter and a freeman of Philadelphia after satisfying his apprenticeship and paying £5 2s. 6d. for the right.[5] Records indicate that in the early eighteenth century, William Crews, Edward Hughes, and Gabriel Thomas had also attained a journeyman's status.

Common redwares remained virtually unchanged in composition throughout the eighteenth and nineteenth centuries in Philadelphia. With only modest variations in form, shape, or decoration, local potters used essentially the same clays, glazes, and techniques that they had learned from their fathers and would pass on to their sons. In

33. *Above:* Paired here to contrast local and foreign production of similar objects are an English white salt-glazed stoneware chamber pot with scratch-blue decoration, *c.* 1740-60, and one of grey salt-glazed stoneware made by Anthony Duché, Sr., Philadelphia, *c.* 1730-62. Both were excavated within the Park's confines.

34. *Far left:* Detail of the touch mark of Anthony Duché, Sr., impressed below the handle of a fragment of the Philadelphia salt-glazed stoneware chamber pot illustrated previously.

35. *Left:* The "R.W." touch mark on the base of a clay-pipe bowl that was excavated in the square behind Independence Hall has been tentatively identified as that of Richard Warder who was making clay pipes in Philadelphia as early as 1716.

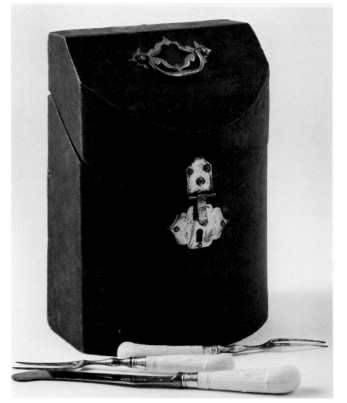

36. *Above (left):* An extraordinary find in the archaeological excavations conducted in Philadelphia's oldest residential area is this locally-made manganese-glazed red earthenware "puzzle jug" of about 1740-60. An object used at parties, its only purpose was entertainment—to fool the drinker into spilling the contents of the jug onto himself or the floor.

37. *Above:* This type of white salt-glazed stoneware, with graceful lines and impressed border decorations, was first introduced in England about the mid-eighteenth century. By the 1760s it was fairly common to American households, a strong and comparatively inexpensive alternative to more costly porcelains.

38. *Left:* The height of fashion for a short period of time after the mid-eighteenth century was ceramic-handled cutlery. The examples here are part of a rare set of twelve knives and forks, with white salt-glazed stoneware handles, together with their equally rare shagreen-covered case or box. The metal parts were made by William Tricket in Sheffield, England, c. 1760-80.

some examples only an expert eye and the assistance of modern technology can differentiate between eighteenth- and nineteenth-century pieces of redware. Potters generally used clays found in and around Philadelphia; a copper, red, black, or brown lead glaze was applied before the piece was fired, and slip decoration was sometimes added later. The poisonous lead glazes commonly used on earthenware became an increasingly recognized health hazard. Later in the century a movement to outlaw them proved unsuccessful.[6] Lead-glazed earthenware continued, nevertheless, to be manufactured in great quantity.

In the latter part of the seventeenth century stoneware was being made in considerable quantity in England and by the early eighteenth century it had been introduced to the colonies. Stoneware has certain advantages over redware in that it is more vitreous and denser. Its special clay body is capable of withstanding firing at high temperature, and in the process it acquires considerable strength and becomes especially suitable for liquid containers. Stoneware also has certain disadvantages. The special clay body is not always readily accessible, and it is more expensive to manufacture. Local craftsmen who were accustomed to red or yellow ware found the clay difficult to handle. It was not always easy to adapt to the forms which they knew, and the new firing techniques required a degree of skill and specialization which many of the craftsmen did not have or did not care to acquire.[7]

Anthony Duché, of Huguenot descent, was probably the first potter to produce salt-glazed stoneware in Philadelphia. He managed to capture a small corner of the monopoly formerly held by importers of German Westerwald and English stonewares. It is unclear if Duché learned his trade from a potter in London or if he was apprenticed in Philadelphia, but it is certain that on May 13, 1717, he was admitted as a freeman of the city of Philadelphia and that his sons worked with him in producing pottery between 1724 and 1730.[8]

In 1730, the Duché family petitioned the Pennsylvania House of Representatives for the "sole privilege" of making stoneware within the province for twenty-one years and asked the House to discourage imports of any stoneware from neighboring provinces. In the petition, the Duchés said that ". . . for several years past they have, with great Industry, applied themselves to the art of making Stoneware, here-to-fore unknown in these parts; and after many chargeable Experiments have attained to the Perfection thereof . . . ." The petition failed to pass the House, and the Duchés did not win the "sole privilege" they sought, although they did, however, ply their trade for some time.[9]

Anthony Duché also worked as a dyer and glovemaker and owned two shops, one on Front Street and one on Chestnut Street, with a pottery behind the latter shop. He sold American and imported ceramics as well as imported textiles and other goods until his death in 1762.[10] Archaeological excavations on Chestnut Street below Fifth Street have documented the kiln site and have turned up numerous examples of the equipment he used, along with examples of his touch mark, "A.D.," surrounded by a rather fancy cartouche. The stoneware he introduced was usually made of a light-brown or gray clay and a clear salt glaze, sometimes with cobalt-blue decoration added. It was almost exclusively shaped and decorated in either the English or German Westerwald traditions. Shards of chamberpots and handled mugs have been excavated in abundance, the former rather crude by Continental standards, but imaginatively decorated with free-flowing and symmetrical floral designs. The inventory of Duché's estate is also of interest for it lists the tools of the potting trade as well as "The Times of 3 Apprentices" at £35 each, "Unburn't Earthenware, Tiles" at £8 5s. 2d., and "2 Clay Mills and 3 Potters Wheels" worth £3 10s. each.[11]

On several occasions Duché's manufactory was put up for sale, perhaps indicating something about the difficulty of competing with importers of stoneware.[12] The potter and his sons continued to make salt-glazed stoneware and other earthenware through the middle of the eighteenth century. One son, Andrew, went to Savannah in the 1730s and made red earthenware pottery. It is said that he learned how to make porcelain and tried to start a factory there. Another son, James, failed in the salt-glaze stoneware potting business in Massachusetts and returned to Philadelphia and the family pottery where he worked until his death in 1751.[13]

A potter's range of products could include anything made from clay, everything from bricks for the construction of buildings to clay pipes for the smoking of tobacco. The *American Weekly Mercury* for May 12 and 19, 1720, advertised "Good long Tavern Pipes" at 4s. a gross, made by Richard Warder "near the Market Place, where also any that have occasion may have their foul Pipes burnt" for 8d. a gross. Warder probably made his clay pipes and fired them at the kiln of his neighbor, Joshua Tittery. As early as 1711, Warder had inherited from his brother John "Clay tools and implements for making Pipes."[14] For finer wares, early Philadelphians had to rely upon imports. Unlike clay pipes or redware pie dishes, these were objects to be treasured and displayed with pride and not to be disposed of when chipped or even broken.

Apparently, very little Oriental porcelain came into Philadelphia before the mid-eighteenth century. It had appeared in England as early as the last half of the fifteenth century, and it seems reasonable to believe that there were examples of it in use in Philadelphia at a very early date. Its absence from archaeological excavations may reflect that such delicate ware was treated with tender care and, if broken, was mended.

Extant estate inventories list comparatively few porcelain objects. One list itemizes ". . . one Japan dish cract, 3 china plates, 1 Japan bowl, 1 china cup and 1 china dram cup."[15] All of these items had been assigned a higher than average valuation for the time, indicating their probable rarity. It is clear that porcelains did not appear in any sizeable amounts until around 1750.

What does appear in this early period are English imitations of Dutch delft—the tin-glazed earthenwares from Lambeth, Bristol, and Liverpool—and pressed molded wares from Staffordshire. Blue-on-blue tin-glazed earthenwares, often polychromed, known in various national terms as majolica, faience, and delft, also came to Philadelphia from Italy, France, and Holland respectively, shipped in English vessels. Along with the English imitations, these became the most widely used finer pottery during the period. The inventories do not indicate, however, whether a particular earthenware delft vessel was imported from Holland via England, nor do they list a particular object as English, Bristol, or Lambeth delft. The terms—"Dutch, Holland," and "Holland ware" give us a bare clue to the origin of the pieces.[16]

Glass for windows and common domestic vessels and medicinal vials were undoubtedly produced locally. Yet evidence of particular glassmakers' work is extremely difficult to pinpoint, especially the sources which are extant, since the objects themselves yield few clues. William Penn had tried hard to attract glass blowers to Pennsylvania. Tittery, mentioned earlier as a potter, had answered the call, as it were, and arrived in Philadelphia on the ship *America* on June 20, 1683. He was described as a servant to "ye Society" of traders and as a "broad glassmaker" (a maker of inexpensive window glass) from New Castle-upon-Tyne who was to serve four years at £88 per year. Minutes of the Philadelphia Yearly Meeting of Friends of April 3, 1685, reveal that Tittery complained of being denied his proper wages. No record has been located to show where the Society of Free Traders carried on the window glass business. Meeting records note that when Tittery married Cicely Wooly on February 4, 1688, he was still described as "Joshua Tittery of Philadelphia Glassmaker."[17]

Penn's hopes for the establishment of a glass industry in Philadelphia proved a bit premature. Most of the early attempts failed, either from lack of support or the high cost of glass manufacture. And, for the time being at least, both England and Europe professed to have the resources to supply the colonies with all the glass products they needed.

Caspar Wistar, an enterprising twenty year old, came to Philadelphia from Hispach near Heidelberg, Germany, in 1717 and became a Quaker in 1725. Despite his German origin, Wistar was eventually assimilated into the city's merchant elite. In 1738, he brought four glass blowers to Philadelphia from Germany. Soon after their arrival, Martin Halter, William Wentzel, Simeon Griesmeyer, and Caspar Halter began construction of a glass house on the Alloway Creek in Salem County, New Jersey.[18] It came to be known as the United Glass Company, or Wistarberg, its major output being window-pane glass, lamp glasses, bottles, and electrical globes and tubes for early experiments. Benjamin Franklin was a close friend of Caspar Wistar and his son Richard. Franklin asked the Wistars to make electrical tubes as early as 1747. As Franklin wrote in his autobiography:

> My house was continually full for some time with people who came to see these new Wonders. To divide a little of this Incumbrance among my Friends, I caused a number of similar Tubes to be blown at our Glasshouse . . . so that we had at length several performers . . . .[19]

39. Educational as well as decorative, such allegorical figurines of polychromed porcelain as this set of the "Four Seasons" are today as fascinating to contemplate and study as they undoubtedly were in eighteenth-century households. They are attributed to Derby, England, c. 1770.

40. Among the discoveries made through archaeological excavations in the Park was early glassware of American origin. The handled mug and spirits or wine bottle shown here have been attributed to the South Jersey glassworks of Caspar and Richard Wistar, c. 1730-60.

The Wistars' factory was the main source of locally-made glass for Philadelphia between 1739 and 1776. Crown glass ("bull's eye" glass, used mainly in windowpanes) was imported and sold by Wistar, but it is doubtful that any was produced at Wistarberg. Caspar Wistar died in 1752, leaving the business to his son who continued the operation into the years of the Revolutionary War. In an advertisement in the *Pennsylvania Gazette* for July 30, 1752, Richard Wistar gave notice that he had "removed from his late father's house in Market-Street, next door to the Spinningwheel, almost opposite to the prison, where may be had glass and bottles, either wholesale or retail." The advertisement also noted that Richard Wistar carried on the trade of making brass buttons and said that "Merchants, Shopkeepers and Others may be supplied as usual."

Bottles of various shapes and sizes formed the chief output of the Wistar factory. A few glass artifacts that can be associated wtih the glassworks were recently retrieved from a well at Franklin Court. These include a few almost complete bottles and a glass mug, the bottles being of a clear pale-green glass with a rather crudely applied lip. The base, or foot, of each is indented with a shallow kick that has a smooth pontil.

As Philadelphia continued to grow and prosper, Wistar's locally-produced glasswares were supplemented by imports of the finer sort. Two advertisements from the *Pennsylvania Gazette* give testimony to their availability. In the issue for August 2, 1750, John David, a "joyner in Second Street, opposite the Black Horse Alley," listed the following as just in from London on the ship *Speedwell:*

> . . . All new, a very curious perspective glass, with 24 cuts, looking glasses, swinging frames and others, hungary water, Stoughton's bitters, Bateman's drops, Daffy's elixir, etc . . . .

Charles Willing and Son, merchants, reported in the issue of December 7, 1752 that their shop had available from London and Bristol:

> . . . Looking glasses, pier-glasses, chimney glasses . . . sash crown, glass 8 x 10 and 11 x 9 . . . double and single flint drinking glasses, decanters, dessert-glasses, pyramids and salvers, Wiltshire and Bristol bottled beer . . . .

Although descriptions of double and single flint drinking glasses often appeared in newspaper advertisements, they are rarely found in archaeological contexts of the mid-eighteenth century. Their absence can be explained, perhaps, by the demand for glass. Once broken, glass was sold to the glass blower and melted down for reuse.

Technological innovations and newer styles introduced to the English ceramics industry between 1750 and 1771 appeared almost immediately among Philadelphia's imports. Archaeological excavations at Franklin Court have produced evidence that a wide variety of wares were imported. These included white salt-glazed stoneware, tin-glazed earthenware, Jackfield-type plain glazed wares, scratch blue stoneware, earthenwares, creamware (Wedgwood and Whieldon), Staffordshire slipwares and brown stonewares, Metropolitan slipware, Staffordshire dipped stonewares, mottled earthenwares, and porcelain. A typical merchant's advertisement of the time is that of James Clulow which appeared in the local newspapers in 1757. He offered "RED lead, literage, magnas, China Delf, Blue and white and White Stone ware, very cheap for ready money."[20]

Many of these newer imports were of forms introduced to meet the demands created by the ceremony of tea drinking, a social custom adopted by the English-speaking peoples in the last quarter of the seventeenth century. The tea equipage, often in the delicate plain and scratch blue salt-glazed stoneware, or soft paste porcelains, imitated

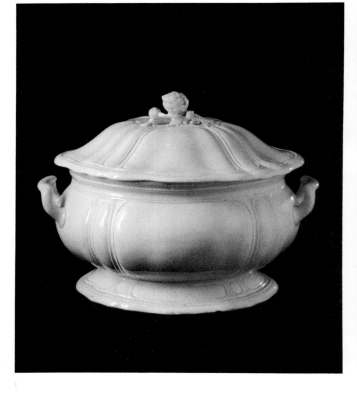

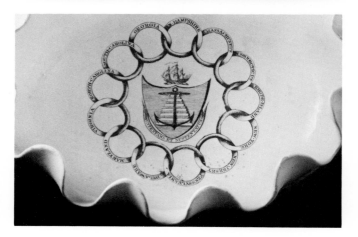

41-45. *Opposite page. Top (left):* This fragment of a clear glass bird feeder is one of two examples retrieved from archaeological excavations in the Park. Both date to the last half of the eighteenth century and may be either English or American in origin. An example in "mint" condition was acquired for a birdcage in the restored home of John and Dolley Todd. *Top (right):* By far the most common of imported English ceramics in the latter third of the eighteenth century and early nineteenth century was cream-colored earthenware (creamware), several forms and patterns of which are shown here. *Center (right):* English creamware lent itself to a wide variety of ceramic shapes and impressed decorations, here illustrated by three desert molds. These late-eighteenth- or early-nineteenth-century forms were, in turn, reproduced in locally-made redwares. *Bottom (left):* European ceramics never presented a challenge to the Staffordshire factories of England in the American trade. Virtually indistinguishable from its English counterpart, this creamware tureen is probably of French manufacture, c. 1770. *Bottom (right):* Prototypes for these miniature ceramic items were retrieved from the privy of the Bishop White House, the playthings, undoubtedly, of one or several of the Bishop's many children and grandchildren. They are green-glazed creamware of the Whieldon type made in Staffordshire, c. 1770-1800.

46-48. *Top:* The specific intention of transfer printing this maxim onto this English creamware beaker of c. 1790-1810 is unknown, but it is safe to assume that it would have appealed to the merchant classes of either America or England. *Center:* Probably the rarest of creamware ceramics in the Park's collection is this monteith that was made in the factory of Josiah Wedgwood, c. 1780-85. It is believed to have been part of a large table service that Robert Morris had made when he was the United States Agent of Marine (1781-85). *Bottom:* Transfer printed onto the bottom of the interior of the monteith is the arms of the Continental Navy, surrounded by a chain of thirteen circles emblematic of the unity of the original American colonies.

forms of prized Chinese porcelains, most of which were withheld from re-export to the colonies. Some porcelains found their way to grace the tables of Philadelphia homes at a very early date, as the inventories of estates reveal.[21] English blue-and-white china was by far the most common everyday ware. Easier and cheaper than salt-glaze to produce, it became very popular in the colonies, outselling white salt-glaze and delft. Chinese export blue-and-white porcelain and Chinese and European famille verte and famille rose enameled wares were owned and used by those who could afford them. Philadelphians also bought Bristol imitations of Oriental porcelain, both early-period Worcester and "powder blue" from the factory at Bow. Some of these English porcelains carried imitation Chinese lake and floral scenes and were often marked on the bottoms as if they had come straight from the Orient.

Many contemporary newspaper advertisements attest to the variety of fine ceramics available to Philadelphians at mid-century:

> . . . Lately imported from London, Bristol and Liverpool, and to be sold by Daniel Benezet . . . at his store in Arch-St . . . boxes of china well sorted, containing blue & white and enamelled tea cups and saucers, coffee cups, plates, bowls, sugar dishes, custard cups, etc. . . .[22]

As long as the English, and not other foreign traders, provided most of the fine ceramics and glass for Philadelphians, merchants on both sides of the Atlantic made a profit and remained content. As long as Philadelphians confined their domestic production to utilitarian wares and did not attempt to compete with English producers, there was little reason for complaint by royal officials. During this time potters like Richard Stanley and Samuel Hale continued to ply their trade in ordinary redware products without much problem. This was, in fact, the time when Philadelphia firmly established itself as a center for the production of very good common utilitarian red earthenwares, a position which it held for many years.[23]

Any local attempt to compete in the manufacture of fine ceramics produced in the factories of Staffordshire would have proven uneconomical, if not totally unnecessary. The importation of luxury goods was an accepted way of life, at least until such time as the British government attempted to raise its revenues from the colonies through taxation. Richard Wistar's advertisement in the *Pennsylvania Chronicle* for July 31, 1769, tells of the growing resentment in the colonies against British trade restrictions, new taxes, and new duties:

> As the above mentioned glass is of American manufacture, it is consequently clear of the duties the Americans so justly complain of; and at present it seems peculiarly the interest of America to encourage her own manufacturers, more especially those upon which duties have been imposed for the sole purpose of raising a revenue . . . .

In response to the Stamp Act of 1765 and the Townshend Acts of 1767, colonists tried to restrict imports through non-importation agreements, although these collapsed in 1771. Often they sought ways to evade the restrictions against colonial manufacture. In 1768 Govenor William Franklin of New Jersey sought advice on how to deal with the British Board of Trade which regulated colonial enterprises, including the Wistar glassworks and similar establishments. Benjamin Franklin instructed his son to minimize the importance of the industries to the Board: ". . . You have only to report a glass-house for coarse window glass and bottles."[24]

William Franklin followed his father's advice, as his account of the glass factory to

Lord Hillsborough shows:

> A Glass House was erected about Twenty years ago in Salem County,
> which makes bottles, and a very coarse green glass for windows, used
> only in some of the Houses of the poorer Sort of People, the Profits
> made by this Work have not hitherto been sufficient it seems to induce
> any Persons to set up more of the like kind in the Colony . . . .[25]

Young Franklin was probably well aware that Wistar operated at the time one of the
more profitable industries in colonial America. Later, the story was different. Wistar,
labeled a Tory, had almost closed his glass factory by 1778, and in 1780 was offering it
for sale with 1500 acres of land adjoining.[26]

The protest against taxation grew through the 1760s and early 1770s. Isaac Gray,
merchant and owner of the Philadelphia Glass Works advertised in the *Pennsylvania
Packet* of March 22, 1773, with patriotic fervor:

> Isaac Gray, In Chestnut-street, near Strawberry-Alley, hath for sale . . .
> a neat assortment of white and green Glass Wares, made at Kensington,
> which are allowed to be equal in quality to those imported from Great
> Britain; it is therefore hoped that the inhabitants of these provinces, and
> of this city in particular, will, in purchasing, give the preference to
> Goods manufactured by their fellow citizens, whereby they may be
> likely to receive again the money they expend, which it is in vain to ex-
> pect when sent beyond the sea . . . .

On October 20, 1774, the First Continental Congress agreed to the suspension of commercial intercourse with England. The delegates agreed unanimously not to import or
consume British goods and, in principle, not to export anything to England. Imports
came to an abrupt halt, except in those areas under British control.

West of Philadelphia, William Henry Stiegel, a German, brought several glass blowers
to Berks and Lancaster counties between 1763 and 1781. Newspaper accounts of the
period convey the impression that Stiegel was a ruthless businessman and harsh task-
master.[27] The *Pennsylvania Packet* for November 11, 1771, carried a bondage challenge, filed by Felix Farrell, who charged Stiegel with paying low wages and failing to
honor his contracts for working time. The discontent of Stiegel's workers was Philadelphia's gain. Those who broke with Stiegel began the production of glass in the Kensington section of Philadelphia. In 1777, Felix Farrell and George Bakeoven begged in the
Pennsylvania Gazette:

> . . . to inform the Public that they have, at a considerable expense,
> brought to Perfection, the Blowing of Glass, and for sale at the Ware
> house in Kensington, and at the House of Mr. Abraham Cloathing, in
> Third-street near Race-street; Quart and Pint Decanters, Quart and Pint
> Tumblers, Wine Glasses and Phials.[27]

Orders for American glass could also be placed through John Elliott in Walnut Street
and through his son, John, Jr., in Market Street. The older Elliott was first a cabinetmaker and then proprietor of a looking-glass store, and sold both imported and local
glass until his death in 1792. Elliott, Jr., continued to make looking glasses throughout
the last quarter of the century.[29]

Probably the most prolific buyer and seller of glass, both imported and local, was
Alexander Bartram. The inventory for 1778 of sundry goods at his house in Market
Street near the Indian King Tavern tells of the enormous range of glass and ceramics

available in Philadelphia. Listed are excerpts from the inventory of his household glass, with the value of each object:

14 vinegar cruets	1 shilling	
9 dram glasses	1 shilling	
4 glass stands	7 shillings,	6 pence
10 ink bottles	1 shilling	
7 decanters	3 shillings,	9 pence
1 box bound beeds	3 shillings,	9 pence
1 bowl decanter stoppers	7 shillings,	6 pence
2 pr glass candlesticks	7 shillings,	6 pence
18 pr glass salt stands	1 shilling	
48 Salt Linings and cupping glasses	2 shillings,	6 pence
8 nippes do	1 shilling	
43 Vinegar Cruets	1 shilling	
15 lamp glasses	1 shilling	
36 glass lamps	1 shilling	
35 vinegar crewitts	1 shilling	
3 bottles Wine Vinegar		
98 pieces of Glass ware in beau sett	2 shillings,	6 pence
15 electrical globes	7 shillings,	6 pence
a basket full of glass ware & ca	5 shillings	
55 groins and comule glasses		1 pence
3 glass stands	3 shillings,	9 pence
a parcel of salts and other glasses on the upper shelf	1 shilling,	10 pence[30]

In addition to the glass inventory, there was a large assortment of ceramic wares which included Queensware bowls, teapots (flowered), plates, cream pots, mustard cups, turned dishes; black teapots, sugar dishes, and cream pots; china covers, old china plates, old china teapots; earthenware jugs, plates, dishes, pots, teapots, flower pots, and chamber pots.

Before and during the Revolution, Philadelphia's potters produced large quantities of earthenwares from kilns usually located in their own backyards. Philadelphia, from its earliest period, had never been wanting for potters. Tax lists for the city for 1769 to 1774 tell us the names of some of the potters working in the city. Listed by year and by wards were: *1769—Mulberry Ward:* Thomas Meyer, Joseph Poynts, Jacob Rhodad, John Thomson, Jacob Utteree; *Dock Ward:* John Snowden. *1774—Mulberry Ward:* Matthias Meyer; *Dock Ward:* William Young and John Snowden; *North Ward:* John Hooke, Thomas Clulow, and William Standley.[31]

The potters' industry was essential to the practical needs of the city, with brickmaking no small part of their production. By the end of the war, Philadelphia had grown to more than 36,000 people and nearly 5,000 dwellings, the majority of which were of brick construction. According to Daniel Topham, a potter, bricks were "very Scarce and Much Wanted." In 1780 he petitioned the Supreme Executive Council of the State of Pennsylvania for the "Privilege of Digging Clay for the purpose of making bricks and Potter's Ware on a Certain Lot Situated on the North Side of Race Street between Tenth and Eleventh Streets." The lot, he said, was then unoccupied and he thought his work would be "of Publick Utility . . . ."[32]

Products of utility were the stock in trade of Philadelphia potters, however much their reputation for making fine earthenwares spread beyond the city's limits. This is well illustrated in the advertisements of two potters. The first, that of Thomas Jackson, in the *Pennsylvania Gazette* of January 5, 1774, tells us that crucibles for the use of other trades were one of many other products of his manufacture. The second, that of Jonathan Dubell, a New York potter, boasted that his wide variety of earthenwares was "far superior to the generality, and equal to the best of any imported from Philadelphia, or elsewhere."[33]

Philadelphia's reputation in the ceramics industry was well deserved. In 1770, America's first successful porcelain factory was founded in the city by Gousse Bonnin and George Anthony Morris. The initiative of these two enterprising men is seen in a historical perspective by Graham Hood as "a colonial manifestation of the contemporary English rage for porcelain, and their initiative . . . as a colonial counterpart of the estimable English porcelain factories of that time."[34]

The China Manufactory was built in a new street appropriately named "China Street" (today Alter Street, between Front and Second Streets near Washington Avenue). South of China Street, Bonnin and Morris built a three-story frame building, eighty feet by fifteen feet, in which, according to the sale notice of October 19, 1774, "the principal branches of the China manufactory were carried on."[35] Initially, the clays used in their product were drawn from the banks of the Delaware between New Castle and Wilmington. It was mixed with calcined bones. In August, 1772, the *Pennsylvania Gazette* told its readers that American china could "stand the Heat beyond any kind of crucibles ever yet made":

> . . . We can with Pleasure acquaint our Readers that the Proprietors of the China Manufactory in the City have lately made experiments with some clay presented to them by a Gentleman of Charles-Town, South Carolina, which produces China superior to any kind brought from the East-Indies.[36]

Products from the China Manufactory were sold at the Bonnin and Morris warehouse on the east side of Second Street, a few doors below Market Street. One newspaper advertisement read:

> . . . AMERICAN CHINA. JUST OPENED, A FRESH ASSORTMENT OF AMERICAN CHINAWARE, by BONNIN and MORRIS, Proprietors of the Manufactory, at their Ware-House . . . —Ladies, by sending their orders, may be supplied with complete sets of Dressing Boxes for the Toilet, either in Blue or Enamel. N. B. Ready Money for broken Flint Glass, at their Ware-House and factory . . . .[37]

That the firm paid "Ready Money for broken Flint Glass" suggests that melted-down glass was used in making the glaze for ceramics. Nevertheless, between 1770 and 1774 the China Manufactory produced a fairly reasonable soft paste porcelain ware.

A letter written by a prominent Philadelphian, Joseph Shippen, to his father, Edward, in 1771, indicates the initial success of the Bonnin and Morris venture:

> . . . I have been at the American China Shop, to procure some of the China which Mammy has an inclination for; and find they have none left of the same kind of cups and saucers bought by Mrs. Penn, which were tea cups with handles and not coffee cups; they are guilted china, and have a border round the edges in imitation of Naking China. There were only one dozen of that sort made, all of which Mrs. Penn bought; but I am told by the seller that more of it will be finished at the factory next week; and Jenny promises herself the pleasure . . . .[38]

Bonnin and Morris were able to sustain their soft paste porcelain production for only three years. Political events and the high cost of labor probably contributed to the manufactory's demise. In the opinion of one authority, the "flood of imported ceramics—after the collapse of the Non-importation Agreements, and labor difficulties must surely have convinced Bonnin of the hopelessness of his task. . . . He was presumably prescient enough to close the factory before losing everything."[39]

Between 1760 and 1764 and again after the non-importation agreements broke down, until 1774, English merchants and manufacturers of ceramics capitalized on the American market. However preeminent Wedgwood was, his was only one of many factories to ship wares to America. Archaeological evidence indicates that the new Black Basalts introduced by Wedgwood in 1767 were quite popular among Philadelphians, and that they liked the different type of Whieldon Ware that came in stone agate, tortoise shell, and "cauliflower" patterns. The lead-glazed Staffordshire and Leeds wares with scalloped and feathered edges were first introduced in Philadelphia in the 1760s and 1770s. Older ceramic types like the brown and gray salt-glazed stonewares, the fine white salt-glazed stoneware, and various forms of delft and tin-glazed earthenwares, retained their popularity.

Such old-style wares arrived again on American shores after the Revolution, but they were soon replaced in popularity by porcelains imported directly from China and by the newer transfer-printed creamwares decorated to appeal to patriotic sentiment. Many tons of tableware were brought into East Coast seaports during the seventy years that the American-China trade in porcelains flourished. Early shipping records report such large quanities as "90 half-chests of china . . . 25 boxes of china . . . 200 roles of chinaware . . . 350 Table Services of China . . . 240 Tea Setts . . . 370 China bowls . . . 600 sets of long china dishes. . . ."[40]

49. A fragment of a fluted bowl, identical to the pristine example shown here, was excavated in the Park. It is English creamware, c. 1780-1820, identical to another example in the collections of the Winterthur Museum that bears the mark of the Leeds factory.

50. The evidence compiled from archaeological digs at the Bishop White House proved conclusively that Chinese export porcelain of the blue-and-white Nanking pattern was the household's fine dinner service. The examples shown date variously between c. 1790-1840.

The archaeological excavations conducted at the Park testify to the impact of the China trade on Philadelphia and even indicate what were the most popular patterns and types. For example, the yield of Fitzhugh, Canton, and Nanking porcelains from the privy pit of Bishop White's house, together with pieces that descended in his family, support the conclusion that these were the preferred dinner wares among people of affluence. The American eagle was a popular decoration for china, especially on the Fitzhugh wares, and those who could afford it could order porcelain emblazoned with a custom design, including initials or family crest.

The Anglo-American ceramics trade was just as vigorous. The well-to-do American consumer needed English goods and wanted the newer creamwares and pearl wares being made by Wedgwood and others. British merchants offered long-term credit to American merchants, who risked debt to give their customers what they wanted. Thus, home manufacture of quality ceramics and glass was discouraged as much by economics after the war as it was before the conflict.[41]

Just as the Chinese exporters had offered wares decorated with the American eagle, English entrepreneurs decorated their creamware and pearl ware with easily applied transfer prints of the eagle and with portraits of such Revolutionary heroes as Washington, Hancock, and Franklin. Thomas Turner's blue willow pottery, produced in the 1780s in designs similar to the Nanking pattern, was also popular in Philadelphia.[42] Staffordshire underglaze blue on white, which followed Oriental patterns as well, was popular in England between 1777 and 1788. Shards of this group appear in Park archaeological excavations and are quite frequently associated with use by the middle class.

The tea tables in Philadelphia's finest homes were laid with Chinese and English ceramics. The custom of setting a tea table returned after falling out of favor during the Revolution, almost as if it had never stopped. An unidentified house inventory for 1791

51-52. *Left:* This tapered body, or "lighthouse"-shaped, coffeepot descended in one Philadelphia family, possibly from the time of its importation from China, c. 1790-1810, to its gift to the Park in 1973. It is porcelain, with gilt and sepia-colored painted decoration. *Above:* All three of these objects of Chinese export porcelain descended in the family of Bishop William White. The plate dates to c. 1750-70; the pair of fruit baskets to c. 1800.

in the Philadelphia Municipal Archives serves as an indication of the important role the
tea table played as a social institution:

1 Tea table sett of pencilled china cream jug and top of sugar dish wanting	4 shillings	10 pence
1 Tea table sett of enamelled china with four cups of same figures but larger— one coffee cup & one saucer wanting	3 shillings	
10 saucers—7 teacups—5 coffee cups pencilled china	1 shilling	
2 Slop bowls, 1 cake plate, 1 tea pot & stand 1 cannister	3 shillings,	5 pence
1 red tea pott	1 shilling	
12 enamelled plates & 1 dish	18 shillings	9 pence
4 enamelled bowls	7 shillings	6 pence[43]

The inventory for 1788 of the household effects of John Penn, Jr., gives us an idea of
the range of ceramics available in Philadelphia:

> . . . China. 1 four quart and 1 three quart blue and white china bowls; 1
> quart and 1 pint china mug; a set of elegant Dresden tea china, contain-
> ing 2 tea pots and trays, 6 breakfast cup and 7 saucers, 5 coffee cups, 2
> tea canisters, 1 sugar dish and stand, 2 cream jugs, 2 slop bowls, 1 spoon
> tray; a set of dining china, containing 2 large tureens and dishes, 2 small
> ditto, 2 large deep salad dishes, 1 deep fish dish and strainer, 13 dishes
> sorted, 1 pudding dish cracked, 11 soup plates, 4 dozen and 3 flat ditto,
> 4 butter boats, 2 sugar dishes, 6 cups and saucers of English china . . . .[44]

One merchant, Joseph Stansbury, while not altogether notable as a person of historical significance, is of some interest for an understanding of post-Revolutionary ceramics and glass and because of the nature of his imports. Before the Revolution Stansbury had kept a store on Second Street above Christ Church where he dealt in a large
range of ceramics and glass.[45] A Loyalist, he was imprisoned in Philadelphia in 1780,
and upon release he removed to Canada.[46] By 1785, however, he was back in the city,
now operating a business on the west side of Front Street near Walnut Street, and the
next year offered a wide range of goods, apparently mostly English:

> . . . Imported in the last vessel from England, a general assortment of—
> China, Glass and Earthen Wares—Among which are—COMPLEAT tea
> table sets of enamelled china richly ornamented, Egyptian or black
> china tea pots, sugar dishes, and creamwares; elegant cane coloured
> ware; cut glass candlesticks, salts, mustard pots, cruets, decanters, and
> wine-glasses, single and double flint glass ware, a few quart tumblers
> and covers, Bohemian pint tumblers, balloon tumblers of several sizes
> and quart decanters, with a variety of common articles for country con-
> sumption. Country orders carefully packed, and executed at the short-
> est notion . . . .[47]

Later, in 1788, Stansbury imported from Liverpool "A GENERAL ASSORTMENT OF—
QUEENS WARE" along with cruet frames, plain and ornamented, and glass and china,
which he offered for sale at still another store, next to the George Tavern on Second
Street.[48]

XXI. This tin-glazed Bristol delft bowl, c. 1730, was excavated in 1972 from a well at Franklin Court in Philadelphia and evidence suggests an association with the Franklin family.

XXII. Showing the human side of one very drowsy English cleric, "The Vicar and Moses" was a popular religious subject in ceramics from the last quarter of the eighteenth century through the first half of the nineteenth. This figure by Ralph Wood of Burslem illustrates that the rector is oblivious to the vicar's lengthy sermon on Moses.

78

XXIII. Beautiful monochromatic English redware coffeepots much like this "Astbury-type" were introduced to the Philadelphia market between 1740 and 1760. The popularity of English redware can be attributed to its stylistic charm and to demand for fine English wares. The sale of such English products did not preclude the production of local utilitarian redwares.

XXIV. Mid-eighteenth-century English brass candlesticks. The swirl base candlestick was one rococo design which English brass founders developed independently. A more usual practice was to copy popular silver prototypes directly in brass. Candles were the most reliable source of light until the end of the eighteenth century, but they were expensive—a fact which forced most families to retire soon after dinner.

XXV. View of kitchen table in the Todd House. The cramped kitchen in the John and Dolley Todd House is typical of kitchens in many middle-class Philadelphia homes. A lack of cupboard space matches the general shortage of kitchen utensils which prevailed throughout the eighteenth century. Many utilitarian cookwares had to be imported, as were the brass "cullender," the comb-patterned redware dish, and the hourglass. Most furniture, on the other hand, was of local manufacture.

In the face of the flood of imports, occasional efforts were made to drum up support for American products. On July 4, 1788, Philadelphia celebrated the adoption of the Constitution of the United States by the ratification of the ninth state, New Hampshire, with a "Grand Federal Procession." The potters carried a flag

> . . . on which was neatly painted a kiln burning, and several men at work in different branches of the business. MOTTO—"The potter hath power over his clay." A four-wheeled carriage drawn by two horses, on which was a potters wheel, and men at work; a number of cups, bowls, mugs, &c. were made during the procession.[49]

Philadelphia potters continued to make utilitarian redwares, but the production of common pottery was becoming an expensive proposition in the center of the city, largely because of higher real estate prices. Sales of potteries for their value as pure real estate mounted and ordinary potters found it difficult to afford to buy or rent new facilities in Philadelphia. John Curtis, for instance, announced in the *Pennsylvania Packet* for July 8, 1790, that the partnership between himself and Jacob Root would be dissolved; he said, however, that he would continue to carry on the business at the "manufactory in

53-54. *Left:* One of 4000 objects that were in the collections of Independence Hall before the establishment of the Park in 1948, this flint wine glass is of English or Irish provenance. It is typical of glasswares imported by Philadelphians about 1790. *Above:* Two English blown wine glasses, c. 1800-20, and four Irish lead glass decanters, c. 1790, reflect the neoclassical style which changed both the form and decoration of virtually all newly-made furnishings after the American Revolution.

Front Street near the corner of Love Lane in Southwark." In 1789 the plight of the city potters had become so desperate that certain manufacturers and vendors of earthenware petitioned the Philadelphia Common Council ". . . praying that they may not be removed from their accustomed Stands . . . ."[50] The potters did not vanish overnight, but there was a pattern emerging—and the common potting industry would nearly disappear from Philadelphia proper by the last quarter of the nineteenth century. As the potting industry started to fade in Philadelphia, it continued to flourish in the outskirts of the city and in the surrounding counties where the cost of land, as well as the cost of many raw materials and foodstuffs, was lower.

The manufacture of glass in the Northern Liberties section of the city, along the Delaware River, provided Philadelphia with yet another industry and supplied some of the domestic glass needed for everyday use. Glass production continued to thrive in the Northern Liberties until the end of the nineteenth century.

Glass was also "imported" from other parts of the new nation. In 1785, the Amelung Glass Works, located near Frederick, Maryland, advertised a variety of glassworks and listed as agents, among others, "Messers Cox and Frazier, Philadelphia."[51] But glass imported from Europe still outsold domestic glass by far, just as it had at the beginning of the eighteenth century. The imported glass available at James Gallagher's store in Second Street in 1781 included:

> . . . single and double Flint, plain and cut. Gallon, half gallon, quart, pint and half pint Decanters. Flowered and plain Goblets, Mugs. Half gallon, quart, pint, half pint and gill and half gill Tumblers. Quart, pint and half pint, cut and stemmed, plain and labelled Punch, Grog, and Beer Glasses, with and without Covers. Cut, flowered and plain Wine Glasses, all sizes. Table Wash Basons, Cream Pots. Vinegar Cruets, Pepper and Mustard Pots and Salts. 11 by 9, 10 by 8, 9 by 7, 8 by 6, English, French and Spanish Window Glass, by the box or smaller quantity . . . .[52]

55. According to family tradition, Bishop William White once owned these two decanters. On the left is an example of a molded cut-glass type that was produced in England, c. 1810; and, on the right, a less ornate example made in either England or Ireland, c. 1780-1800.

The dependence on local goods which the Revolution had necessitated quickly ended along with the War. English and American merchants reestablished trade ties which, in many cases, had never been completely severed. Americans of this period proudly proclaimed themselves confident of their place alongside the other sovereign states of the world and of their status as a self-sufficient nation, but, with the possible exception of the American-China trade, this "independence" did not manifest itself in glass and ceramics: England's production of these goods and importation of them to her former colonies was greater than ever, and the production of local wares increasingly declined.

The development of Philadelphia glass and ceramics has been surveyed against the economic and political background from the time Penn wrote of the "fast fat Earth" until the beginning of the nineteenth century. Despite encouragement from the Quaker founders, those potters and artisans in glass who succeeded economically in the New World did so, primarily, as makers of utilitarian wares. A sizeable number of these American craftsmen were as active in purveying their goods as they were in producing them. Only in America, perhaps, could such artisans and merchants as Anthony Duché and Alexander Bartram rise so rapidly into the merchant class. Many of these same potters served as agents for the sale of fine English wares. Philadelphians able to afford such objects grew rapidly in number during the Colonial period. Only during periods of unusual political and economic stress, as in the pre-Revolutionary years and during the War itself, did they accept, if not encouarge, home production of porcelain and highly decorative wares. And when peace came again, they returned to English ways as well as to a passion for things Oriental.

Most of the craftsmen and merchants who lived and worked in Philadelphia in the seventeenth and eighteenth centuries are forgotten. Their shops, homes, and potteries were replaced with larger nineteenth-century dwellings and factories. The glass and china objects—many of them in fragments—remain, however, to tell us what they can.

56-57. *Left:* Olive and green-colored glass case bottles of c. 1790 fill a compartmented wooden chest of the same period. Once broken, common glass items of this sort provided local glassmakers with a ready supply of materials to be reused. *Above:* America's nationalism was exploited by enterprising English manufacturers of ceramics, primarily by decorating their wares with transfer prints of American scenes and symbols. Enoch Wood & Son of Burslem even utilized the American eagle as a ceramic mark, as illustrated on this hand-decorated pearl ware dish of c. 1818-46.

3. It Is Mete and Right So to Do: Metal Craftsmen in an Emerging City
by JANE BENTLEY KOLTER

A few streets filled with two-, three-, and four-story brick houses huddled along the banks of the Delaware River, resembling not in the least the "greene countrie town" of William Penn's agrarian dreams. By 1730 the pioneering phase was nearly over, and Philadelphians could begin to take a more leisurely view of the world. Their view was urban and remarkably English.

The city had been modeled on the areas of London where the middle class, or "middling sorts," had rebuilt after the Great Fire. Streets and alleys were a little wider, but, as in the capital, they were usually dirty. Rather than building on the western edge of town, the colonials had crowded everything together near the wharves of the Delaware, causing more than one tourist in the area to lament the loss of the greens and parks which Londoners found so convivial. Penn's plan had designated four public squares, and the long city lots were designed for orchards and gardens behind every house; but many settlers, with an eye to profit, not aesthetics, chose instead to fill their gardens with a row of smaller houses fronting on the alley.

In a reconstructed London, the colonists pursued their basically English lives. An unsettled country naturally demanded some adjustments, but Pennsylvanians ordered their routines to the new circumstances. The British mental framework of habits, customs, and traditions persisted, though slightly modified by contact with the Swedes, Dutch, and Palatines who also considered Penn's colony their home.

In Philadelphia, nearly everyone lived above his place of business. Shops or offices filled the front rooms, while artisans worked at their trades at the rear of the first floor or in a separate building in the small back yard. One of the two first-floor rooms was reserved, when possible, for a combined parlor and dining room. Kitchens were either in attached brick "back buildings" or, frequently, in the cellar. Many homes were so short on space that the master's bedchamber was the only spot left for entertaining. This could be fitted up for its dual role with a tea table and chairs drawn close to the fireplace

Opposite page: English hogscraper candlesticks (detail), c. 1730-
c. 1840. *See* fig. 69.

and with an imposing bed with hangings pushed against a wall.

Furniture ranged from serviceable to elegant. If it lagged a little behind the latest London mode, only a few colonists were inclined to complain. Wealthy Americans, like the merchant class of England, rarely attempted to set fashions in home furnishings. That was risky business while the established taste always remained unimpeachable, a wise investment, and a testimonial to traditional values and gentlemanly aspirations. Stylish dress, on the other hand, held more attraction for the newly affluent. Although clothing was very expensive in the eighteenth century, many Philadelphians succumbed to ostentation but still rejected the extremes of fashion. More than one visitor to the city remarked on a disposition to dress to the hilt:

> One sees the meanest city people—or particularly their wives and daughters—going about dressed according to the best and newest French taste. Wearing the most expensive silk, calico, and chintz, they go around daily with their hair dressed and powdered.[1]

Before fashion plates became available, changing tastes in women's clothing were generally transmitted by letter or by dressed wax dolls. The arrival of these fashion babies, "which, silent, give the law of the mode," was likely to be greeted with a squeeze of eager ladies clamoring to see the dolls that sat in state at local dressmaking establishments.[2] Very few people were exempt from the attraction of the *monde*. Even the Quakers, who consciously dressed more simply, only modified the extravagances of fashion by avoiding frills and wearing more sober clothing made in the finest fabrics they could obtain; the men eliminated showy buttons and lace cuffs, while women generally simplified the garment's lines. Peter Kalm, a Swedish scientist who chronicled his travels through the Delaware Valley, wryly mentioned that "although they censure all ornament I have seen [the ladies] wear just as gaudy shoes as other English women."[3]

Men's clothing and shoes were generally somewhat plainer, but sartorial impact might be achieved with lively, even shocking, color combinations, a novel waistcoat, or the indispensible buckle. Buckles for knees and shoes were made in several metals, fancy or plain. Gold, silver, and paste proclaimed the wearer a gentleman of some distinction, and many Philadelphians aspired to that station. Shoe buckles grew larger as the century progressed, and by the 1770s, they had achieved such magnificent proportions that the great playwright Richard Brinsley Sheridan was moved to complain:

> Formerly, indeed, the buckle was a sort of machine intended to keep on the shoe; but the case is now quite reversed, and the shoe is of no earthly use but to keep on the buckle.[4]

At the dining table, as in matters of dress, colonists followed the British lead. Early in the century, the main meal of the day was a dinner, served at midday, followed by a lighter supper about seven o'clock in the evening. In wealthier homes, the dinner hour was gradually pushed back; by the beginning of the nineteenth century, today's luncheon and dinner hours generally prevailed.

Where money was scarce, the staples were bread, grain porridge or gruel, and salt pork or fish, supplemented by whatever fruits and vegetables were cheap and easy to grow. On the other hand, when the financial situation was comfortable, no Philadelphian would hesitate to treat his family and guests to as much culinary elegance and volume as he could provide. Breakfasts were hearty; eggs and coffee were served with a full complement of meats, including beef, ham, stewed kidneys, or even salt fish. Small portions of everything that pleased were the rule. One could expect two or three courses at dinner, with a dessert of fruit and cheese. Wine was almost always served

58. Hand mirror, possibly American, c. 1800-25. The "vanity glass" provided multiple images on one side and a clear view of the user's face on the other. For some, the variety of views must have been pleasing, if less than useful.

59. Silver shoe buckles by Joseph, Jr., and Nathaniel Richardson, Philadelphia, c. 1785-90, and paste and enamel mounted silver shoe buckles, possibly English, late eighteenth century. Chaste, almost "Quakerish," silver shoe buckles on the left appealed to classical tastes of the late eighteenth century. Each is marked "I · NR" by Joseph, Jr., and Nathaniel Richardson. When the brothers dissolved their partnership in 1790, their shop inventory listed "94 pair Silver Shoe Buckles"—an indication of continuing popularity. The paste buckles are imports of an earlier period.

60. Pewter dish and drainer by Samuel Ellis, London, 1721-65. Many Americans ordered "long" or oval dishes from English pewterers since few American pewterers seemed to produce these serving pieces. Only one American oval dish has come to light (illustrated in Charles F. Montgomery, *A History of American Pewter,* p. 140).

throughout the meal, causing numerous interruptions for toasts or "drinking of healths." A Frenchman visiting in the 1780s grumbled that the toasting made dinners "extremely long." More appalling to him were the table settings found in the new country:

> A table in the American style would seem extraordinary in France. The table is covered with a cloth, which also serves for napkins; it is ordinarily large enough to overflow on all sides, and each one wipes in front of himself (unhappily, they do not change it very often).[5]

The amount of food served in wealthier homes seems astonishing. A family dinner might consist only of "a rump of beef, apple pie and vegetables," but on company occasions the victuals were more elaborate: "First rock fish, next mock turtle, ducks, ham and boiled turkey, with plenty of vegetables, and after these were removed, we had floating island, several kinds of pies with oranges and preserves."[6] This order and succession, with slight variation, had served wealthy Englishmen in their town and country residences since the end of the Puritan regime. Cookery books, while less than illuminating on recipes and preparation, were very decided in their instructions for serving. Every season had its appropriate dishes for each course, and drawings of a well-laid table, with the proper placement of main and side dishes, accompanied most books.

61-62 .*Left:* Iron coffee mill, "Bruerton Warranted 6c," probably English, nineteenth century. Life without Mr. Coffee was a trial. Whole coffee beans were purchased by the pound, then roasted in a hand-turned roaster over the kitchen fire. A quick grinding just before brewing guaranteed a fresh cup; nevertheless, the coffee frequently resembled mud. *Above:* Iron-and-brass ladle marked "I. WITMAN," probably Reading, Pennsylvania, early nineteenth century, with bone-handled steel cutlery, marked "MARSHES & SHEPHERD," Sheffield, England, c. 1825-45. Craftsmen sometimes marked their wares as a guarantee of quality. More often the marks served as advertising devices. While cooking or dining, one was constantly reminded that I. Witman made the ladle and Marshes & Shepherd, an English firm, furnished the cutlery.

Books printed fifty years apart were likely to prescribe exactly the same seasonal dishes and placement, indicating either a severe case of literary piracy or an ingrained monotony in English eating habits.

The pies, roasts, and breads served in many Philadelphia households came from a nearby bake shop or confectioner's. Both custom and tiny kitchens without ovens had combined in Philadelphia, as in London, to make these bake houses an expected element of the city scene. Early in the morning the housewife would stop at the baker's, bringing her pies and roasts to be cooked alongside the bakery products.

Needless to say, even with the baker's help, the daily preparation of meals was a far more time-consuming task in the eighteenth century than it is today. The housewife, or her cook, not only had to content with the whim or mischance at the bake shop, but she also had to struggle with reluctant fires and expensive fuel. She had vague cookbooks, or none at all; there was little storage space; and the selection of cooking equipment was extremely limited. Most homes would contain one or two large iron pots, a kettle or two —preferably of copper—and a few miscellaneous skillets, gridirons, toasters, and saucepans. Most of the pots and pans were imported, as mercantile policy dictated, but some of the wrought- and cast-iron utensils were fashioned in the colonies. Local blacksmiths could bend their creative impulses to these utilitarian objects without violating anything more serious than the spirit of the Navigation Acts.

63-64. *Left:* Steel chopper, American, c. 1796. Hector St. Jean de Crèvecoeur remarked that Americans ". . . habitually prefer the useful to the beautiful . . . ," which failed to account for little embellishments which Pennsylvanians, especially, were prone to add to functional objects. Even vegetable choppers did not escape the decorator's hand. *Above:* Wrought-iron toaster, probably Pennsylvania, last quarter eighteenth century. Most of the utilitarian wrought iron from Pennsylvania shows a mingling of Germanic and English design vocabularies. It departs from strictly English traditions and, like the toaster, reflects the process of a culture unconsciously moving toward a unique synthesis of expression.

Marketing, if not a form of entertainment, was a lively element of urban social life. Most housewives, or their servants, were out at least twice weekly in one of the city's two market areas, where meeting friends and enjoying some gossip seemed as much a part of the market complex as buying and selling. Here was a neutral meeting ground which loosened constraints and opened channels of communication between artisans, merchants, and farmers—who equally depended upon the market for their livelihood. Here, too, the effects of English mercantile policy were readily noticed and often discussed. Restrictions imposed on trade became increasingly irritating as Philadelphia's business activities expanded, and this irritant proved to be a major agent in the transformation of a loosely-knit community of dependent colonials into a cohesive group of Pennsylvanians. In a sense, the market bred those men who finally opposed with violence all British attempts to meddle with their trade.

Peter Kalm recognized Philadelphia as a city of merchants when he visited Penn's town in the 1750s. He reported that "England supplies almost all stuffs and articles which are wanted here," but he warned even then that Britain's mercantile system was crumbling. ". . . It is much to be feared that the trade of Philadelphia and all the English colonies will rather decrease than increase . . . [;] the town not only furnishes most of the inhabitants of Pennsylvania with the goods they want, but several inhabitants of New Jersey come every day to trade."[7]

Indeed, Philadelphia served an increasingly wide area with the "conveniences and necessaries" of the eighteenth century. Though no group had a monopoly on trade in the city, Quakers certainly seemed to dominate it. Penn encouraged English Friends to settle in Pennsylvania, but most of these immigrants were relatively poor artisans and farmers who had little effect on the economic prospects of the colony. The merchant families who arrived at the beginning of the eighteenth century generally came from other British colonies in the West Indies. These Friends brought mercantile connections and, as William Fishbourne chronicled in 1739, "quantities of coined silver and gold."[8] The triangle trade among various English colonies and the mother country, which these immigrants established, together with an infusion of cash, assured Philadelphia's success as an entreprenurial center supreme in the New World and envied in the Old. Moreover, these wealthy families arrived with the values and the highly developed tastes of a rising and increasingly powerful middle class. In effect, they helped accelerate a change, begun in Europe with the Reformation, toward the materially-oriented society and capitalistic economy which would flourish in America.

What distinctions there were between "monetary" aristocrats and immigrant artisans were initially blurred by day-to-day problems of living in the New World. The success of each depended upon the success of the community as a whole. Labor was in short supply, so tradesmen and laborers were paid considerably more than they had earned in Europe. Foodstuffs and provisions could be had "very cheap."[9] Land, too, was available at a reasonable price. Hundreds of unclaimed acres and Penn's liberal policies made it possible for many immigrants, even indentured servants, to become landowners. Moreover, minimal voting requirements guaranteed that some measure of participation in the colony's government was within reach of any freeman who met the two-year residency requirement and had accumulated either 50 acres or £50 in personal property.[10] These advantages gave Philadelphia artisans a rank in society which few in the Old World could hope to equal.

If necessity conferred a certain dignity to the craftsman, other aspects of a new order combined to further equalize the emerging Pennsylvania society. Economic success insured a degree of respectability not usually achieved in England or the Continent, where the traditions of a hierarchical society were more ingrained. Belief in the established

65-67. *Above (left):* Hickory splint market basket, American, nineteenth century. Food spoiled quickly, and storage was a problem in small kitchens, making frequent shopping trips for provisions a necessity. Briggs's *New Art of London Cookery* recommended that "You must be particularly careful in the choice of pork, for when it is measly it is very dangerous . . . ." Most cook books gave explicit instructions for choosing fresh meats, and some detailed means to preserve them in crocks, like the assorted examples of American stoneware crocks shown here. *Left:* Silvered-brass wall-light or sconce, English, c. 1705-15. Cast brass was often silver coated, using mercury to float a thin layer of precious metal over the brass. This process was exceptionally deadly to craftsmen, who breathed vaporized mercury given off when the piece was heated to deposit the silver. *Above:* Walnut ballot box, Delaware Valley, eighteenth century. William Penn made his original *Frame of Government* (1682) short and to the point. He assumed that everyone understood the ground rules of voting, since they were based on centuries of English precedent. He wrote: "For particular Frames and Models, it will become one to say little; and comperatively I will say nothing." Penn only required that the Freemen "chuse" a Provincial Council and "yearly chuse members to serve in a General Assembly as their Representatives." The Constitution of 1776 was more specific: "The members of the House of Representatives shall be chosen annually by ballot . . . ."

order certainly persisted in America, but two elements were missing—the hereditary nobility and a church dedicated to preserving the status quo. The total lack of a state church in Penn's colony further encouraged social mobility.

The trappings of the upper class, land and material possessions, were accessible to most colonists, and mobility was a fact of life. Bolstered by prospects, if not by cold cash, Philadelphians, and especially the artisans, embraced John Locke's theories of property rights and liberty. Locke's assertions—that common citizens had legitimate claims to ownership of property and to freedoms which the nobility had secured in the Magna Charta—were startlingly novel in the seventeenth century. In the next century they formed the basic tenets of English Whig philosophy, a philosophy which flourished in the New World. When Whig radicalism clashed with trade restrictions created by mercantile policy, seeds for the revolution were sown.

In spite of all the freedom colonial life promised, a move to America had its negative side. However much the artisans earned, they paid higher prices for imported items which they could not grow, commandeer, or fashion themselves. There was a scarcity of specie or any regulated form of money, so much of their business had to be conducted through bookkeeping or in the awkward medium of barter. Housing was expensive and in short supply. Many craftsmen were forced to rent one of the combined shops and dwellings near the marketplace, sometimes because they could not afford to buy a house, or, more frequently, because a cabal of merchants had purchased and improved the area's lots as income-producing properties.[11]

The guild system which some artisans left Europe to escape could still haunt them from across the Atlantic. The Worshipful Company of Pewterers in England, for example, could refuse reinstatement to any pewterer who returned from abroad.[12] Moreover,

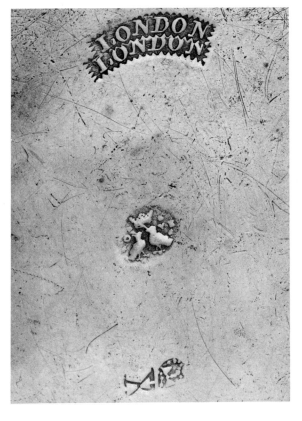

68. "LOVE" touchmark and "LONDON" marks on pewter basin, Philadelphia, last half eighteenth century. London's Worshipful Company of Pewterers ruled that guild members working outside the capital could not stamp "LONDON" on their wares, but "LONDON" was struck in spite of all restrictions. Rural craftsmen knew that they could usually escape detection; in America, impunity was assured. A group of enterprising Philadelphia pewterers probably used these marks during the last half of the eighteenth century.

this guild acquired a strangle hold on the pewterer's raw materials when it convinced the Board of Trade to sponsor several measures to protect the English craft: export of tin was greatly restricted; excise on worked pewter was eliminated; and the Company was granted an exclusive patent on the pewter alloy.[13] Similar legal barriers to colonial manufacture played havoc with the other crafts.

The mercantile policy, in effect, forced the American artisans to diversify. Many combined their craft activity with an import business, selling a variety of English products alongside those of their own shops. Others turned to an additional trade, sometimes working in two or three related materials. Whichever solution they chose, they removed themselves from the traditional craft patterns established in the Old World—a step, in fact, away from the industrial revolution with its narrowing of specialties, but a step which would draw them further into the value system and conservative interests of the merchant community.

In America, the ascent through the ranks of the bourgeoisie was likely to be rapid. Aspirations were not dampened by traditional social structure, and a tendency toward display was inflamed by the heady atmosphere of a city just beginning to draw on its cloak of gentility. Franklin whimsically described this situation in his own home:

> Our Table was plain and simple, our Furniture of the cheapest. For instance, my Breakfast was a long time Bread and Milk, (no Tea) and I ate

69. Group of English hogscraper candlesticks, from c. 1730-c. 1840. Hogscraper candlesticks appealed to the miserly. The push-up handle squeezed the last ounce of use from a candle stub. This feature was particularly appreciated in England, where candle taxes were strictly enforced.

it out of a two-penny earthen Porringer with a Pewter Spoon. But mark how Luxury will enter Families, and make a Progress, in Spite of Principle. Being call'd one Morning to Breakfast, I found it in a China Bowl with a Spoon of Silver. They had been bought for me without my Knowledge by my Wife, and had cost the enormous Sum of three and twenty Shillings, for which she had no other Excuse or Apology to make, but that she thought her Husband deserv'd a Silver Spoon and China Bowl as well as any of his Neighbors.[14]

By the 1730s, when the Franklins were having this domestic crisis, Philadelphia had developed a sophisticated community of consumers. Advertisements in the city's newspapers appealed to discriminating tastes:

To all Lovers of Decency, Neatness, and
TEA-TABLE DECORUM.

JUST arrived from London, *all Sizes of the best White-metal Pewter Tea-Pots; likewise Tea-Stands, Cream Sauce-Pans, Tea-Spoons, and other Curiosities; all of which are the newest Fashion, and so very neat, as not easily to be distuinguish'd from Silver, either by the Workmanship or Colour; and will be sold very* Cheap, *by* Retail, *at Mr. Stone's, next Door to Mr. Samuel Par's in Front-Street, Philadelphia, by the Importer* JOHN SACHEVERELL.[15]

Sacheverell's droll appeal to snobbery was one of many which peppered the Philadelphia newspapers, but he catered more explicitly to those who wanted ostentation. Most merchants straightforwardly listed fabrics, tools, and several sorts of utilitarian metalwares.

Pewter, however, was a great leveler. In spite of its expense, 2s. 8d. for a tankard, or the equal of a day's earnings for a skilled craftsman, pewter appeared in homes of every economic station.[16] The metal had distinct advantages: it was practically unbreakable; it could be easily cleaned; it could be melted down and remade whenever fashions changed or the piece was damaged; finally, it was a decorative asset and a substitute for silver on shelves and cupboards. From another viewpoint, that of the important merchant, it was seen as a ship's ballast which did not spoil or corrode too much and, more pertinently, as a large profit.

Many British pewterers enjoyed a lively American trade. As early as 1697 pewter shipments valued at over £3,000 were sent to the colonies.[17] By the 1740s, nearly £8,000 worth of pewter arrived annually in American ports.[18] Some of the imported forms were rarely or never made in the colonies. American pewterers were probably unwilling to compete with their English counterparts for the few customers who needed a specialized form. Instead they tended to produce those conservatively-styled necessities which were in great demand. Simpler pewter was profitable and easier to produce. Since every article was made of one or more cast pieces, the pewterer could reduce the number of molds he had to fashion by eliminating frills and by limiting himself to the more functional vessels.

At first, much of the pewterers' business was in reworking old pewter and repairing damaged pieces, a service Simon Wyer obligingly offered in an issue of the *Pennsylvania Gazette* of 1746:

all sorts of old pewter dishes and plates, &c. that by long use or neglect of servants are batter'd, bruised, melted or damaged, shall be mended (if possible) neat and cheap.[19]

On the other hand, a craftsman with capital to spare would opt for a commercial venture, as Thomas Biles (Byles) seems to have done:

> *Just Imported from London . . . and to be sold very*
> *cheap by Wholesale or Retail, three Doors be-*
> *low the Post-Office, in Market Street.*
> All Sorts of Pewter, Hard Metal and
> common, Brass, Copper and Tin-ware of all Sorts;
> where is also given the highest Price in Cash, for any
> Quantity of Old Pewter, Copper or Brass, by
>
> THOMAS BILES.[20]

70. Pewter nursing bottle, funnel, and strainer, probably English, late eighteenth-early nineteenth century. While Thomas Byles's inventory, made in 1771 when the Philadelphia pewterer died, listed "15 Sucking bottles and 1 funnel," Byles himself may have imported some of his stock for resale.

71. Pewter plate by Thomas Byles, probably Philadelphia, 1738-71. Much "Batter'd and bruised," this pewter plate by Thomas Byles nonetheless survives. Philadelphians seemed to prefer large plates. This measures a comfortable nine inches in diameter.

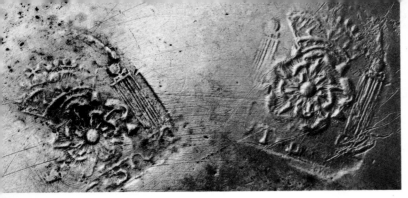

72. Byles's marks on the back of the plate illustrated on the previous page. Byles consciously adopted the mark which London pewterers had squabbled over since 1564—when the crowned Tudor rose was declared off limits for common use. A few craftsmen were granted special patents to strike the motif, but this was an accolade for quality workmanship. By the eighteenth century, the London Company of Pewterers relaxed its control of the use of touchmarks. The craft was too widespread for the guildhall to regulate.

73. Group of pewter inkstands, probably English, from c. 1740-c. 1870. While serving as chaplain to Congress during the Revolution, Reverend William White quipped, "You have been treating yourselves, I perceive, to new inkstands." The wry reply was, "Yes, and private credit had to be pledged for the payment."

Thomas Byles, a Philadelphia pewterer whose name was variously spelled, arrived in the Quaker City by 1738. In that year he purchased property on High Street, also called Market Street. Byles came from the Boston area, and, in a sort of pilgrim's progress, he moved to Newport, Rhode Island, then migrated south to Philadelphia. His pewter business seems to have been extremely successful, for when he died in 1771 Benjamin Harbeson and William Will took an inventory of his shop which was valued at more than £1500.[21] There were hundreds of tools and nearly 1200 pounds of brass molds listed in this shop inventory. The molds, particularly, represent the basic livelihood of the pewterer. The inventory is also a revealing document of those pewter forms which Philadelphians used in their homes and businesses. However commonplace it is to say that there were purchasers for everything that Byles sold, this fact, nevertheless, points out the direct relationship between stock listed in a business inventory and the domestic scene of the eighteenth century. Byles carried hundreds of items for the household.

If the housewife was well supplied, the man of business was not neglected by pewterers or by silversmiths. Byles had a variety of writing accessories, including, in lead, the

XXVI. *Opposite:* View of the kitchen bedchamber at the Todd House. Not every household could boast a tall-post bed complete with textile bed hangings. When these luxuries were present, they were usually reserved for the master's bedchamber—often the best room in the house. Simple, painted low-post beds generally served the less-well-to-do, transients, children, and servants.

XXVII. *Above:* Silver coffeepot by William Hollingshead, Philadelphia, c. 1780-85. Income received from the "incomparable chocolate and mustard works" owned by Mary Crathorne's family provided her with an ample dowry when she married John Montgomery in November, 1785. She must have acquired this silver coffeepot about that time, perhaps as a betrothal gift. It is engraved with script initials, "*MC,*" on one side. Though the form is conservative, a pineapple finial proclaims the newest Federal fashion.

XXVIII. *Left:* Silver inkstand by John White, London, 1730/31 and silver taperjack by John Langford, II, and John Sebille, 1765/66. American silversmiths did not reap all the benefits of the quest for gentility; a great deal of silver was imported from England. At mid-century, a secretary or desk equipped in the most modern taste was likely to boast English silver accessories.

XXIX. *Above:* Cowhide-covered trunk by James Anderson, Philadelphia, c. 1795. James Anderson labeled his cowhide-covered trunk discursively, but, then, he plied a number of trades. As "Saddler, Harness-Maker, and Trunk-Maker," he could provide all sorts of riding accoutrements and traveling cases. He closed his list of products with the statement that "he flatters himself, from the execution of his work, and the quality of the materials, he shall be able to give his employers the greatest satisfaction. *Philadelphia;* April 24, 1795." Even the label printer had his bid at advertising: "PRINTED BY WRIGLEY & BERRIMAN, NO. 149, CHESTNUT-STREET."

XXX. *Left:* Brass andirons, American or possibly English, c. 1765-85. Daniel King offered "curious . . . Brass Fier Dogs neater and more to Order than any yet made on the continent" in the *Pennsylvania Chronicle* of April 20, 1767. Certainly his reference to the classical taste, which England was just adopting, is among the earliest made by any American craftsman. These Doric andirons, which may be American, seem to be a close equal of the expensive Corinthian models King made for John Cadwalader in 1770. Each stop flute, here, was cast separately and is removable.

XXXI. *Top:* Japanned wood jewel casket, English or French, c. 1800-14. In the early years of the republic, classical decoration appeared everywhere. The self-reliance fostered by a successful revolution found an outlet in every area of the decorative arts. Even jewelry cases reflected this phenomenon. Ironically, Americans imported their tastes and many of their accessories from England and France, where the same fashion reigned without moral imperatives. "Joseph Anthony, Philadelphia silver-smith, and son," as the label records, imported this particular japanned wood casket and sold it from their High Street shop, sometime between 1811 and 1814.

XXXII. *Above:* Painted and stenciled bellows by Eckstein and Richardson, Philadel-phia, 1819-23. Bellows and brushmakers John Eckstein and Ross Richardson made bellows to suit the several tastes and pocketbooks of Philadelphians. In 1819, they advertised that their newly-formed partnership could supply ". . . common bellows of various sizes; Bird-eye, curled Maple, Mahogany, Cherry, Satin-Wood . . . and a varie-ty of lower priced Parlour Bellows" similar to this painted and stenciled pair.

ubiquitous office inkstand. Strictly utilitarian, the "office" or "treasury" inkstand was a small masterpiece of organization, and it was common enough to become symbolic of commmercial and public life, appearing in a number of period portraits and prints as an indication of the sitter's profession.

The form of the inkstand is one of those which is so appropriate and so adaptable that it continued unchanged through several revolutions of fashion. However, while such everyday accessories of business were conservative and barely affected by the vagaries of style, ceremonial pieces, which graced the desks of wealthy men and rulers, were usually made in the newest taste. What governor, or even gentleman, would wish to commit anything to paper unless his words were backed by the weight of silver and fashion, if not that of authority? So in 1752, the Pennsylvania Assembly invested over £25 in a silver inkstand made by Philip Syng, Jr.—an early and deliberate appeal to the authority of silver.

Pewter and silver carried the same sort of social authority at the tea table. The shining accoutrements proclaimed their owners men of taste and discrimination, and, incidentally, displayed whatever wealth a family could boast. The need for these implements developed quickly, for the American predilection for hot drinks was already well remarked by the 1750s.[22] Although tea, coffee, and chocolate were novelties, even in England, at the beginning of the century, fifty years later a tourist in America would comment that the beverages

> are so general as to be found in the most remote cabins, if not for daily
> use, yet for visitors, [are] mixed with muscovado, or raw sugar.[23]

Visitors, tea, and the leisure to enjoy both were not that rare in many Philadelphia homes by mid-century. Indentured servants and slaves were available to minimize labor in well-circumstanced homes, so some were able to enjoy carelessly the time-consuming ritual which surrounded tea and coffee. Families of smaller means took tea with less formality. In any case, this social ceremony generated a need for a whole spectrum of new utensils which pewterers and silversmiths quickly exploited.

American silver and pewter mimicked the British middle-class styles but lagged somewhat behind. This hiatus in the transmission of the latest London fashions was greater in the first half of the century, and it was most noticeable in silver. By the 1750s, the gap had considerably narrowed; after the war for independence, it practically ceased to exist. Communication between the Old and the New Worlds had improved dramatically in three-quarters of a century, and those who could afford silver, particularly, were demanding that their trophies equal the standards set by affluent English merchants. As Graham Hood explains in *American Silver: A History of Style,* the wealthiest urban Americans saw themselves as counterparts of these London merchants, and they preferred the same solid evidence of their status. Suburbanites, like those along the Schuylkill banks, might just as easily identify with the prosperous country squire. Neither English group was a leader in silver fashions, and, generally speaking, they tested and approved every style before Americans adopted it. In Philadelphia, especially, conservatism reigned. Both the Friends who commissioned silver and those who worked it tended to prefer the same broad, linear elements which made Philadelphia furniture so distinctive. The English models were followed plainly, for silversmiths were obliged to cater to entrenched tastes which they found in the colonies.[24]

Several Philadelphia silversmiths, among them Joseph Richardson and his family, did their own importing of London silver. They had factors, or English business representatives, and sold the English wares at a price which was probably slightly higher than that asked for their own work. English marks were, after all, a guarantee of all that was prop-

74-76. *Above (left):* Tin chocolate pot, probably American, c. 1780-1840. The conical or "lighthouse" shape was a common one for coffee and chocolate pots. It was easy to make with soldered sheet metal. Chocolate pots usually had the handle at right angles to the spout and always had a hole in the top for the "chocolate mill," a rod used to stir the loose chocolate shavings when pouring. *Above:* Pewter teapot by Samuel Ellis, London, 1721-65. Samuel Ellis produced pewter teapots with and without hoofed feet. Apparently, Philadelphians preferred the legless versions, for Daniel Wister, an area merchant, specifically asked John Townsend, his main supplier of English pewter, to send this type. Philadelphia pewterers William Will and Cornelius Bradford made similar teapots in the Queen Anne style, with and without legs. *Left:* Mid-eighteenth-century English brass candlesticks. Brass and silver shared the same design sources Thomas Chippendale tapped for furniture. Birmingham brass manufactories extended their market by circulating unmarked trade catalogues which found their way to American merchants. These catalogues and other pattern books provided inspiration for colonial silversmiths adopting London styles.

er. The high favor which the rococo coffeepot enjoyed in Philadelphia is one case in point of the influence of imports on the local market. Richardson, and later his sons, imported several single- and double-bellied coffeepots each year, specifically requesting these styles from 1759 to 1773.[25] At the same time, they were also producing their American counterparts in the Richardson workshop.

Other silversmiths improvised on the same visual theme. Philip Syng, Jr., Joseph Lownes, and William Hollingshead are a few of the well-known Philadelphia silversmiths who produced surprisingly similar pieces. The rococo pots were not only what might be called a stock item for area silversmiths, but these pots would also prove to be a popular form for a number of years. Throughout the last half of the eighteenth century, this style became a basic idiom, surviving long after it had been supplanted with neoclassical designs in England. Philadelphia craftsmen experimented with the newest fashions in ornament, but they left the basic lines of the pieces unchanged; in fact, bellied coffeepots were almost as persistent as the office inkstand. Great-granddaughters of the earliest buyers might have purchased a very similar coffeepot from a Philadelphia firm in the 1840s.[26]

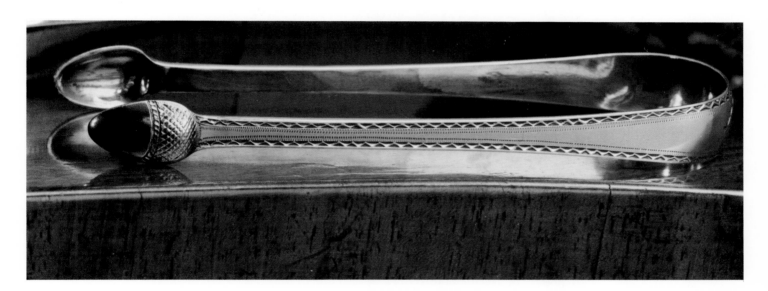

77. Silver sugar tongs by Joseph Richardson, Jr., Philadelphia, c. 1790. Household inventories of the 1790s indicate that tea was no longer the sole property of the wealthy. Ordinary people—blacksmiths, potters, and tailors—could and did serve tea. They might offer it with a jumble of earthenware, pewter, and china serving pieces, but serve it they did. Silver teaspoons or sugar tongs added elegance at an affordable price. This pair by Joseph Richardson, Jr., was made soon after the partnership with his brother Nathaniel was dissolved in 1790.

William Hollingshead created several rococo pots which are variants of the single-bellied example (c. 1785), seen in plate XXVII. Hollingshead is one of those Philadelphia artisans known mainly through extant examples of their work. In point of fact, all that is truly certain about him is that he worked in the Quaker City from about 1754 until 1785.[27] He was probably related to a family of Quaker clockmakers in Burlington, New Jersey—a city with strong ties to the Philadelphia community.[28] Hollingshead's silver apparently needed no advertisement, for he only used the newspapers to announce "a Plantation" in Kensington to let and, in 1774, he offered his fellow craftsmen "A Good Assortment of Black Lead Crucibles, made by . . . Jackson, in Philadelphia, and found to be much better than any imported."[29]

Evidently Hollingshead supported the home industry movement. On the other hand, either he objected to local non-importation agreements, or more probably, he did not trade in London silver. Unlike Philip Syng Jr., and Joseph Richardson, he was not among the Philadelphia firms and craftsmen who signed the Non-Importation Agreement of 1765 or who were listed on a broadside— . . . *to the Merchants and Manufacturers of Great Britain*—announcing the second trial of non-importation. Hollingshead's 1774 tax assessment shows that the silversmith was reasonably prosperous. Moreover, he took his civic duties seriously, as did many craftsmen, and served on at least two juries between 1773 and 1775.[30]

Hollingshead and the Richardsons received a great deal of business from the area Quakers. Kalm remarked that the church members "cling together very close . . . and the more well-to-do employ only Quaker artisans, if they can be found."[31] Many Friends with strict interpretations of the creed's simplicity found a tendency "to outward show and greatness"[32] disturbing. Nevertheless, even among Friends, silver became more common as the century advanced and wealth accumulated. It was, after all, a wise investment. Currency fluctuated wildly and was easily stolen. Pieces of plate, as silver was called, were easily convertible if cash was direly needed and were more easily identified.

Philip Syng, Jr., another silversmith and close associate of Benjamin Franklin, also profited from the local demand. Today, however, his mark on the whole spectrum of Philadelphia life seems more important than the marks which he left on silver. Syng was born in Ireland and immigrated with his parents, Philip and Alicia Murdock Syng, in 1714. The family arrived in Philadelphia, and the elder Syng set up in the goldsmith's business "near the Market Place."[33] The younger Syng, as was characteristic of many of the craftsmen or "mechanicks," became involved in nearly every aspect of the greater Philadelphia community. He was an original member of Franklin's Junto and assisted Franklin with several particulars of the electrical experiments of the 1740s. He served on the vestry of Christ Church, was a founding member and director of the Library Company of Philadelphia, acted as a city warden and as a trustee of the College and Academy of Philadelphia. Syng was also one of the directors of the Philadelphia Contributionship Insurance Company, a treasurer of the City and County of Philadelphia for over ten years, and still managed to enjoy some sort of family life with his wife, Elizabeth, and twenty-one children.[34]

Perhaps it was through the Library Company of Philadelphia that Lynford Lardner became acquainted with Philip Syng, Jr. Lardner, the attorney to the Penns, arrived in 1740 and over the next few years, commissioned several pieces of silver from Syng.[35] Both the lawyer and the silversmith served as directors of the Library Company at various times, where each was working toward the same end—providing the community with the means to knowledge.[36]

The Library Company was one of the Philadelphia organizations where all sorts of men mixed freely, with little concern for wealth or self-perceived status. Artisans, including Franklin and Syng, were instrumental in founding the library, but the unqualified support of several wealthy merchants helped it to grow rapidly. The corporate library they developed provided Philadelphians with access to the standard references and the more recent publications in many fields. Other library companies, founded about the same time, and the personal libraries of wealthy men which were occasional-

78-80. *Above:* Silver half-pint cann by Philip Syng, Jr., Philadelphia, 1749-61. When Lynford Lardner married Elizabeth Branson in October of 1749, she wore a wedding ring made by Philip Syng which Lardner recorded in his manuscript account book. Syng also made a half-pint cann, engraved with the Lardner-Branson arms, sometime before Elizabeth's death in 1769. Lardner, an attorney to the Penns, occupied an important place in the social hierarchy of the colony. *Above (right):* Hickory splint basket, probably American, possibly nineteenth century, with oak stocking stretchers, American, late eighteenth or early nineteenth century. Large families and lots of laundry are unfortunate corollaries. Wood forms, or stocking driers, were made in every size to keep knit stockings from shrinking—another thrifty device which answered Franklin's admonition to "waste not, want not." *Right:* Stick barometer and mahogany case, labeled "Printed and Sold by John Saddler, Liverpool," England, mid-eighteenth century. With all their sophisticated equipment, today's meteorologists often fail to predict tomorrow's weather. The eighteenth-century barometer had a similar track record, but never told jokes.

ly opened to interested "mechanicks," served a generally literate community.[37]

Philadelphians shared that spirit of inquiry so characteristic of the eighteenth century. They hoped to distill the mysteries of nature into practical knowledge by applying what is now called the scientific method. The keys to this method were patient observation and careful analysis of observed phenomena; from this, one could generate theories which further experiment would prove or disprove. This system appealed to Philadelphians, who had enough wealth and curiosity to underwrite experiments. Moreover, they saw their surroundings and, more importantly, their situations as circumstances which could be explained, reasoned through, and controlled. Their spirit of exploration was directed at any possible object—the weather, indigenous plants, animals and people —and towards the movements of the heavens. Philadelphia's two philosophical societies encouraged the members to expand the boundaries of useful knowledge. Spurred by the inquiring climate of the age and of the city, gentlemen and artisans alike contributed to the aim.

Not every men's club and society was directed towards the pursuit of knowledge. Numerous groups met for purely social reasons and, as in London, flourished in the city's taverns and coffeehouses. Here men could discuss trade and politics, "feast upon Phyladelphia Beer and Porter," while putting down "ten thousand delicacies."[38] Some clubs met in private homes, and at least one built a refuge where, having slipped the

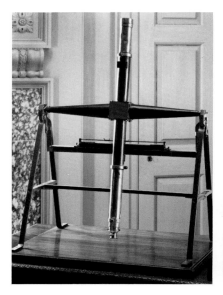 

81-82. *Above (left):* Astronomical transit instrument, by John Bird, London, c. 1760. The transit of Venus across the sun piqued the curiosity of scientifically-inclined Philadelphians. Proprietor-Governor Thomas Penn supplied an instrument—also called a transit—to observe this phenomenon. A wooden platform was erected in the State House Square and manned by members of the American Philosophical Society. John Bird, official instrument maker for the observatory at Greenwich, England, made this transit, reportedly used on that occasion and later used to establish Philadelphia's mean time. Perhaps that was when the transit was mounted in the tower of Independence Hall, where it was discovered in 1914. *Above (right):* Mahogany tall-post bed, probably English, c. 1770. The high water table caused many problems for Philadelphia residents. Those who could not leave the city for the summer usually slept behind gauze curtains to escape bloodthirsty bugs, while those who did adjourn to country houses along the Schuylkill River often kept their windows closed to avoid "miasmas" brought on by the damp night air.

domestic leash for an evening, the members could amuse themselves by cooking their freshly caught fish. Silversmiths John Leacock and Philip Syng, Jr., were among those Philadelphians who made up the Fishing Company of the Colony of Schuylkill.[39] The culinary traditions begun in 1732 continue today, and the deadliest, perhaps, is the infamous "Fish House punch."

Punch in all its several variations was the hospitable offering of the eighteenth and early nineteenth centuries. A little lemon, some sugar, wine, rum, and hot water were standard ingredients, or:

> One sour,
> Two sweet,
> Four strong,
> And eight weak,[40]

mixed in a burnt china punchbowl. Several sorts of imported wines were offered in the homes of the wealthy. Ratafia, an almond-flavored liqueur, was a favorite of the ladies. Beer and cider were used by everyone, rich and poor.

Anything, it seems, was preferable to water. Philadelphians shared the Englishman's distrust of the liquid—and well they might. The city's water system was less than perfect. Several community pumps were available on every block, but a fire in the neighborhood could exhaust them.[41] Some households had private wells in the yard, all located perilously near the "necessary." Moreover, the city was bounded by two rivers and had a fairly high water table. A few day's rain would create a sodden swamp in every low spot in the city. On the whole, there was probably good reason for the popularity of beer and cider.

Just as alcoholic potations were the most common beverages of the eighteenth century, so the ritual of drinking served as a common denominator in certain other ways. Taverns were forums where colonists discussed moral and political philosophy. Through casual associations formed over the tankard, merchants, artisans and laborers explored common interests and beliefs. Initially, all agreed that they were virtuous members, though at a distance, of the English mixed government. They accepted the delicate balance of order and liberty which John Locke's contractual theory had popularized, but soon they found that colonial interests were overlooked, even ignored, by policymakers in England. The contract was failing.

While they enjoyed greater freedom in their loosely-structured colonial society, Americans had little means to participate in political decisions which affected them. They were excluded, by distance and design, from the system of implicit checks and balances which a two-house Parliament and monarchy exerted. This clashing of personal liberty and imposed order became a breeding ground for dissension which gradually eroded British authority, and measures of control became more and more oppressive.

Some sought to achieve Parliamentary recognition of their rights as citizens and, also, their economic power by adopting a policy of non-importation, but the mention of boycott created confusion and conflict. Every American perceived the results of such drastic action differently, and each reacted according to his perceptions. Artisans were caught up in the conlict in sundry ways. Some were obliged to change their business orientation, relying on their own production, not importation, for their income. Others, including William Will, opened inns to augment the returns from their craft.[42] Many must have viewed the widening breech between the colonies and England as a chance to better their community standing. Non-importation would surely diminish the influence of the merchant oligarchy which dominated the provincial government as well as the marketplace. Local manufacture further guaranteed the craftsmen a number of new

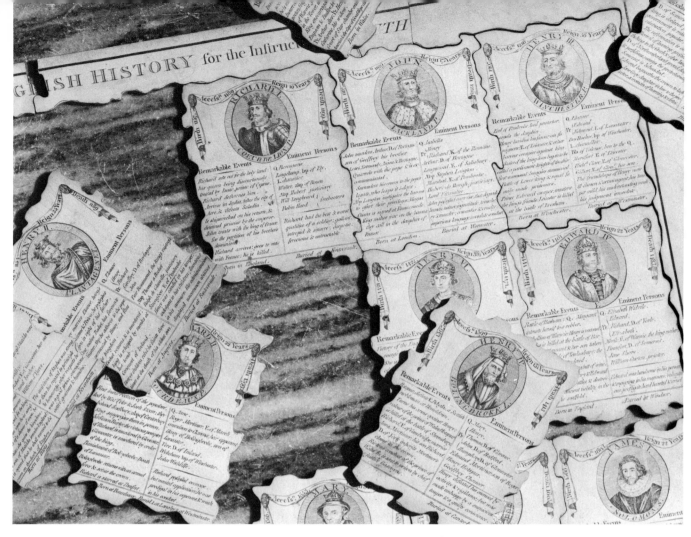

83-84. *Above:* Children's puzzle or "dissected picture" with box, sold by John Wallis, London, 1788. Restrictions on trade were difficult for colonists to swallow, but England's attempts at internal taxation, like the Stamp Act, were intolerable. The process of dissolving ties with the mother country was painful. Everything that English colonists had inherited with their culture had to be tested and adapted to their new situation. The monarchy was one institution that did not survive, though the children's puzzle, engraved in 1788, was still a favorite teaching toy in post-revolutionary America. *Left:* Pewter sugar bowl, attributed to William Will, Philadelphia, 1785-98. This sugar bowl, like many everyday accessories, received hard use. It was probably fashioned with a matching lid, now lost, and it may have been made by William Will, since the alloyed metal is consistent with that of other known Will pieces. Similar unmarked bowls, complete with lid, have been attributed to Will's shop.

customers who had previously purchased imported items. In the distance loomed the possibility of a break with England, and, perhaps, a restructuring of the social order. In this, craftsmen planned an active part.

In point of fact, American artisans had lived at the outer edge of England's social structure long enough to develop a different set of standards. New World experiences subtly transformed colonial craftsmen. The new circumstances fostered spirits of independence and enterprise, a willingness to adapt, and a host of aspirations which were alien to their European counterparts.

Even traditional institutions like the apprenticeship system were affected, although most American craftsmen took their responsibilities to the apprenticeship system fairly seriously. Apprenticeship, after all, was the established means of acquiring a trade, and it applied to nearly every occupation. Neophytes learned from the ground up, during the seven years when they were legally bound to a master craftsman, businessman, or merchant. Even without the supervision which guilds provided in the Old World, many Americans maintained the traditions, standards of workmanship, and teaching roles which had been the set in England and Europe. Some, however, did not. Apprentices ran away, or masters failed to teach their craft. More disturbing to the well-defined European establishment was the American tendency to expand profit-making activities to a variety of fields not within the usual sphere of an Old World craftsman.[43]

For instance, John Hyatt, a brass founder advertising in Philadephia newspapers in 1720, sold lampblack—used in making ink and paints—as well as foundry items.[44] Other brass founders pursued a wholly mercantile route. The import business not only attracted customers who wanted English fashions, but also provided the craftsman with patterns and metal which he might eventually recover to melt and recast.

Brass was a great commercial success. Like pewter it was decorative, durable, and inexpensive, but its strength and high melting point made it more suitable for many household objects. British mercantile policymakers had earmarked the metal as a major export product and carefully protected it, for most brass items, as small necessities, made ideal venture cargo. The brass exports, especially candlesticks of the early eighteenth century, reflect a significant Huguenot influence in the English brass industry. Throughout the century, moreover, other French influences were incorporated into Birmingham products.

Many English brass wares were mass produced and so inexpensive that American brass founders chose not to encroach upon what amounted to an English monopoly. That was certainly the case wtih candlestick production until long after the Revolution. American attentions were directed elsewhere—towards more profitable markets. Colonial founders perceived a vacuum in the English brass industry, a vacuum caused by England's dependence on coal for fuel. While firewood might be dear in Philadelphia, England had experienced a critical shortage of wood, even for household use, since the end of the seventeenth century. The better homes of England used basket grates for burning sea coal by the 1720s, so high-fashion brass andirons were never in great demand.[45] Some Birmingham foundries undoubtedly produced andirons for export to the colonies, where wood was widely used.[46] In fact, since coal had not been exploited in America, wood was the fuel of choice. New World craftsmen responded to local necessity, developing the andiron in unique American patterns. While England still supplied the boundaries of fashion within which the colonial craftsmen worked, local interpretations were original.

Most eighteenth-century Philadelphia brass founders are anonymous, or, more precisely, the names of those who advertised in that trade can rarely be associated with any particular pieces. While no pairs of early brass-topped iron fire dogs, or andirons, have

85. Brass candle box, probably English, c. 1767. 1767 was an ominous date for British manufacturers. Americans were becoming increasingly determined to enforce non-importation and gain some recognition of their problems. Unfortunately, the spirit was willing but the flesh was weak. Homespuns quickly lost their appeal, and such necessities as nails were always needed. Many brass products continued to cross the Atlantic, and pieces like this "bark," or candle box, which were used for saving purposes were likely candidates.

been identified with a specific craftsman, a number of pairs were produced in Pennsylvania. Only Daniel King (1731-1806), who did not begin working in the area until the mid-1750s, marked a few pieces. It might be expected that someone who would claim to have invented door knockers "which will stand proof against the united attacks of those nocturnal sons of violence" (a rowdy group of local vandals) would be inclined to sign his work.[47]

King's andirons are superlative, as he fully realized. He charged John Cadwalader over £25 for a "pare of the Best Rote fier Dogs with Corinthen Coloms,"[48] a sum considerably more than the average value of under £6 assigned to used brass andirons in household inventories.[49] Brass often graced the best room of a house, but brass-topped iron dogs served the remaining fireplaces. Utilitarian wrought iron was the usual choice for kitchens.

Like pewterers, braizers or brass founders cast most of the articles which they sold.

86. Brass-topped andirons, probably Pennsylvania, c. 1720-30. The brass finials on these early andirons were sand cast in wood or iron-bound forms called flasks. These were filled with a special type of fine dampened sand which was tamped firm before a pattern was pressed into it. Metal filled the hollowed impression. Though worn considerably, these finials show fine detail achieved with this process.

87. Imported Queen Anne brass candlesticks, English and French, c. 1700-40. Several technological improvements were made in candlesticks during the seventeenth and eighteenth century—each aimed at saving metal. Before 1670, stem and socket were cast in one solid piece. Then the process of hollow casting became common, and sticks were cast in two halves and braized together. Finally, core casting, which was introduced about 1780, was used at even greater savings of time and materials.

Candlesticks, andiron columns, finials, and the like were made in two halves with a hollow core and braized together. Everything was cast in sand, a method which can reproduce surprisingly detailed patterns. Other objects were made from hammered brass sheets.

When the entire scope of Philadelphia's social and economic life is considered, brass founders stand out for their work with the tools, scientific instruments, and molds which other craftsmen and gentlemen required. The braizers' role was a pivotal one in the eighteenth-century community. They made a variety of items for the cabinetmaker, who, in turn, supplied the braizer with many of the carved wood patterns for finials or andiron legs (which often exhibit regional characteristics seen in Philadelphia furniture.)[50] Some pewterers relied on brass founders for mold-making. Innkeepers ordered spigots and cocks, and mill owners purchased several types of machine parts. On a more mundane level, the braizer often provided scales for merchants and house-

88. Brass-topped andirons, probably Pennsylvania, second quarter eighteenth century. The best Pennsylvania andirons before 1750 were usually combinations of brass and iron. Brass was still exceedingly dear, but was available in ingot form. Amos Strettell advertised in a mid-February *Pennsylvania Gazette* that "All manufacturers of plate copper, ingot brass, and block tin, may be supplied . . . on the best terms."

wives who needed to weigh coins or the ingredients for some culinary triumph.

Finally, in the prosecution of the war, the brass founders' skills proved indispensable. Since America could not depend on continued shipments of French weapons, local craftsmen tried to supply the troops. In what must have been the old Bonnin and Morris china manufactory in Southwark, "Mr. Biers [Byers], late of New York," supervised the casting of brass six-pounders. Daniel King produced "Patterara's and Howitzers" closer to the center of town.[51]

Non-importation was an issue which colonial merchants and craftsmen could generally support, or so it seemed in 1765 and again in 1767. Anglicans and Friends believed that economic coercion would peacefully solve the problems with England. Quaker silversmiths like David Hall, Sr., and Joseph Richardson, Sr., added their names to the agreement. Philip Syng, Jr., John Bayly [Bayley], John Leacock, and Benjamin Harbeson, coppersmith, also signed.[52] The first trials of non-importation seemed productive, but gradually it became apparent that boycott would never achieve everything the colonists wanted.

As war became inevitable, sides were drawn in Philadelphia—often on religious grounds. Quakers were generally aligned with their pacifistic creed and attempted to remain neutral. Many Friends, like Joseph Richardson, Sr., remained aloof from the conflict. Richardson's sons, on the other hand, were on the rolls of the second battallion of the Philadelphia County Militia, but they may not have served actively.[53] Anglicans, too, suffered from divided loyalties. Philip Syng, Jr., who might be excused by his age, "retired into the country," while John Leacock entered the pamphlet warfare from his vineyard outside the city.[54] Members of the Protestant reformed churches usually supported a revolution wholeheartedly, as they often had the most to gain. William Will, the pewterer, and Benjamin Harbeson, coppersmith, both actively participated in the American cause.[55]

Harbeson was a member of the Second Committee of Correspondence,[56] the intercolonial news service formed, as Charles Thompson said, to insure that "any intelligence of importance" would be "quickly disseminated to the whole body of the people."[57] Harbeson served in the rank of captain in the Second Battalion of Philadelphia Associators,[58] but perhaps not too actively, since he carried on the coppersmith's trade in Lancaster, Pennsylvania, during the British occupation of Philadelphia. An advertisement in the *Pennsylvania Gazette* of April 11, 1778 showed him at a Lancaster address. By August of that year, the British had left the city, and Harbeson was back in Philadelphia, still pursuing his crafts.[59]

From at least 1755 through 1765, Harbeson augmented his income with retail sales of London imports.[60] Significantly, he marked his own early tea kettles, apparently those produced before the war, with "HARBESON," crowned. Later kettles omit the crown—a likely indication of a shrewd and enterprising character. Harbeson changed his mark to suit the political atmosphere; he carried on his trade during his temporary remove to Lancaster. In another instance, for some unknown reason, he neglected at least one apprentice, George Laub. Laub subsequently sued Harbeson at the January, 1763, session of the Mayor's Court for what amounted to breach of contract. Laub claimed that, in spite of four years service to "Tin-Plate Maker and Copper-Plate Worker" Harbeson, his master had taught him nothing about copperplate work. Harbeson was charged to go ahead with this training, but six months later the complaint surfaced once more. Harbeson was admonished again—apparently with more success.[61]

As war became a reality, Pennsylvanians scrambled to reorganize the government, which, in point of fact, had no authority from the moment independence was declared. All the Lockian assumptions and Whig principles so long discussed were made specific

89-91. *Top (left):* Brass andirons, probably Philadelphia, c. 1785-1800. Several similar pairs of urn and acorn-tipped andirons from Philadelphia and New York have survived—with and without engraving on the plinth. The ball-and-claw feet are the robust Philadelphia type with a "squashed tomato" ball. Whoever carved the pattern for the brass founder was certainly well acquainted with the genre and probably supplied a number of area brass founders and cabinetmakers with legs on a piece-work basis. *Top (right):* Pennsylvania copper tea kettles, eighteenth and nineteenth century. The tea kettle, as made in Pennsylvania, borrows heavily from English and Dutch prototypes. Benjamin Harbeson's trade card pictured an idealized tea kettle which is quite similar to the English cast brass example centered here. But craftsmen made their pieces from soldered copper sheets, and construction largely determined form. The globular-shape gooseneck spouts were derived from English sources, while the flat, bowed handle is borrowed from Dutch design. Harbeson made the kettle at far left. *Above:* Crowned touch mark of Benjamin Harbeson, Philadelphia coppersmith. Benjamin Harbeson must have made tea kettles with this "crowned" touch mark before America's break with England. Crowned marks on English pieces were often used by metalsmiths producing pieces for the reigning monarch and were otherwise added to signify high quality. Perhaps that's what Harbeson had in mind. He always prided himself on quality.

by Jefferson's Declaration. The exclusive rule held by wealthy merchants and Quaker families abruptly ended when artisans and western farmers allied to force a test oath upon Pennsylvania citizens. This oath of allegiance to a new state effectively disbarred Loyalists and Friends, whose religion prohibited the swearing of oaths. With this accomplished, the remaining citizens created a "democratical government" which "admits of no superiority."[62]

The state constitution of 1776 was a radical departure from many British traditions. Like the Declaration of Independence, it affirmed Locke's theory of natural rights. It explicitly guaranteed to every freeman of the commonwealth freedom of conscience and speech, the right to a speedy public trial by his peers, protection against unwarranted search and seizure, the right to bear arms, and the right to participate in his own governance. In the new order, any male taxpayer, and his sons who had reached majority, could vote. Representatives were elected annually to a single-house legislature. Likewise, members of the Supreme Executive Council—which had no veto power and could merely expedite laws—were also elected by the freemen. These constraints insured that no individual or junto could seize or abuse power. Moreover, Pennsylvanians, long concerned with the problems of life tenure in the judiciary, limited judges' terms to seven years.[63]

Under the new constitution the concerns of Philadelphia artisans were satisfied to the detriment of the merchants. Neither group, however, approved of the national state of affairs, which was disastrous from a financial standpoint. Inflation had reached a crisis point in the city, with interest from the war debts compounding at a furious rate. The Articles of Confederation were obviously inadequate, but strengthening them might raise again a strong and tyrannical government. The problem was dissected in the Philadelphia press—the war had been a success, but the country was foundering.

The constitution of 1787 was first tested in Pennsylvania. The legislature hastily arranged for a constituent convention to decide on the national plan. Surprisingly, artisans and mechanics supported the Constitution. Their fears of subjection to a new aristocracy were somewhat allayed. The need for a government which could regulate trade

92-93. *Left:* Cherry writing box sold by N. Middleton, London, late eighteenth-early nineteenth century. "Bought of N. Middleton Original Black L[edger?] & POCKET BOOK MAKER to the KING and PRINCE of WALES, at Nº162 the corner of Strand Lane opposite the New Church in Ye Strand. N.B. Writing & Dressing Desks & Boxes of every Kind"; obviously this box migrated westward to America. *Below (left):* Sheffield-plate candle snuffer and tray, Sheffield, England, c. 1800-10. Guttering candles were a constant source of evening annoyance until the mid 1820s, when braided wicks were invented. Early wicks were wooden splints, rush, or string which smoked and sizzled because they burned more slowly than the tallow or wax fuel. About every half hour, the burning wick needed trimming. One could do it quite elegantly with Sheffield snuffers—imported, of course, from England. Fancy items, like these, rarely cut into American craftsmen's business.

had become critical. British manufactured goods once again flooded the city, captured the market, and drained the state of specie.[64] Artisans sought the most likely means to eliminate this competition—a government capable of enforcing imposts.

The Constitution was ratified by a two-to-one margin in Pennsylvania. On July 4th, 1788, its ratification by ten states (and guaranteed adoption) was celebrated with the Grand Federal Procession. Members of several military troops marched through the city streets, between groups of craftsmen. Several of the craft "societies" were accompanied by horse-drawn floats depicting each group's shop in action. The coppersmiths marched "under the direction of Benjamin Harbeson"; Daniel King, led the brass founders; William Ball, carrying a silver urn, was first among silversmiths; even the stay-makers marched, "represented by Mr. Francis Serre, with his first journeyman carrying an elegant pair of ladies' stays."[65]

As the seat of government during the war years, Philadelphia rapidly expanded and acquired her complement of gentility. After a brief remove to New York, the Federal Government returned. The attendant activity put a burden on the city, and nearly every resident responded. Several new buildings were completed in the two decades between 1774 and 1794. City Tavern, "the most genteel one in America,"[66] the Philadelphia County Courthouse, which would serve as a temporary home for the Congress of the United States, the Bank of North America, as well as unnumbered dwellings became a part of the urban scene. In each building, the new classical taste was well represented. What fashion could be more appropriate to a new republic, descended, as was believed, from those of Greece and Rome?

Advertisements of the period, like those of silversmith and "fancy shop" proprietor Joseph Anthony, Jr., in the *Pennsylvania Packet,* show something of this prevalence of the classical. "Plated and bronzed tea and coffee urns" and "Oval and round sugar and cream basons" are specific allusions to the new taste which appear in a list of over 130 articles.[67] His "Plated-Wares" were no longer solid silver, but Sheffield plate—a fusion of copper and silver which sandwiched a thick layer of copper between two thin sheets of the precious metal. Anthony paid a substantial duty to import this English product; his lengthy advertisements, however, suggest that he found a good market for the metal. At last nearly everyone could purchase on common ground. The less than wealthy could have the look of silver without paying high prices, and even luminaries like President Washington did not disdain this affordable substitute.[68]

On the other hand, exclusive use of imports would destroy the economic stability of the new nation, and it was clear that the government and elected officials must encourage American production. Washington did his part by buying several pieces made by Joseph Anthony. The president also patronized Joseph Richardson, Jr., and subsequently appointed the silversmith Assayer of the United States Mint.[69] Alexander Hamilton publicized the several infant industries, as did the local newspapers.

Gradually, the exports from Philadelphia's manufactories began to balance the imports to some degree. Windsor chairs, copper tea kettles, and books were shipped down the American coast and out to the West Indies.[70] A local rolling mill, the American Bullion and Refining Office, began operation in 1789 to supply the area metalsmiths with raw materials in workable form,[71] while quantities of fabrics, stockings and wallpapers were produced in the city and in Germantown, six miles away.

Self-sufficiency was still several years away, but belief in prosperity proved to be an unquenchable American trait. A general euphoria, coupled with relief that events had passed so well, seized the city. In the upper ranks, a hectic pace was set. Abigail Adams complained in 1791:

> I should spend a very dissipated winter, if I were to accept of one half

the invitations I receive, particularly to the routes, or tea and cards . . . I have been to one assembly. The dancing was very good . . . but the room despicable; the etiquette,—it was difficult to say where any was to be found.[72]

A similar euphoria and a unique perception of liberty affected the artisans and laborers somewhat differently. English visitors were appalled to find that the system of deference to which they had grown accustomed could change so drastically:

In the United States, however, the lower classes of people will return rude and impertinent answers to questions couched in the most civil terms, and will insult a person that bears the appearance of a gentleman, on purpose to show how much they consider themselves upon an equality with him . . . they seem to think that . . . there is no other way of convincing a stranger that he is really in a land of liberty . . . .[73]

Was it a land of liberty? Certainly, the artisans who had supported the Revolution perceived it so, for they were among "the quality" now. They were replaced, however, by younger men who never shared the unifying experiences of building and protecting a community. These young men and their merchant counterparts faced a difficult climb through a social hierarchy which had become nearly as impenetrable as any found in Europe. In effect, they and each succeeding generation would fight their own revolutions on a different scale.

94. Japanned tin sewing box with ivory implements, box labeled "J.T.&c./LONDON," c. 1820-40. While men were agitating in the political arena, women realized their own changes in the home. Many echoed Abigail Adams's plaintive request that ". . . I desire you would Remember the Ladies, and be more generous and favourable to them than your ancestors. Do not put such unlimited power into the hands of Husbands, Remember all Men would be tyrants if they could. If perticuliar care and attention is not paid to the Laidies we are determined to foment a Rebelion, and will not hold ourselves bound by any Laws in which we have no voice, or Representation." Fancy sewing, the genteel accomplishment, wiled away the hours spent waiting for this social revolution.

95. Sheffield-plate hot water urn, Sheffield, England, c. 1790-1800. Henry Wansey, an English visitor, reported that "Mrs. Washington herself made tea and coffee for us. On the table were two small plates of sliced tongue, dry toast, bread and butter, &c. but no broiled fish as is the general custom . . . There was but little appearance of form; one servant, only attended, who had no livery; a silver urn for hot water was the only article of expense on the table." A list of items purchased for the President in 1789, which included two plated coffee urns—one with heater and one without—indicates, however, that Wansey may have underestimated Washington's frugality.

XXXIII. The Governor's Council Chamber. In this room, with its impressive architectural detail and elegant appointments, the chief executives of the Province of Pennsylvania—appointed by the Penn Family with the King's approval—officiated from 1741 to 1775. Fine furniture, "Venetian" curtains, and silver accessories were designed to impress the visitor with the importance of the Penn family in the local scheme of things. The "French" elbow chairs on each side of the fireplace are two of a suite of twelve made for Governor John Penn by cabinetmaker Thomas Affleck.

118

XXXIV. The Morris family desk and bookcase, Philadelphia, c. 1740. The scallop shell carved in high relief above the "glass shutters," with undulating "grasses" at each side, relates in form and date of execution to the shell-carved frieze above the Speaker's chair in the Assembly Room. Behind the upper doors of the desk is one range of drawers and shelving above; the desk interior is fitted with shell-carved, shaped and "secret" drawers.

XXXV. An eight-day brass musical clock with a silvered dial made by Peter Stretch in Philadelphia, c. 1740. This carved mahogany case is of exceptional quality. With its acanthus leafage, composite Corinthian columns, egg and dart moldings, blind fret and baroque urns, it illustrates both the competence of the cabinetmaker-carver and the urbanity of the patron who ordered it.

XXXVI. *Above:* A pair of Philadelphia Chippendale mahogany "French" elbow chairs from a group of twelve made about 1768 for Governor John Penn by Thomas Affleck. Today, the chairs, with their rococo arm terminals, palm frond carved arm supports, and Chinese trellis blind fretwork carved front legs, set a tone of elegance and affluence in the Governor's Council Chamber similar to that originally provided in the Penn town house on Third Street.

XXXVII. *Left:* Two mahogany desks with holly line inlay and a part of a third have survived from the furnishings of Congress Hall in the 1790s in use by the Federal legislature. These were removed to Lancaster in 1799 and later to Harrisburg in 1812 and were used by the State Senate. The one illustrated was returned to Philadelphia in 1867 identified as the desk upon which the Declaration of Independence had been signed, a fictitious claim. Because of its long association with the Congress Hall furniture and similarity of style and construction, the desk may be attributed to Thomas Affleck, the Philadelphia cabinetmaker who furnished armchairs and desks for the building in 1790 and again in 1793.

XXXVIII. Tiger-stripe maple cellarette with lid and two simulated drawers upon a stand with a drawer, pierced brackets, crossed stretchers and Marlborough legs with block feet. The interior has compartments for wine bottles. Philadelphia, c. 1770.

THE

GENTLEMAN and CABINET-MAKER's
DIRECTOR:

Being a large COLLECTION of the

Moſt ELEGANT and USEFUL DESIGNS
OF

HOUSEHOLD FURNITURE,

In the Moſt FASHIONABLE TASTE.

Including a great VARIETY of

CHAIRS, SOFAS, BEDS, and COUCHES; CHINA-TABLES, DRESSING-TABLES, SHAVING-TABLES, BASON-STANDS, and TEAKETTLE-STANDS; FRAMES for MARBLE-SLABS, BUREAU-DRESSING-TABLES, and COMMODES; WRITING-TABLES, and LIBRARY-TABLES; LIBRARY-BOOK-CASES, ORGAN-CASES for private Rooms, or Churches, DESKS, and BOOK-CASES; DRESSING and WRITING-TABLES with BOOK-CASES, TOILETS, CABINETS, and CLOATHS-PRESSES; CHINA-CASES, CHINA-SHELVES, and BOOK-SHELVES; CANDLE-STANDS, TERMS for BUSTS, STANDS for CHINA JARS, and PEDESTALS; CISTERNS for WATER, LANTHORNS, and CHANDELIERS; FIRE-SCREENS, BRACKETS, and CLOCK-CASES; PIER-GLASSES, and TABLE-FRAMES; GIRANDOLES, CHIMNEY-PIECES, and PICTURE-FRAMES; STOVE-GRATES, BOARDERS, FRETS, CHINESE-RAILING, and BRASS-WORK, for Furniture.

AND OTHER

ORNAMENTS.

TO WHICH IS PREFIXED,

A Short EXPLANATION of the Five ORDERS of ARCHITECTURE;

WITH

Proper DIRECTIONS for executing the moſt difficult Pieces, the Mouldings being exhibited at large, and the Dimenſions of each DESIGN ſpecified.

The Whole comprehended in TWO HUNDRED COPPER-PLATES, neatly engraved.

Calculated to improve and refine the preſent TASTE, and ſuited to the Fancy and Circumſtances of Perſons in all Degrees of Life.

By THOMAS CHIPPENDALE,

CABINET-MAKER and UPHOLSTERER, in St. Martin's Lane, London.

THE THIRD EDITION.

LONDON:

Printed for the AUTHOR, and ſold at his Houſe, in St. Martin's Lane; Alſo by T. BECKET and P. A. DE HONDT, in the Strand.

MDCCLXII.

Title page, *The Gentleman and Cabinet-Maker's Director* by Thomas Chippendale, 3rd edition, London, 1762. Chippendale's designs, as presented in this enlarged edition, were extremely popular among Philadelphia cabinetmakers. *See* p. 131.

4. Philadelphia Furniture: "Of the Best Sort . . ."
by Charles G. Dorman

The "Philadelphia style" in furniture took time to evolve, and its beginnings were inherent in the furniture used in the first settled areas of the Delaware Valley. These pieces carried the marks of Swedish, Dutch, English, and German-trained craftsmen. Because of the admixture of cultures, a regional style appeared that eventually became representative of the Philadelphia area.

William Penn, proprietor of Pennsylvania, was interested in the manner and style of dwellings to be built in his new city, and he guided, by example, the furnishing of them. On October 6, 1685, he wrote to his overseer:

> Here comes a Dutchman, a Joyner, and a Carpenter . . . let him wain-
> scot and make tables and stands for some of the rooms, but chiefly help
> with the Outhouses, because we shall bring much furniture[1]

Although shipping costs were expensive, some of the early settlers imported furniture nonetheless. Penn owned his own ship and was able to bring furniture for his country house, Pennsbury Manor, in present day Morrisville, Pennsylvania, and for his rented town house in Philadelphia.[2] Ideally, the importations for Pennsbury Manor, extending as they did from 1682 to 1700, would serve the furniture historian seeking prototypes of the introduction of the Anglo-Dutch mode along the Delaware River, but few identifiable pieces have survived.

Under Penn's leadership Philadelphia was a cross section of seventeenth-century society: Quakers seeking a haven from religious persecution; poor farmers from the Palatinate fleeing their war-torn homeland; English entrepreneurs venturing their fortunes in the New World. But they all had some skill which, Penn hoped, would soon contribute to their own, and to the colony's benefit. This steadily growing emigration was not happenstance, but a carefully calculated campaign on the part of the Proprietor who traveled throughout England, Ireland, the Netherlands, and the cities along the

96. Walnut gate-leg table, Pennsylvania, c. 1720-40. Early gate-leg tables may have first been used in an all-purpose dining parlor. By the nineteenth century, however, they had been relegated to the kitchen, the back porch, or, in lucky instances for today's antiquarians, the attic.

Rhine recruiting settlers.

But Penn knew that if the new colony, Pennsylvania, was to be a sound business proposition, money had to cross the Atlantic with the settlers. He drew on his Quaker acquaintances in London and Bristol for the funds and for organizational talents. So to Philadelphia, "named before it was born,"[3] came prosperous Englishmen determined to make a city flourish in the wilderness.

Some of these "First Purchasers" had to endure living in caves overlooking the Delaware, but only long enough for newly-arrived carpenters and joiners to provide shelter according to the purses and inclinations of the new arrivals. As the settlers moved into the new homes, the caves were requisitioned or rented to less fortunate later arrivals.[4] Penn and his deputies were aware of the advantage of city planning and brick construction; the experience of the Great London Fire of 1666 had influenced their thinking. By the end of the seventeenth century there were many two- and three-story brick houses facing the river, some having balconies as well as pent eaves.[5] It was only natural that the major portion of these houses would be furnished with the most comfortable furniture possible.

William Penn became a Quaker in 1665, but, before he decided to follow the "inner light," he had been a worldly courtier, with an eye and an ear toward material advancement. Penn would never have been able to advance his scheme for the "Holy Experiment" if he had abandoned all his diplomatic skill at finding favor with the King and his ministers. Thus, it is the founder himself whose attitudes epitomize a people who professed belief in the simple life, but produced the elegance in the decorative arts for which the city has been famous for over two centuries.

Quakers believed in thrift and simplicity in their private lives and forbade any extravagance in dress or furniture. As early as 1698, the Philadelphia Monthly Meeting put on record its admonition

> that no superflous furniture be in your houses, as great fringes about your valances, and double valances, or double courtains, and many such needless things.[6]

Quakers, in Great Britain, in some cases, had even put away

> our fine veneered and garnished cases of drawers, tables, stands, cabinet escritoires, &c . . . or exchanged for decent plain ones of solid wood, without superfluous garnishing or ornamental work; our wainscots or woodwork we had painted one plain colour; our large mouldings or finishings of panelling, &c, our swelling chimney pieces, curiously twisted bannisters, we took down and replaced with useful plain woodwork, &c., our large looking-glasses with decorated frames we sold or made them into smaller ones.[7]

An estimated eighty percent of the furniture craftsmen in Philadelphia between 1685 and 1785 were Quakers.[8] Quaker craftsmen were also at work in all the cities of the eastern seaboard from Newport to Charleston, and they all turned out products "adorned with simplicity" for their relatives and, at the same time, produced astonishingly beautiful concoctions for merchant princes and colonial governors. But even Quakers did not maintain rigid observance of the rules of simplicity for themselves. Curator Beatrice Garvan explains the dichotomy in this manner: "During the formative period . . . , Quakers still preferred to celebrate worldly success with learning and land, but eventually the protests of strict Friends against gleaming mahogany, shiny plate, elegant bright-colored silks, and gilded looking-glasses were voices in a wilderness."[9]

It would appear, then, that the much-quoted phrase, "Of the best sort, but plain," was an ideal which received never-failing lip service. A Philadelphian in popular legend is a Quaker gentleman in a silk suit carrying a gold watch, who lives in a Georgian mansion, sits in a Queen Anne chair, sleeps in a Chippendale bed, and uses silver utensils. A contemporary anecdotal conformation of this image is that of Isaac Norris, Speaker of the Assembly, who chose to appear at Meeting one day in a new suit of clothes that was "of the best sort" and then some. His retort to the raised eyebrows: "But you don't expect me to dress like a shoemaker, do you?"[10]

Quaker tenets notwithstanding, early Philadelphians liked color in their surroundings, including furniture, so great quantities of japanned furniture were imported. By 1720, Quaker merchant Thomas Chalkley, wishing to capitalize on the popularity of lacquered furniture, departed from his customary West Indies trade and imported from London japanned corner cupboards, looking glasses with japanned frames, dressing tables, and two tall case clocks with japanned cases, one blue with gilt highlights and the other black with gold.[11]

William MacPherson Horner in his *Blue Book of Philadelphia Furniture* can give us only one example of a locally-made lacquered furniture which has survived the centuries. Perhaps there are others which lost their regional identity; but the greatest attrition would be the desire of a latter-day owner to "freshen up" the surface by stripping it down to its primary wood.

Furniture makers, known from the seventeenth century to the end of the eighteenth variously as "joyners," "shop joyners," and "cabinetmakers," arrived in Pennsylvania among the first craftsmen, and, since the success of Philadelphia as a world port was an exciting upward spiral for over a century, with ships from London appearing almost daily on the River, they came in increasing numbers. With all this activity there did not have to be a cultural lag at all. Cultural lags are for the isolated or the uninspired; stylistically, one would expect the products of Philadelphia cabinet shops to be as modish as those of

97-99. *Top left:* Tiger-stripe maple tall-case clock, Chester County, Pennsylvania, c. 1740. Joseph Wills, a Philadelphia clockmaker of the first half of the eighteenth century, produced the works for this clock, as well as some of the finest clocks with brass or silver-washed and engraved dial faces made locally. The clock is said to have been made for Mahlon Dickinson, an ancestor of the donor. *Above:* Walnut dressing table, possibly New Jersey, c. 1750. Plain but handsome and of good proportions, this dressing table was taken to California in the nineteenth century by a family of Philadelphia origin. *Left:* Pole screen, Pennsylvania, c. 1765. Eighteenth-century fireplaces gave one the option of freezing on one side and roasting on the other. A seated lady or gentleman, busy with needlework or reading, could be made comfortable by adjusting the fabric screen to head height.

London. As a matter of personal preference, however, some Philadelphians were still ordering furniture in the transitional Queen Anne-Chippendale style as late as 1800.

Hornor lists one hundred joiners and turners who were at work in Philadelphia between 1682 and 1722. Joiners made clock cases, tables, coffins, packing chests, chests of drawers, cupboards, bottle racks and presses.[12] Turners made bedposts, balusters, legs, stretchers, and stiles. These craftsmen made the kinds of furniture they had known in England or had worked on wherever they had served their apprenticeship—wainscot and bannister back chairs with handsome turnings, bold moldings, ball-footed chests and gateleg tables. Each one incorporated a bit of himself in his product, as was inevitable in this age of hand craftsmanship. The early craftsman usually did not have pattern books to refer to; but invariably, as part of his stock in trade, had templates or patterns of pieces which had appealed to him in his training or were of proven popularity. These, and a patron's examples, could be copied or adapted.

During the eighteenth century, Philadelphia, like its sister cities along the East Coast, became a center for the training of craftsmen, and the apprentice system provided a common link between seventeenth- and eighteenth-century artisans. By this system, unchanged since medieval times, craft skills were passed from one generation to another, and so the quality of the product was assured. The apprentice was

> to learn the art, trade, and mastery of a Shop Joyner, and after the Manner of Apprentice to Serve him his said Master from the date hereof . . . During Which term the Said Apprentice his said Master faithfully shall serve [,] his secrets keep, & his Lawful Commands obey, he shall do no Damage to his said Master nor see it done by others, Without giving notice thereof to his said Master, he shall not Commit fornication nor contract matrimony . . . .[13]

100. Walnut gate-leg table, Chester County, Pennsylvania, c. 1740. Tables with falling leaves were the practical answer in the eighteenth century for small rooms put to varied uses.

101. Mahogany candlestand, Philadelphia, c. 1765. The Philadelphia craftsman's attention to detail is especially evident here in the entasis and stop-fluting of the post of this candlestand.

102. Windsor high-back armchair, Delaware Valley, Pennsylvania, c. 1750. This might be the earliest form of what became renowned in the colonies as the "Philadelphia Windsor."

Socially and sexually, it was a dull life, but if the apprentice was industrious, he got a new suit, a small sum of money, and some tools. His skills and the freedom to strike out on his own were the greatest rewards.

While the acculturation of peoples of diverse nationalities may explain the origin of distinctly regional furniture styles, it is certainly the locally-trained artisan who perpetuated them. It must be so, for how else can we explain the furniture of Philadelphia which is English in inspiration, but totally Philadelphian in execution? With such a melting pot of craftsmen and trades how could an identifiable Philadelphia style evolve? Why in this transitional, even embryonic period of local furniture development can the turnings of the ubiquitous "table with falling leaves" of the Delaware Valley be distinguished from those not only of old England, but of New England and even New York? Surely there was no guild laying down the rules, or community of craftsmen choosing a logo. Charles F. Montgomery gives credit for the regional touch to the specialist, such as a wood turner, in a city where there were a number of craftsmen who would employ him. The turned posts for a tea table or a candlestand for all of his cabinetmakers would bear the particular mark of his expertise.[14] All that is known is that there is a regional look, a robustness and definition of the turned parts in Philadelphia furniture that one does not find in that of New England, and that years of familiarity have made discernible. Pride of craft would have governed the finesse of the local turner. Even a novice reacts to a "gutsy" as opposed to a weak turning, and turnings appeared in much of the environment that surrounded the eighteenth-century Philadelphian: balusters of a staircase; arm supports, legs, and stretchers of a Windsor armchair; canes, bedposts, chair stiles and legs; spinning wheels; the columns of a clock hood; even billiard sticks.

Penn's city flourished and attracted not only craftsmen, but customers as well.[15] Affluent clients wanted furniture in "the latest fashion," although the international high style might have its source in classical antiquity. The word "antique" to an eighteenth-century gentleman anywhere in the western world, however, often meant a marble bust with a missing nose. Sometimes it would be the real thing from ancient Rome, but frequently it was a fabrication of more recent Italian origin. In their quest for fashion early Philadelphians provided the patronage for furniture craftsmen which in turn produced much more furniture than necessity required.[16]

The customer entered the creative process of furniture production in a way that would seem strange to today's consumer, accustomed to store-bought products. In an eighteenth-century cabinetmaker's shop, "ready made" was more the exception than the rule. The purchase of a piece of furniture required personal contact with the producer, discussion of the basic form and material, choice of decorative options, and agreement upon the delivery date and cost.

The William and Mary style was brought to England from the Netherlands in 1689 by Queen Mary and her husband, William of Orange. Examples of the new fashion reached Philadelphia soon thereafter, and colonial interpretations were simplified in form. Important pieces of furniture in this style have survived in local families, and a few, to date, have been found bearing the name of the "joyner" or cabinetmaker and the date of completion. An imposing and documented piece is a 1707 fall-front writing desk, now at Williamsburg, signed Edward Evans. Evans (1679-1754) was a joiner patronized by William Penn and his daughter, Letitia. He is a link in one of those three-generation chains of training encountered again and again in studying Philadelphia furniture. His father, William Evans, was a London-trained carpenter, and his son, Thomas Evans, became a carpenter, too.[17]

Equally impressive is the double-arched-top desk and bookcase at the Philadelphia Museum of Art which bears the chalk inscription "D JOHN 6/20," which has been assigned by Beatrice Garvan to David or Daniel John, both residents of Philadelphia County.[18] More prosaic in form, but bearing the inscription "William Beakes 1711," is a walnut chest of drawers upon ball feet which is in a private collection. In 1709 Beakes was an apprentice to William Till (d. 1711), one of the city's earliest furniture craftsmen.

The William and Mary style, with its bulbous cup-and-trumpet turnings, stayed in vogue even while Philadelphia furniture craftsmen were experimenting with other forms. They were turning out, for example, prototypes of the Delaware Valley rush-seat chair and the Philadelphia Windsor. At the same time, cabinetmakers in the city were creating their version of a cabriole leg, or "crookt leg," in the Queen Anne style.[19]

The shift from the somewhat ponderous furniture in the William and Mary style to the carefully calculated curves of Queen Anne was "the happiest change in English furniture in hundreds of years," according to one authority.[20] The Queen Anne style did not become popular in America until some time after the English monarch's death in 1714, but for the next forty years, until 1760, it was the fashion and standard for fine furniture. Hogarth's cyma or "S" curve, the "line of beauty," was the Queen Anne style's major feature, but it was often embellished with scallop shell, acanthus leaf, and trailing grass carving.

One of the visual joys of the Park Collection is the Humphreys-Archer Queen Anne armchair (pl. XL). We are assured by a most astute writer on the subject of the Philadelphia chair that there is no English prototype for it.[21] How a Philadelphia cabinetmaker of the third or fourth decades of the eighteenth century in Philadelphia came upon the orchestration of curves found in this example we do not know, nor do we know who he was. It is quite clear, however, that the piece is a local bit of genius known only in a few examples from the same locale and era. The only straight line in such a chair is the rear seat rail; all else is a carefully contrived interplay of sweeping curves in the legs, the seat, and arm supports and back. It is not only pleasing to the eye, but it happily meets the basic requirement of seating furniture: it is extremely comfortable.

More architectural than sculptural in conception is a walnut desk and bookcase of the Philadelphia Queen Anne style (pl. XXXIV). This piece, with its mirrored doors, shell-carved interior, and scallop shell in relief within the scroll top, epitomizes the cabinet-work done at this time for a prosperous and sophisticated clientele; and it is consistent with the known elaborateness of the Governor's Council Chamber in the old Pennsylvania State House.[22]

Equally consistent with the elaborateness of the room is the silver-dialed tall case clock made by Peter Stretch (1670-1746), who had come to Philadelphia from England in 1702 and was the father of Thomas Stretch (1695-1765), maker of the first State House tower clock in 1753. The Peter Stretch clock is a most versatile mechanism for it not on-

103-104. Below (left): Mahogany slant-front knee-hole desk, Philadelphia, c. 1755. This is possibly the first of a number of desks Benjamin Franklin acquired for use in his home, Franklin Court. A desk with drawers for candles is referred to in a piece of Franklin correspondence. *Below (right):* Upholstered mahogany armchair, English, c. 1765-70. While resident in London, Franklin purchased a set of locally-made chairs in the latest "French" fashion, of which this is one example. He brought the furniture to Franklin Court upon his first return to Philadelphia in 1775.

ly does all the things normally expected of a clock, but also tells the time of high tide in the Port of Philadelphia and plays a tune every three hours. Its mahogany case, nearly ten feet in height, incorporates a veritable lexicon of early Georgian carving used with a trained eye and a sure hand. Peter Stretch was perhaps Philadelphia's first great clockmaker, but surely the city's and the nation's most famous clockmaker was the native genius David Rittenhouse (1732-94). By the time Rittenhouse was seventeen he was making accurate clocks, and seven years later he was running a flourishing clockmaking enterprise at his family's farm in Norristown ("Norriton" as it appears on his clock faces), and it was here that he made the clock in the Park collection (fig. 105).

Only the Governor's Council Chamber exuded a feudal opulence; most of the furnishings in the other rooms of the State House were for legislative and judicial use and so were provided with basics in the way of tables and seating furniture.

The State House, designed by Andrew Hamilton, gentleman architect, and Edmund Woolley, carpenter, was begun in 1732; the building, with sashless windows, was up by 1736, but it was not until 1741 that it was truly ready for occupancy and reasonably well furnished. Among the seating furniture provided by the Pennsylvania Assembly for its own use were rush-seat and Windsor chairs, so that by the time of the American Revolution the Assembly Room in the State House contained an unintentionally representative collection of locally-made chairs. Documentation for the presence of rush-seat chairs in the room precedes that for Windsors, for on December 26, 1760, Thomas Acherly, a maker of rush-seat chairs, rendered a bill to the "Province of Pennsylvania" for "12 Rush bottom Chairs for the State House [at 5s. per chair] £ 3.0.0,"[23] while one year later he was paid the same amount for twelve more chairs.[24] In 1776 the Assembly paid for re-rushing Delaware Valley slat-back chairs,[25] like those in figure 107, which had been worn out

105-106. *Far left:* Walnut tall-case clock, made by David Rittenhouse, Norristown, Pennsylvania, c. 1760. This clock is typical of those made by Rittenhouse for his former neighbors in Bucks County before he removed to Philadelphia, where his fame became world-wide as an astronomer. *Left:* Persimmon tall-case clock, made by Frederick Maus, Philadelphia, c. 1785. The lively carved crowing cockerel—nature's alarm clock—is rarely found employed as a finial on locally-made furniture, nor is the use of persimmon as the primary wood.

107-108. *Opposite page. Left:* Maple slat-back side chair (left), Delaware Valley, Pennsylvania, c. 1750-80, and maple slat-back armchair, Delaware Valley, Pennsylvania, c. 1750-80. Characteristic of the Pennsylvania slat-back armchair is its bulbous, turned front stretcher, undercut arm rests, and finely-turned arm supports. *Right:* Mahogany side chair, Philadelphia, c. 1770. Originally owned by Captain Samuel Morris, Sr., (1711-82), the chair is transitional in style between the Philadelphia Queen Anne and Chippendale.

by long use in its meeting room. One scholar ascribes the origin of the Delaware Valley rush-seat armchair—with its graduated splats, undercut arms, and bulbous turned front stretcher—to the German provinces from which so many new Philadelphians of the early eighteenth century had emigrated.[26]

One book that had a great deal of influence on what happened to furniture design in Philadelphia in the second half of the eighteenth century was *The Gentleman and Cabinetmaker's Director* by the London cabinetmaker Thomas Chippendale. It was published in 1754 and republished in 1755. The enlarged third edition of 1762 was on the shelves of Philadelphia's Library Company in 1764, and craftsmen Thomas Affleck and Benjamin Randolph had copies of their own.

The Director, with its plates of designs which could be endlessly varied, stimulated Philadelphia cabinetmakers at a period when, because of a rising tide of resentment toward Great Britain and its mercantile policies, patriotic Philadelphians turned to home-town craftsmen more than ever before. As Captain Samuel Morris wrote to his nephew, Samuel Powel, Jr., away on a European Grand Tour, in 1765:

> Household goods may be had here as cheap and as well made from English patterns. In the humour the people are in here, a man is in danger of becoming Invidiously distinguished, who buys anything in England which our Tradesmen can furnish . . . I have heard the joiners here object this against Dr. Morgan and others who brought their furnishings with them . . . .[27]

The availability of the *Director,* combined with the climate of the times and the astuteness of the Quaker and "worldly" craftsmen, gave the decorative arts of the New World

what we now call Philadelphia Chippendale. It was a time in the history of local furniture craftsmanship—generally the period between 1745 and 1789—which Hornor prefers to call a "golden age."[28]

Philadelphia craftsmen took Thomas Chippendale's designs and copied some of them, altered others in various ways, and simplified some to reduce the cost. The overall result was a flood of rococo-inspired mahogany furniture—chests, tables, side chairs, upholstered wing chairs, and tall post beds—that has not been equalled before or since. The high chest was a peculiarly American product, and "the Philadelphia highboy," as it came to be known, is in some ways the culmination of Philadelphia Chippendale, with its flamboyant carving that could include carved heads or wooden urns filled with wooden flowers on the pediment, fretwork, scallop shells, or even illustrations from Aesop's *Fables*. All the furniture makers on the East Coast from Boston to Charleston were ready for experimentation when Chippendale's book came out, but Philadelphia led the way in elegance and production.

Premier Philadelphia cabinetmakers who worked in the Chippendale mode were Thomas Affleck, Benjamin Randolph, John Folwell, Jonathan Gostelowe, Edward James, Thomas Tuft, James Gillingham, John Elliott, Jonathan Shoemaker, William Wayne, Joseph Deleveau, and Henry Clifton.[29] Some, like William Savery, did work that spanned both the Queen Anne and Chippendale periods.[30] Among the carvers who embellished the furniture were Hercules Courtenay, James Reynolds, Nicholas Bernard, and Martin Jugiez. All told, there were hundreds of men working on furniture in Philadelphia at this time.[31]

Jonathan Gostelowe (1744-1806) made mahogany furniture, including chests on chests, card tables, and ladder-back chairs, of high craftsmanship and often in a mode he himself had evolved; in particular, a serpentine-front chest of drawers in which the broad canted front corner is continued down into the full ogee bracket foot.[32] He was born in Philadelphia and kept his shop in Church Alley "about midway between Second and Third Streets."[33] Gostelowe was not a Quaker; he was, in fact, a vestryman of Christ Church and made and donated the baptismal font and communion table. During the Revolution he was first a major in the corps of Artillery Artificers and later ran the commissary of military stores. After the war, he became chairman of the Society of Gentlemen Cabinet and Chairmakers, and, on July 4, 1788, he led the members of this group in a grand public procession that celebrated the adoption of the United States Constitution. The newspaper account of the parade informs us that all the notable craftsmen of the city were represented and that among their number was "Mr Jonathan Gostelowe at the head of the Gentlemen Cabinet and Chair Makers,

> carrying the Scale and Dividers, insignia of the craft, followed by Jedediah Snowden with the Rules of Architecture; four of the oldest Masters; Mr. James Lee, attended by three Masters bearing the standard or cabinet makers' arms, elegantly painted and gilt on a blue field . . . below the arms, two hands united. Motto: By Unity We Support Society . . . The masters six abreast wearing linen aprons, and bucks tails in their hats. The workshop, seventeen feet long by nine feet eight inches wide, and fourteen feet high, on a carriage drawn by four horses; at each end of the shop ten stars . . . two signs inscribed Federal Cabinet and Chair Shop; Mr. John Brown, with journeymen and apprentices, at work in the shop."[34]

Benjamin Randolph (1721-91), the proprietor of a furniture-making establishment in Chestnut Street at the sign of the Golden Eagle, was prominent in pre-Revolutionary

109-111. *Above (left):* Looking glass, Philadelphia, c. 1765. Capable native cabinetmakers and carvers, well-versed in the latest London fashions, were able to provide elegant furnishings for their Philadelphia patrons, as exemplified by this painted looking glass with gilt highlights. *Left:* Cherry high chest of drawers, made by Ziba Ferris, Sr., Wilmington, Delaware, c. 1770. A plain but finely-made piece of furniture, this high chest of drawers descended in the family of the cabinetmaker. *Above:* Mahogany tea table, Philadelphia, c. 1765. A typical Philadelphia tilt-top tea table, this example is said to have descended in the family of James Smith, a Signer of the Declaration of Independence.

112-114. *Above (left):* Looking glass, made by John Elliott, Philadelphia, c. 1763. Pasted to the back of this looking glass is the printed label of John Elliott, which he had prepared bilingually to overcome any problems of communication he might encounter in his business dealings with either the English- or German-speaking peoples of Philadelphia. *Left:* Pier glass, possibly made by John Elliott, Philadelphia, c. 1770-80. Pier glasses, by their very name, are made to hang between the windows of a large room. There, they reflect light to brighten the room and at the same time break up the expansiveness of wall space. *Above:* Pair of walnut side chairs, Philadelphia, c. 1745. Chairs incorporating the best features of the Queen Anne and Chippendale styles were extremely popular in Philadelphia and in the Delaware Valley from their inception about 1745 until the end of the century.

115-116. *Left:* Walnut scroll-top document cabinet, Lancaster, Pennsylvania, c. 1770. The largest inland city in the United States at the time of the American Revolution, Lancaster had resident craftsmen who produced such fine furniture as this cabinet, which is comparable to fine pieces in Philadelphia. *Below:* Mahogany breakfast table, made by Jonathan Gostelowe, Philadelphia, c. 1789. Referred to generically as a "Pembroke table," this example contains a portion of a printed label, pasted inside the drawer, which has been identified as that used by the cabinetmaker Gostelowe when his shop was located in Church Alley.

Philadelphia.[35] Randolph was born in Monmouth County, New Jersey, and came to Philadelphia where he was first known as a "joiner," then as "cabinet maker," and, finally, as "merchant." He employed several very talented carvers in his shop, including Hercules Courtenay and John Pollard, and provided furniture for the mighty moguls of the era: John Dickinson, John Cadwalader, and others in the city, and for Vincent Loockerman in Dover, in "the lower counties on Delaware."[36]

Thomas Affleck (1740-95) was as important a cabinetmaker of the time as Randolph. He was born in a Quaker family in Aberdeen, Scotland, and learned his trade in Edinburgh and London. He came to Philadelphia in 1763 on the same boat on which John Penn, Wiliam's grandson and eventual governor, was traveling.[37] Affleck's first shop was on Union Street and later on Second Street "a little below the Drawbridge."[38] A pair of elbow chairs originally owned by John Penn (pl. XXXVI) can be attributed to Affleck. These are only two of the twelve believed to have been made in the 1760s for Governor Penn's town house. [39] Affleck was responsible for the introduction of the Marlborough style in Philadelphia, a reaction consisting variously of straight legs, some with blind fret carving and block feet, and rectilinear lines to counteract the curves of the Rococo. He was a complete craftsman, however, and could produce extravagant whimsies in any

117. Mahogany upholstered armchair, attributed to Thomas Affleck, c. 1790. This commodious armchair is one of four presently known from an original group of six or more that were probably used by the presiding officers of various legislative and judicial bodies which convened in the buildings of Independence Square.

118. Mahogany upholstered armchair, made by Thomas Affleck, Philadelphia, 1790-93. Erroneously referred to as "Signer's chairs" earlier in this century, chairs of this type have been correctly identified as those made by Thomas Affleck for Congress Hall when it became the nation's capitol.

XXXIX. The mahogany lyre base center table with drop leaves has two real and two simulated drawers, acanthus carved legs, and brass paw casters. One drawer contains the name "Buffington" incised on its inner left side, apparently to identify an early owner. Philadelphia, c. 1815.

XL. This outstanding walnut armchair with its shell and volute carved crest rail, carved splat, scrolled arms, balloon seat, and trifid feet, was made about 1745 by an anonymous, but accomplished and inventive Philadelphia cabinetmaker. The piece descended in the family of Joshua Humphreys, the shipbuilder of Southwark.

XLI. This painted Windsor armchair, with unpainted mahogany arms, c. 1806, is part of a set of chairs said to have been used in the Director's Room of Stephen Girard's Bank (formerly the First Bank of the United States). Independence Park has five of the original set. Under the seat is a paper label which reads in part: "ROBERT T. TAYLOR,/WINDSOR & FANCY CHAIR MAKER,/ . . . / At No. 99 South Front-Street (near Walnut-Street.)"

XLII. Limited facilities for the storage of linens and small clothes in an eighteenth-century house could be extended by the use of a chest of drawers. Such mahogany chest-on-chests as this one were popular in the homes of wealthy families. This fine example was made about 1770 and was originally owned by the von Kisselman family.

style the patron was able to pay for. Affleck also made the leather-upholstered arm-chairs and desks in 1790 and 1793 for both the House of Representatives and the Senate Chamber of Congress Hall, the west flanking building of the State House complex.[40]

John Folwell (working, c. 1762-82) is a Philadelphia cabinetmaker who is renowned for a chair he made and for a book he didn't publish. Folwell and John Norman, a Philadelphia engraver, and a group of sponsoring booksellers along the Atlantic coast planned to publish a book called *The Gentleman and Cabinet-Maker's Assistant, Containing A Great Variety of Useful and Ornamental Household Furniture. The Whole Being Illustrated with Upwards of Two Hundred Curious Designs, Elegantly Engraved on Sixty Folio Copper Plates. The Drawing, by the Ingenious John Folwell, Cabinet-Maker, and the Engravings by John Norman.*[41] But the Revolution began, and the project was abandoned. Unfortunately, all the drawings and plates have disappeared, and, until some come to light, we can only guess at the treasures that would have been in the book.

Folwell's famous chair for the Pennsylvania Assembly [pl. IV] gives us more than an inkling of his talents and is one of the most extravagant productions of an eighteenth-century American cabinetmaker's shop. The chair was made to replace the original Speaker's chair of the Pennsylvania Assembly, probably destroyed during the British occupation.[42] It was later to be used by General Washington in 1787 as presiding officer of the Constitutional Convention.

Folwell decided to incorporate as many patriotic and optimistic New-World decorative devices as would look well on the high back of the chair. The most prominent devices, a liberty cap and sunrise, were carved on the crest rail and gilded for emphasis. When the chair was comparatively new, and the gilded surfaces bright, they were observed by Benjamin Franklin at the successful conclusion of the Convention:

> Whilst the members were signing . . . Doctr. Franklin looking towards the Presidents Chair, at the back of which a rising sun happened to be painted, observed to a few members near him, that Painters had found it difficult to distinguish in their art a rising from a setting sun. I have, said he, often and often in the course of the Session, and the vicissitudes of my hopes and fears as to its issue looked at that behind the President without being able to tell whether it was rising or setting: But now at length I have the happiness to know it is a rising and not a setting Sun.[43]

Hornor, with customary perception, notes the difference in execution between Folwell's armchair and the French elbow chairs made by Affleck for Governor John Penn's home, two of which are now in the Governor's Council Chamber. Neither artisan suffers in comparison, for the chairs were made for different purposes and under different circumstances.

Thomas Tuft (died 1788) is less well known than some of the other cabinetmakers of this period, but one of his clients kept extensive records of his work, and from those records a great deal can be learned about the types of objects produced in this era. Tuft was established as a cabinetmaker by 1772, and bought his shop "four doors from the corner of Walnut Street in Second Street" in 1780. He did a great deal of work for a widow, Mrs. Mary Morris of Fair Hill, including repairs to various pieces of furniture.[44] When Mrs. Morris's daughter, Deborah, married George Logan, Tuft was commissioned to make all of Deborah's furniture. It took more than a year, possibly two years, to make a little breakfast table, a carved top highboy (which cost £ 45), a rolling pin (1s. 6d.), an ironing board, a mahogany sofa, a dozen dining room chairs, a tilt-top table, a dining table, a knife box, a high post mahogany bedstead with scalloped cornices and pulleys for drawing the curtains, a mahogany basin stand, and a large "Mahogany Drawers with fret & Dentels & (carved) Table to suit."[45] This lot of furniture cannot be readily identified, but it is possible that the carved-top high chest is the one auctioned with Logan furniture at Samuel T. Freeman & Co. in 1974 and now one of the treasures of the American Wing of the Metropolitan Museum of Art. At any rate, it could certainly have resembled the von Kisselman chest-on-chest with its dentils, frets, and scrolls (pl. XLII) in the Park collection and now in the Bishop White House bedroom.

While Philadelphia was celebrated for its creation of sophisticated Chippendale-style furniture, it was also the center for the production of turned wooden chairs that were comfortable, durable, and cheap. The Windsor chair in its early English-influenced form must have come to Philadelphia in the first quarter of the eighteenth century, but once it arrived in town it flourished as never before. The list of Philadelphia Windsor chair makers is impressively long, but surely one of the earliest artisans in the line must have been Thomas Gilpin (1700-66).[46] It is also quite likely that he had much more than an incidental part in bringing "The Philadelphia Chair"—as it became known all along the East Coast—to its state of perfection. Because Windsors played such an important part in the furnishing of the buildings in the area now encompassing the Park, both before and

119-121. *Above:* Painted poplar low-post bed, Pennsylvania, late-eighteenth or early-nineteenth century. Low-post beds were not only for the lowly on the social scale. Personal option, room space, and other circumstances determined whether or not one purchased a tall- or low-post bed. *Right:* High- or comb-back Windsor armchair, made by Thomas Gilpin, Philadelphia, c. 1750. Branded into the underside of the seat of the Gilpin armchair is the name of its maker.

after the Revolution, an incomparable assemblage of locally-made Windsor furniture is to be found here. The result of the research done for the furnishing plans for each historic structure in the Park indicated the widespread use of Windsor furniture, and so this form, particularly chairs, constitutes a significant part of the Park's collections. Since Francis Trumble (c. 1716-98), cabinetmaker and Windsor chair maker, is known to have supplied Windsor armchairs before and after the 1777-78 British occupation of Philadelphia,[47] he would represent the transition from bulbous-turned Windsor furniture to the end-of-the-century bamboo turnings of the furniture known to have been provided for Congress Hall by William Cox (active 1767-c. 1804).[48]

After the Revolution, trade with England resumed and new design books became available to supplement the earlier Chippendale-style volumes. Philadelphia furniture began to show evidence of a new "Federal" style and to demonstrate the influences of Hepplewhite and Sheraton. Americans traveled to England and the Continent and returned with the latest furniture. Edward Shippend Burd brought back from France a famous set of "Louis XVI" chairs, and there is a legend that when Dr. William White, rector of Christ Church and Saint Peter's, went to London in 1786 to be consecrated a bishop, he attended a sale after the death of George Hepplewhite and bought shield-

122-124. *Top:* Low-back Windsor settee, Pennsylvania, c. 1770. The basic form of a Windsor chair lent itself to adaptation as a settee, an especially useful furniture form for use in public buildings. *Right:* Sack-back Windsor armchair, made by Francis Trumble, Philadelphia, c. 1775. Trumble is noted as a chairmaker who provided seating furniture for the Pennsylvania State House both prior to, and subsequent to, the British occupation, 1777-78. On the underside of the Trumble chair is branded the name of its maker.

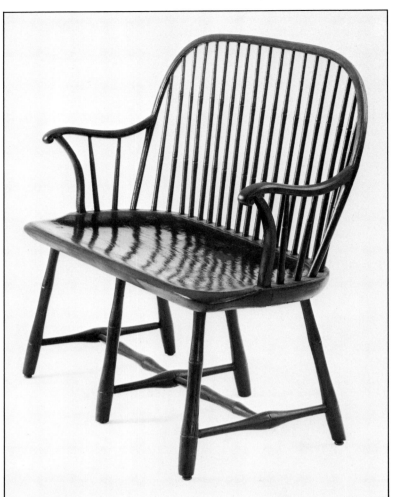

125-127. *Left:* Bow-back Windsor settee, made by John Letchworth, Philadelphia, c. 1790. Possibly a unique survivor, this settee of love-seat size is one of a pair now in the Park's collections. *Below (left):* Pair of bow-back Windsor armchairs, made by John Brientnall Ackley, Philadelphia, c. 1800. The Windsor chair was not without its variations on the theme of a spindled back, as here illustrated by a pair of chairs that might be termed "ribbon backs." *Below:* Pair of bow-back Windsor side chairs, Philadelphia, c. 1795. Part of a set of seven chairs, these examples illustrate a late-eighteenth-century innovation of sometimes upholstering the seat of a Windsor chair for additional comfort.

128-129. *Opposite page. Left:* Bow-back Windsor armchair, by John Letchworth, Philadelphia, c. 1800. This chair, which descended in the family of Bishop William White, is identical to the chair which appears in the foreground of John Sartain's painting of the Bishop's study (*see* pl. V). *Right:* Mahogany desk-on-frame, attributed to Jonathan Gostelowe, Philadelphia, c. 1787. Bishop White's house on Walnut Street, new in 1787, received many pieces of furniture from the shop of his friend and vestryman, Gostelowe. This desk appears prominently in the painting of the Bishop's study (*see* pl. V) and is very likely the work of this maker.

back chairs for his new dining room on Walnut Street.[49] The truth is that Bishop and Mrs. White were indeed aware of the latest fashion in fitting up a dining room, but they purchased the contents locally, probably from Jonathan Gostelowe.

A close patron-cabinetmaker relationship can be documented between Bishop White and Gostelowe. Gostelowe's first shop was in Church Alley in the shadow of the Bishop's chief charge. It is not surprising that, when the Bishop needed furniture for his new home, he would enlist the aid of his friend. Mrs. White's taste probably influenced the furnishings. She was the daughter of a former mayor and, as the well-to-do spouse of the state's newly consecrated Episcopal bishop, she certainly had no desire to be unfashionable.

Bishop White's study,[50] the scholarly male preserve at the rear of the second floor, was meticulously delineated by John Sartain in the painting commissioned by the Bishop's granddaughters after his death in July 1836 (*see* pl. V). With the graphic documentation of the painting, and the preservation of so many of the items portrayed by descendants, it has been possible in recent years to reproduce the study as it appears in the painting. The picture documents the unself-conscious use of high-style Chippendale chairs and Windsor chairs in the same room. Also seen is that library shelving was added at random, with more thought to convenience than aesthetics.

While Bishop White's house was under construction, with former Mayor Samuel Powel as volunteer Clerk of the Works, Benjamin Franklin returned at last from abroad and began enlarging his home, Franklin Court, under his own personal supervision. It was a period of growth for the city, for by Congressional compromise, Philadelphia became the nation's capital for the ten years between 1790 and 1800. The State House

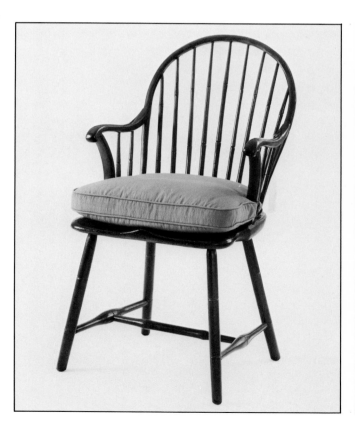

which had played a national role since the opening of the Second Continental Congress in the Assembly Room on May 10, 1775, was now serving as capitol of the commonwealth. Two new flanking buildings were turned over to the Federal authorities, the County Court House later known as Congress Hall to serve the Federal Congress and City Hall to be used by the United States Supreme Court.

Philadelphia never lost its drawing power for the ambitious and industrious. After the Revolution there were more native and foreign-trained furniture craftsmen than ever before and a patronage to keep them employed. The more prosperous members of Congress could afford to lease a house and have their families in residence, and the first families of the city vied with each other to entertain the politically-oriented residents of the new capital. The "Republican court" was in full swing.

In 1791 George Washington leased Robert Morris's mansion at 190 High (Market) Street, one block north of the State House, and proceeded to have it renovated and enlarged. As it was larger than his New York residence, which had been furnished with the household contents of the retiring French Minister, the Count de Moustier, and with New York furniture in the latest fashion (shield back chairs, Hepplewhite tables, etc.),[51] Washington furnished it lavishly by exchange and purchase. When he neared the end of his second term he purchased items for Mount Vernon, particularly for the "New Room," also called the Banquet hall: twenty-four side chairs in the Sheraton style and a

desk and bookcase with a tambour roll lid, the latter being for the General's Office-Library.[52] This furniture was purchased from the cabinetmaker John Aitken (working, 1790-1814), who assured the public in a newspaper advertisement that "he has for sale, chairs of various patterns, some of which are entirely new, never before seen in this city . . . Likewise, desks, bureaus, bookcases, bedsteads, tea tables, card, dining, ditto &c."[53]

The Presidential Mansion was splendid, but was outshone by the newest and most elegant domestic establishment in the city, the residence of William and Anne Willing Bingham at Third and Spruce Streets, just below the Samuel Powel house. This residence was as much like a London establishment as the wishes and resources of its owners could make it, and it was furnished lavishly from London furniture emporiums.[54]

All over town, younger men were building houses in the Federal style, and often they turned to local craftsmen to complete the homes in proper form. The new furniture was less robust than that in various colonial styles. The elaborate inlays that became popular required different techniques, a special knowledge of the idiosyncracies of exotic woods, and a sure hand with cutting tools.

Daniel Trotter (working, c. 1778-1800), chairmaker and cabinetmaker of Elfreth's Alley,[55] was one of the older Philadelphia craftsmen who was innovative enough to bridge styles and contribute his own version of what was "in the latest fashion." He

130. *Opposite page:* Pianoforte, made by Charles Albrecht, Philadelphia, c. 1790. The contrasting veneers of white pine, tiger-stripe maple, mahogany, and cherry woods make this instrument an especially handsome piece of case furniture. The mahogany piano stool is English in origin and is of the same period as the pianoforte.

131. *Left:* Bracket clock, Philadelphia, 1793-1809. The resumption of trade with England after the Revolution brought economic opportunities to urban artisan "mechanicks," including clockmakers, who, like Thomas Parker, could import clock parts from London and sell the assembled timepiece at a profit after he had put his own name on the dial. The works of this clock are signed by William Stephenson of London.

made so-called "pretzel splat" chairs for merchant prince Stephen Girard as well as tall post beds and other furniture for the upper rooms of Girard's house. A particular form of double swag ladder-back chair has been attributed to him. He had both apprentices and journeymen working in his shop. Thomas Janvier (working c. 1790-96), of Cantwell's Bridge (now Odessa), Delaware, was doing job lots in pieces for Trotter, apparently as a journeyman in the shop, while Ephraim Haines apprenticed to him in 1791 and became his son-in-law and partner in 1799.[60] Together they did much to popularize the Sheraton style in Philadelphia. The chief exponent of the Sheraton style in the city, however, was Henry Connelly (1770-1826).[57] About 1800 Connelly was established at 16 Chestnut Street, but he was working at other locations until he retired in 1824. The works of Haines and Connelly are so similar in style that it is difficult to differentiate between their unsigned pieces.

By the 1820s, Philadelphia was losing its position of leadership in furniture-making. With the ascendancy of New York City as the financial capital of the country and Washington as the political capital, Philadelphia seemed satisfied with its solid accomplishments, but the impetus which had been provided by the successes of the eighteenth century did not wane; on the contrary it flourished to the extent that there were sixteen times more men involved in the furniture trade by 1840 than could be found in 1760.[58] The fame of Philadelphia craftsmen as producers of what was both fashionable and innovative gave the city the domestic and foreign patronage that would warrant such an extensive body of craftsmen.

In order to survive as a craftsman, a cabinetmaker must please his clientele by creating useful objects in the latest fashion. Fashion, however, does not always denote purity of line or inherent good taste. One wonders, then, what some cabinetmakers whose working period spanned the late eighteenth and the early nineteenth centuries must have thought privately of the furniture forms requested by their nineteenth-century patrons. Duncan Phyfe, working in New York City from the last decade of the eighteenth century until the fourth decade of the nineteenth, chose to call his later productions his "butcher furniture." One wonders what his peers in Philadelphia—Henry Connelly, John Barry, Mathew Bouvier, Anthony Quervelle, and others—thought of the late Federal and the Greek Revival or Empire phases of their careers as accomplished cabinetmakers. The last mentioned, Quervelle, flourished in the second quarter of the nineteenth century and was responsible for the production of some of the most extravagant Philadelphia furniture in the Empire style.[59]

Until the middle of the century handwork for details was the rule locally, thus avoiding the banal duplication of the machine-filled factory. A visitor to the White House at Washington would have found much furniture therein of Philadelphia origin; for Presidents Monroe, Jackson and Buchanan had called upon Philadelphia artisans to supply furniture for the gaps produced by hard usage. Quality was the winning factor, and style and distinction were assured. Philadelphia could rest on its laurels, secure in the knowledge that it had never, even though a great city, lost its human scale. And that much that met the eye was of the best sort . . . and on a very high plane.

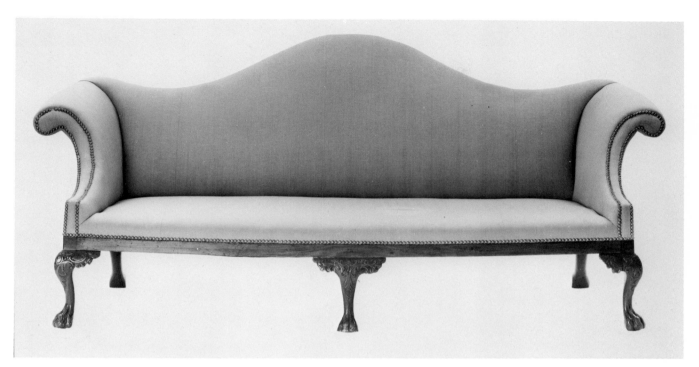

132-33. *Above:* Sofa, Philadelphia, c. 1765-70. This may be the only extant Philadelphia-made sofa with "hairy paw" feet. Adding to its importance is the sofa's history of ownership by Robert Morris and President George Washington, respectively. *Left:* Mahogany card table, Philadelphia, c. 1810. One of a pair in the Park's collection, this card table is characteristic of the understated carving on furniture of the Federal period in Philadelphia. Sheraton in style, the pair is attributed to what has been generically referred to as the Haines-Connelly School of cabinetmakers.

5. Portraiture: Commemorative and Symbolic
by John C. Milley

A museum of portraits has a forbidding ring to the general public of today—a mausoleum perhaps better left to dust and mummies than be entered into for education and rational entertainment, two of its most important reasons for being. Historically, the principal purpose of a portrait was commemorative. It preserved for present and future generations the likeness of an individual whose acts and deeds in life were deemed worthy of remembrance and emulation. It was, therefore, symbolic, a signpost to what people of a given time and place held to be an honorable conduct of life. Grouped together for either private or public contemplation, portraiture further helped foster either familial or national unity and conveyed a sense of security through one's identification with a tradition or heritage.

There can be little doubt that these purposes and precedents were foremost in the mind of Charles Willson Peale (1741-1827)—the painter whose works constitute the nucleus of the portrait collections of Independence National Historical Park—when he first conceived a gallery of "celebrated personages" associated with the American Revolution. It was in the same context that the Second Bank of the United States, a historic structure, was adapted in 1974 to serve as a portrait gallery dedicated to the founders of the United States. With no intention to signify a differentiation between the "decorative arts" and what we are disposed to call the "fine arts," the painting collections of the Park were consolidated in one building. The fortuitous marriage of one of the great examples of the Greek Revival style of architecture in America and a collection of portraits dating predominantly from the late eighteenth and early nineteenth centuries brought two arts together of similar ideological origin. Each in its own way was symbolic of the unification achieved through the American Revolution and of the country's need following that epical time to both commemorate its accomplishments and to give visual expression to the stability of its government.[1]

Portraiture, like other art forms, tells us of a time. It is datable and attributable to a

134. *Opposite page:* George Washington (1732-99), by Rembrandt Peale, c. 1824.

place of origin through stylistic and technological characteristics. The distinctiveness of
the recorded image of an individual is, however, in the subject portrayed, for that lends
itself to a personal association with, or a more intimate understanding of, a time past.
While a chair, a basket, a coverlet definitely tell us something about a culture, and may
delight us in sensuous ways, they often leave us wanting to know something more than
vital statistics about the person or persons who created or used them. Portraiture,
braced by interpretive biography, helps to supply such information. The maps and
prints, the furniture, the ceramics, the everyday household things all become more
meaningful in our identification with them of persons who used them or, indeed, caused
them to be made. Nevertheless, a portrait remains an abstraction of reality, and, aesthetic considerations aside, it can only speak to us in symbolic ways, provided, of
course, that we are equipped with knowledge of the historical and ideological frames of
reference in which the likeness was conceived, knowledge enhanced immeasurably by
an understanding of what purposes it served from one age to the next.

"In a historical point of view, this collection is *unique,* and very interesting, being composed of distinguished persons, whose names are inseparably connected with achievement of our Independence, and the foundation of our Institutions." So wrote the Messrs.
Thomas, the auctioneers who handled the sale of portraits from the Philadelphia
Museum of Charles Willson Peale in 1854. In the preface to the sale catalogue they went
on to say with some truth that they doubted that a comparable collection existed in any
country, and that it was their hope that it would become the basis for a national gallery.
They hit upon the commemorative nature of the paintings, isolating the various cate-
gories of fame for which the subjects were honored, but they fell far short of giving the
prospective purchaser any more justification for indulgence than that.[2]

Interest in the collection was overwhelmingly local. Failing, as Peale himself had
failed years earlier to awaken a national consciousness to the educational potentials of
the collection, the auctioneers hammered down the paintings piecemeal. Quite evident
at the auction, however, were a few public-spirited citizens who represented the City of
Philadelphia and who acquired a sizeable number of the portraits for the express purpose of placing them in Independence Hall. The selection of paintings is significant, for it
gave emphasis to the portraits of persons who were in some way associated with the
historical events which either took place in Philadelphia or made up the fabric of the city's history. Landscapes, still lifes, and more ambitious or personal forms of portraiture
were sacrificed by the city to other buyers. Clearly, those who guided the city's purchases preferred history to art, and in that respect they may have been closer to an
understanding of the traditional purposes of preserving one's likeness than later teach-
ings of aesthetics might have us believe. This is not to say that aesthetic considerations
were of no concern to the city's counselors in this matter, or to artists like Peale. Rather,
it underscores a basic difference in the conception and perception of these paintings
from one age to another.[3]

Conditioned as we are in the twentieth century to the candidness of the photographic
image, and to looking for the "Art" in a painting through generations of teaching, we
tend to look upon the hand-crafted likeness as bereft of other significance. Historical
tracts are replete with references to portraiture, its methodology and purposes, although all such commentaries must be weighed against other forms of visual and written evidence to ascertain their most probable meaning. An aesthetician of today might
tell us one thing about the portrait arts of Rome of the first century A.D., for instance, but
Pliny the Elder tells us something different. Lodged in his compendious work on *Natural
History* is his explicit condemnation of contemporary art as virtually unrecognizable in
person. Moreover, he criticized harshly the collecting of portraits for no other purpose

than the display of wealth. "Thus it is," he lamented, "that we possess the portraits of no living individuals [as his ancestors had] and leave behind us the picture of our wealth, not of our persons." Indolence had destroyed the arts.[4]

Pliny's words are not without their relevance to the portrait art of Charles Willson Peale. Pliny propounded a preference for verisimilitude in portrait art; he implied that there was a moral purpose to artistic endeavors; and he cast disdain by inference upon the pursuit of sensual pleasure without any other purpose. Revived during the Renaissance, and transmitted to America through England, the insistence upon fidelity to nature was the portraitist's charge. The phrase "to be like," however, meant something quite different from one end of the eighteenth century to the other. Where Roger de Piles in 1708 could concoct a recipe of equal parts of deportment, temperament, attitude and costume, which made the subject more recognizable, more "true" by station in society than in fact, Sir Joshua Reynolds would lecture between 1767-80 on a methodology for truth in portraiture that transmuted reality to idealization. The polarity of these extremes is exemplified in the contrast between the work of such American artists as Robert Feke and Thomas Sully.[5]

To advance the hypothesis that American artists of the first half of the eighteenth century possessed much more than a superficial acquaintance with the polemics of art theory, all having been publicized contemporaneously in London, may be to do both them and us an injustice. Rather, the assimilation of ways transmitted through the medium of prints and the perpetuation of inherited customs placed the work of American artists within a unified community of English art.

For all the similarities that researchers have found between the work of artists in America and provincial England, there were the differences of time and place. If anything, American portraiture of the first half of the eighteenth century was more *retardataire* than the arts of silversmithing and cabinetmaking. The portrait style of Feke is comparable to that produced in England almost a century earlier. What we find in the work of someone like Feke is what Roy Strong, the director of the National Portrait Gallery in London, finds in earlier work of provincial England, "the transmission of the baroque vocabulary into a two-dimensional Jacobean icon."[6] In other words, in areas removed from the style-setting centers, artists tended to cling tenaciously to older cus-

135. William Allen (1704-80), attributed to Robert Feke, c. 1750. The portrait of Allen was more true-to-life in its reflection of his social status in Philadelphia than in its recording of his actual appearance.

toms. The situation would reverse itself dramatically in America with the turn of the century (as in Sully's work, for example) and as a result of more frequent and direct contact with the style centers of London, Rome, and Paris.

Somewhere between the extremes of date and style of Feke and Sully were those who held that a person's character is revealed directly in the face and that to "be like" the portrait should approach a mirrored exactness. The eminent Dr. Samuel Johnson was of this thinking, adding that it was especially important in the portraits of ancestors that they be shown in the costume of their time, whereby the portrait became an historical document.[7] It was this kind of thinking that suited best the pragmatic mind of Charles Willson Peale, and it synchronized or harmonized well with his craftsman-oriented training.

By the time of Peale's adulthood, ideas of this kind flew on all sides of him, both in Philadelphia and in London, where he was training in the atelier of Benjamin West during the very years that Reynolds initiated his annual discourses. Art theory was heady stuff for a saddler from far-off provincial Annapolis, Maryland. Try as he may, even to the point of executing a print laden with symbolism of classical origin, he could not quite digest thinking of a philosophical kind. Although Peale never shied from mouthing in all sincerity his master's stance on the respect due the professional artist or the premier position assigned to the painting of history, or working tirelessly toward the establishment of an academy of art in Philadelphia, he had to confess that "My enthusiastic mind forms some idea of it, but I have not the execution . . . what little I do is by mear [sic] imitation."[8] The idea that art is imitation, and more specifically, the "Imitation of Nature, and therefore, of God," was one of ancient derivation. According to Dr. Charles Coleman Sellers, Peale's biographer and descendant, such thinking "was probably sifted to Peale through West's teaching, or it would not have taken so well."[9]

Dr. Sellers, as well as other scholars, recognized the pragmatic nature of Peale's thought, although what that may mean in terms of his painting style needs to be explored further. "He loved construction," Dr. Sellers revealingly writes of Peale, "the balancing of cause and effect, bringing together of elements into a harmonious whole, whether for sight or sound or practical service. Hammer and pliers filled his hand as readily as a brush, and the word 'engineer' not yet having currency, he was wont to speak of a skilled mechanic as an 'artist.'"[10] We tend to forget that Peale was an artisan and twenty-six years of age when he went to England, and that he lacked an educational background which might have influenced his receptivity to study substantively. Both West and Copley were considerably better prepared for study abroad, the former a precocious youth introduced quite early to art history and classical literature; the latter, equally precocious and the stepson of a London-trained engraver. In a word, both were more *au courant* in matters of art than Peale could possibly have been.

The Renaissance concept of an artist as something distinct from and superior to a craftsman in intellectual prowess, and consequently deserving of a higher standing in social esteem, was again something relatively new to Peale's thinking, having hardly had the time to filter down from the courts of royalty in England to the level of vernacular much before the mid-eighteenth century.[11] Buried in the subconscious of a culture, but pursued with conviction by artist and artisan alike, was the classical heritage of an art-craft equation. With reference to its origins in Greek philosophy, Professor Harold Osborne has written:

> Since through the greater part of human history the so-called fine arts
> were regarded as handcrafts among others . . . and since art objects
> like other products of human industry were designed to serve a purpose

136. Artemus Ward (1727-1800), by Charles Willson Peale, c. 1794-95. The incisiveness of this portrait indicates that it is a reliable likeness of the practical and puritanical-minded Revolutionary commander.

137. Baron von Steuben (1730-94), by Charles Willson Peale, c. 1781-82. Draftsmanship was the basis of art for Peale, an artistic principle which undoubtedly contributed to the hardness of his early portrait work.

recognized and approved by the society in which they arose, this practical interest in the purposes of the arts is the most general and in a sense the most natural of all.[12]

While the findings of a scholar working in a related field of inquiry may be shunted aside as not directly applicable to the subject at hand, one cannot dismiss as readily the evidence as manifested in the objects themselves. It would be hard to deny, for example, that the sculptural quality of the Humphreys-Archer armchair (*see* pl. XL) was not conceived as an artful production of execution just as aesthetically rewarding to its maker as the portrait of Rebecca Doz was to James Claypoole, Jr., its maker.

"In an age without machine industry," observes Harold Osborne, "people were keenly conscious of standards of workmanship."[13] The question was not so much one of whether an object was "art" or not, but whether it was well executed and was "useful" to society. Peale's craftsmanlike approach to portrait painting, and his dependence upon classical precedents, becomes patently clear as one follows the development of his museum plans and critically examines the "museum portrait" in particular. What he absorbed in England was put to maximum advantage and in ingenious ways.

Charles Willson Peale, who epitomizes the American artist bent on useful purposes, is looked upon by many who have but an acquaintance with his name as an eighteenth-century Mr. Blandings. The reasons for such misunderstanding are the humor we find in the way some of his well-meant endeavors ran afoul, the curious nature of some things he introduced into his museums (albeit for "rational entertainment"), and the way others have written about him. John Neal, for example, one of our earliest but most caustic critics, branded Peale as "One of the best men that God ever made," adding "although he will paint portraits with a chisel, marry a fifth or sixth wife every few years, and outlive all the rest of the world."[14] What Neal's wordplay referred to was the comparative hardness of Peale's portrait style, his passion for life, and his intense interest in all things affecting life.

Having little or no money, having absorbed as much as he could or cared to in and of England, Peale returned to America in 1769, a man determined to succeed in painting. The political strife that engulfed the colonies, Peale's move to Philadelphia in 1776, his roles as politician and military man in the Revolutionary War effort, and his encampment at Valley Forge, illustrate how inextricably his life was bound up with the events and people it became his purpose to chronicle in paint. How, when, and why he came to

138-39. *Right:* Benjamin Franklin (1706-90), possibly by Joseph Siffred Duplessis, c. 1779. For reasons now unknown, Peale's "museum portrait" of Franklin was not purchased by the City of Philadelphia at the 1854 sale. The ingenious Dr. Franklin is represented in the Park's collection, however, by this portrait, the gift of President Harry S. Truman in 1954. *Far right:* George Glentworth (1735-92), by Charles Willson Peale, 1794. The lilies of the valley and cut pink roses, together with the medical books, identify the subject as a surgeon who was recently diseased. The use of such symbolism was employed by Peale in the majority of his privately commissioned works.

XLIII. *Opposite (above):* Thomas Jefferson (1743-1826); Richard Henry Lee (1732-94); John Adams (1735-1826); all painted by Charles Willson Peale in 1791, 1784, and c. 1791-94, respectively. American statesmen of the Revolutionary period, especially those who were Signers of the Declaration of Independence, were the subjects of fame commemorated by Peale.

XLIV. *Opposite (center):* John Hanson (1721-83); William Bartram (1739-1823); Charles Thomson (1729-1824); all painted by Charles Willson Peale in c. 1781-82, 1808, and c. 1782-83, respectively. Hanson, the first president of the Continental Congress under the Articles of Confederation; Thomson, its secretary; and Bartram, a Philadelphian of international acclaim as a botanist, are typical of the portrait subjects purchased by the City at the sale of 1854.

XLV. *Opposite (below):* John Paul Jones (1747-92); Samuel Smith (1752-1839); Daniel Morgan (1736-1802); all painted by Charles Willson Peale in c. 1781, c. 1788-93, and c. 1794, respectively. Officers of the American Revolution were possibly the first among those Peale chose to commemorate with a "museum portrait."

XLVI. *Above (left):* Thayendanegea, Christened "Joseph Brant" (1742-1807), by Charles Willson Peale, 1797. When painted, Brant was in Philadelphia to press the need for an enlightened Indian policy, an appeal which fell on deaf ears. Knowing that, Peale's portrait of him becomes more meaningful in the perception it shows of Brant's intellect, compassion, and determination.

XLVII. *Above (right):* Marquis de Lafayette (1757-1834), by Thomas Sully, 1825-26. In contrast to the portrait of William Allen (*see* fig. 136), that of Lafayette is a generalization, romanticized purposefully to convey the aura of the revolutionary hero.

XLVIII. *Opposite:* Rebecca Doz (1759-75), attributed to James Claypoole, Jr., c. 1768-70. Painstaking care was taken with the construction of this portrait as revealed in its form and coloring, a masterful showing of the painter's craft in colonial America.

160

XLIX. James Madison (1751-1836), attributed to James Sharples, Sr., c. 1796-97. A typical Sharples pastel portrait of exceptional quality in its life-likeness, this painting records the actual appearance of Madison when he was a congressman.

L. William Floyd (1734-1821), by Ralph Earl, c. 1793. This painting provided a source for engravings incorporated into virtually all later publications treating the lives of the Signers of the Declaration of Independence.

the decision to develop a gallery of portraits of "eminent" men of the Revolutionary period are questions that may never be answered other than speculatively. That Philadelphia was a veritable gold mine for the head hunter may have been incentive enough. The important point, however, is that he did develop the idea, although it was far from being a new one. The fact that Peale's museum grew to incorporate natural history, even to the point of it taking precedence over the portraits in his attentions, was likewise neither novel nor new. What was new were the details of *how* he did these things.

The relationship of natural history to the portraits of man is of utmost importance to understanding both the times and Peale's points of reference. That the association is of classical origin has already been suggested in the reference to Pliny. It found full flower, however, in the *Kunstkammern,* or "cabinets of curiosities," which sprang up all over Europe in the sixteenth and seventeenth centuries—the dawn of scientific enlightenment. Numerous examples of such "cabinets" may be cited, but one is of particular interest because it produced a most important publication. In 1727, Neickelius of Leipzig published a book entitled *Museographia,* in which he offered a kind of blueprint for a scholarly collection, with shelves placed along opposite walls of a gallery for the *naturalia* and *artificialia,* respectively, and with the space over the shelves reserved for the portraits of famous men. Neickelius was telling of a fairly common practice—the establishment of cabinets as small encyclopedias of knowledge, following the sequential arrangement of man-animals-plants-rocks in a rational order of descending importance. In the Galleria Palatina in Rome (and other examples may be cited) systemization became aesthetic in form by placing all paintings in frames of a uniform style and size and hanging them according to the rules of symmetry.[15]

The keepers, caretakers, or curators, as they were variously called, who affiliated themselves with the *curiosi, otiosi,* and *virtuosi,* as the academicians and the collectors of the sixteenth and seventeenth centuries fashioned themselves, were learned men who seized upon every advance in science to better help classify the world of *naturalia* and *artificialia.* Having shaken the fetters of theological superstition prevalent in medieval thinking, men of the Renaissance and Enlightenment turned their thinking with increasing intensity to their own natural environment, human ingenuity, and artistic skills. Equally significant, as it runs through Peale's own words, is that there was a moral purpose attached to such endeavors—it was useful. Peale was in perfect accord with Neickelius, who believed that "idleness creates wickedness" and that collecting was a good and proper preventive to laziness.[16]

When Peale tells us in his writings that his museum was to be "a world in miniature," he does not say that the idea originated with him. Where he tells us that he would follow a system of classification, he does not say that Linnaeus was the source of his museum plans. Knowledge of such things was widespread and certainly not lost upon the educated classes of either England or America. If Peale was not personally familiar with the *Museographia,* he most certainly was conversant with its contents. If he did not see first-hand the collections of the great Ashmolean Museum in Oxford, there certainly was no dearth of others in and about London. The preceding essays in this book comment on the highly intellectual thinking of a scientific and cultural nature in Philadelphia of this time, and of scores of persons both resident and visiting, any number of whom might be expected to have had intimate knowledge of well-worn ideas respecting "cabinets of curiosity." Finally, Peale gives us his own tangible documentation of indebtedness to predecessors like Neickelius in his monumental self-portrait entitled *The Artist in His Museum.* Here, in every particular, is a museum of European ancestry, and in every particular it bears a startling resemblance to the portrait of *Cardinal Mazarin in His Gallery,* a painting that was engraved for distribution in the seventeenth century.[17]

We are told in tracts like the *Museographia* that the portrait was to represent the genus man in the great scheme of things, the highest form of primate—which is why paintings were placed uppermost on the walls in early museums. This was the museum arrangement later adopted by Peale sometime after he opened his gallery of portraits of eminent men in his home on Lombard Street in 1784, and before the addition of specimens of natural history. *Freeman's Journal* of 1784, the first catalogue of the collection, lists no fewer than forty-four subjects. The form this portraiture took tells us that its purpose was something different from either aesthetic enjoyment or education that required book-knowledge to be understood.

The majority of these paintings were executed in a more or less standard size and on rectangular-shaped canvas. They were bust portraits, with the subjects usually set against a neutral ground free of any accessory. And they were conceived to receive a gilded frame equipped with an oval spandrel. Evidence for the frames having been an integral part of Peale's creation of this, the characteristic "museum portrait," is contained on many of the canvases where the four corners are left unfinished.[18]

These portraits represent a radical departure from the majority of Peale's commissions of a private nature in which he almost invariably included some personal accessory, attribute, or symbol that would help identify the subject. Allegory was also a convention for the life-size public portrait, such as that of Monsieur Alexandre Gérard, commissioned from Peale in 1779 by the Continental Congress to honor the services rendered by the first foreign minister to the United States. The illusion of statuary in the upper right-hand corner of this painting, symbolic of the alliance formed between the two countries, has an obviously classical point of reference. More revealing, perhaps, with respect to Peale's thinking, is the portrait of Mary White Morris, painted in 1782, in which we find sculptured busts (among which is one of George Washington) placed upon pedestals in a formal garden setting. That the sculptured bust was the genesis of Peale's "museum portrait," either directly or indirectly, seems highly probable. He was thoroughly conversant with this form of portraiture, and no doubt its meaning. While in England he executed at least three plaster busts—one of Benjamin West, his teacher and master; one of Edmund Jennings, a patron of the arts and colonial sympathizer; and one of himself, the student—all three of which he later incorporated into the painting of his family.[19]

"Sculpture . . . in a sense," writes one scholar most tellingly, "is ever the portrait of immortals, for a bust portrait is often stripped to the essential to represent but the dominant trait which, though particularly that of one man, yet is nevertheless of universal value: grandeur, nobility, courage, force of character, profundity of thought, esprit, genius, intelligence . . . ."[20] Its potential realized during the Renaissance under the influence of humanist thinking, the sculptured bust was transposed to the painted surface. "The reasons for this practice," John Pope-Hennessy finds in his researches on the subject, "is that initially the role of the Renaissance portrait was commemorative; it was consciously directed to the future . . . . If the individual's reputation sprang from his character, and character as classical physiognomical treatises insisted, was directly mirrored in the face, it was in this way that he [the subject] should be commemorated." In the hands of a master like Botticelli, the portrait became a tour de force; "it stemmed from a tenuous web of Neoplatonic thinking whereby reality came to be accepted as a symbol and the depiction of reality took on symbolic overtones." Somewhat later, Giorgione was to give a sense of mysteriousness to the bust portrait by substituting a neutral background for the painted sky and giving less definition to the features.[21]

Thus we find ingeniously combined in the "museum portrait" by Peale almost all of the components that made for a new commemorative portrait style. It told of the virtues

140-42. *Above:* Conrad Alexandre Gérard (1729-90), by Charles Willson Peale, 1779. *Above (right):* Mrs. Robert Morris (née Mary White), (c. 1747-1827), by Charles Willson Peale, c. 1782. *Right:* Alexander Hamilton (1755-1804), by Charles Willson Peale, c. 1791. The adoption of the Constitution, and the location of the capital in Philadelphia provided Peale with subjects of political eminence, illustrated here with the first Secretary of the Treasury.

of the subject, it depicted one deserving of immortal fame, it was consciously directed to the future, it was realistically rendered (and in contemporary costume to make it a piece of history), and it had a foundation in the authority of antiquity. But to make the "museum portrait" more meaningful to Peale's own generation, something else was needed. That something else resided in the frame.

A classical source of origin is once again suggested in the form the frames took, although the inspiration for them came via a more circuitous route of transmittal and with slightly different connotations. Where the commemorative portrait of the Renaissance is often found framed with a rondel, as are the busts on Ghiberti's *Gates of Paradise* in Florence, here Peale adopted an oval. Not that oval framing in itself was anything new with Peale, either as a separate entity or painted in grisaille upon the canvas. When the oval is combined with other elements of design in the Peale frames, however, then it is something more than a trite essay. The moldings to the outer rectangular frame are light in proportion, and are carved with delicate strings of husks. The lightness, the carving, the oval are all so characteristic of the work of Robert Adam as to constitute something of a hallmark.[22] The revolution in design which the Adam brothers ushered into England upon their return from prolonged study abroad in 1758 was all-pervasive, profoundly effecting virtually every category of arts and crafts. It was in full sway in England, during Peale's sojourn there, and it washed America like a "nor'easter" with the cessation of armed conflict. Homogeneity of style in all its constituent parts of interior furnishings and design was yet another characteristic of this, the neoclassical style. The orchestration which the "museum portrait" represented was consistent with that and was one that Americans of the time could listen to with appreciative ears. They knew its meaning, they understood the rational thinking that went into its composition, and although the subjects were of quite diverse national origins, religious persuasions, and social standings, they were as one in this uniform presentation. It made "common sense," didn't it?

Peale's portrait collection grew in number to eighty-seven by 1795, at a time when Philadelphia was the nation's capital, and by this time he had broadened the base of those deserving of his particular stamp of recognition: those whose lives had been devoted to the humanities, jurisprudence, and the sciences. But by this time, too, any comparison of artist and craftsman was fast becoming an archaic kind of thinking as Americans were told more and more what "art" was all about and what special gifts of talent the artist was endowed with from birth. That kind of thinking was something Peale could never swallow wholeheartedly, insisting that painting was a teachable art which required but diligence and perseverance to master, a simplistic, even idealistic point of view to be sure. And he proceeded to make his point through his own example and by siring one of America's dynasties of painters.

The Peale "museum portrait" takes center stage in the Park's Portrait Gallery, accompanied there by yet a second and complementary collection of commemorative portraiture. Much, much less is known about its originator, James Sharples, an English painter of pastels.[23] Sharples was attracted to Philadelphia in 1796-97, during his first visit to the United States, by the promise of a lucrative and concentrated business. What he intended as the ultimate disposition of his collection of American worthies is unknown, but the immediate purpose it served was income through copy work. One suspects that he entertained a more lofty opinion of art and artists than did Peale, but we cannot be sure of that since very little in the way of records has been found concerning his personal traits.

His wife, Ellen, was no Samuel Sewell, but she penned a few cryptic comments about her husband which tell us that he did not have the perseverance of Peale. One suspects, too, that he may not have been on the best of terms with the senior Peale, since there is virtually no record of a correspondence between them, and they were competitors in a way for much the same clientele. Be that as it may, and given the difference between pastels and oils, and even the diminutive size of a Sharples portrait (7″ x 9″), the work of both has much in common. Each concentrated on the portrait bust, each ignored background in a commemorative portrait, and each approached his subject as objectively as possible. Sharples also adopted a uniform framing for his pictures, but probably more for the convenience of conveyance than anything else.

The medium of chalk, and the small size of a Sharples pastel, lends a sense of intimacy to his work, which in a Peale comes out more as a result of his personal acquaintance with his subjects than through the technique he favored. Both were masters at capturing the salient features of their sitters, an art which Sharples studied through a concentration upon the profile image, a portrait form he resorted to with some frequency. Also of classical derivation, the profile was effective in conveying a realistic vision. The oblique projection of the body, so that both shoulders are seen, gave solidity to the figure and strengthened its sense of being true-to-life.

Sharples left Philadelphia in 1797 to resume his itinerary of travel, taking baggage, family, and paintings with him. Except for its exhibit in Bath, England, in 1802, when a catalogue of the contents was printed, the Sharples collection received little public

143. Albert Gallatin (1761-1849), by Rembrandt Peale, 1805. The younger Peale added several works in the "museum portrait" vein to those of his father.

144. Benjamin Rush (1745-1813), possibly by Ellen Sharples after an original by James Sharples, Sr., c. 1803. That Ellen Sharples was personally acquainted with Dr. Rush explains the fidelity of this copy of the original, which is probably that in the Bristol Art Gallery, Bristol, England.

145. William Clark (1770-1838), by Charles Willson Peale, 1810. The Louisiana Purchase, and the success of the Lewis and Clark Expedition, contributed immeasurably to the American sense of self-sufficiency.

notice until it was advertised for sale better than fifty years later. The importance of the collection was left to another day, although its ultimate fate was identical to that of Peale's portrait grouping.

As time advances our perspectives change; the values of this generation are not necessarily, and most likely are not, those of the next; what was one era's symbol becomes a bauble to the next. That is a truism based on "the authority of fact," an apt phrase coined by Nicholas Biddle in another context. Or as one great curator wrote, ". . . nothing can properly be called a 'sign' that is not significant of something other than itself, and for the sake of which it exists."[24] The significance, then, of something like the "museum portrait," once lost, can only spell disaster—either to the painting's total destruction, or to its neglect for a period of time. Once its meaning is rediscovered, a painting may be reevaluated in terms of its meaning to the needs of that time, practically, metaphysically, or otherwise.

This situation obtained in the early nineteenth century. The frustrations which Peale experienced in his attempt to gain the approbation and appreciation of Congress for his museum, the strident cries of artists against what appeared an unappreciative patronage, America's harkening back to Greece for an architectural style that might best express its own self-confidence, the flirtations with utopian experiments, and Emerson's outpouring of transcendental thinking—all, and much more, were signs of restlessness, change, and uncertainty in the young nation.

Reason, or what was believed by those of Peale's generation to be that which gave order to everything, was being challenged as not all so reasonable. Everything might have a place in the order of things, but, then again, it might not. Man's passion was really

146. William Rush (1756-1833), by Rembrandt Peale, c. 1810-13. A woodcarver turned sculptor, Rush was one of the founders, together with Peale and others, of the Pennsylvania Academy of the Fine Arts in 1805.

not predictable at all. Quite the contrary, in fact, the passions of man could dictate his actions with little or no reasonableness of thought. What to do about slavery? What to do about states' rights? What to do about foreign intervention? The stream of questions that presented themselves as a new century dawned was seemingly endless. The dilemma such questions presented to thinking people could hardly be expected to have affected the body politic until it manifested itself in some material, pecuniary, or personal way. But for the thinkers it offered but one of three choices: to escape, join the bandwagon, or "bite the bullet." Americans attempted all three, spitting bullets back at anyone who dared malign their destiny, their sovereignty, or their culture.

The surge of industrial and territorial expansion had to spell the neglect or discard of one thing or another, anything superfluous to the task at hand. For Peale's museum it spelled doom, and for the "museum portrait" it spelled disinterest. No metaphysical need of national magnitude was felt to commemorate the lives of those but recently deceased or still alive; the portraits were old-fashioned but certainly not sufficiently old enough to be held up for veneration; and they were either not "art" or of the lowest order of an artist's concerns. But art in the "grand manner" was culture, and that must be acquired—quickly.[25]

It is now believed, as one scholar puts it succinctly, "that America's fascination with art, stemmed from her lack of art."[26] Early in the nineteenth century a crusade was mounting that would culminate in the idealization of art and the development of reproductive media for the propagation of art, and that would spurn the development of our treasure-laden museums and foster a faith in art as an entity unto itself.

The museum movement and the development of aesthetics as a branch of philosophy are voluminous stories unto themselves, but insofar as they bear upon the resurgence of interest in our material past their influence need be noted. Peale's collection of portraits, however, was preserved, for the most part, for a different reason—as we have seen. Behind it was a bombastic spurt of nationalism. Success in the bogus War of 1812, and the return visit of the Marquis de Lafayette in 1824, have been recognized as catalysts, if not the turning points of America's awakening to matters of historic preservation. The phenomenon did not spring full grown from the head of Zeus, and it took a century or more for the cumulative effects of knowledge to give it a rational direction. One of its earliest manifestations was a stream of publications dealing with the lives of leaders in the Revolutionary War, many of them illustrated with engravings taken from the portraits of Peale, Trumbull, Stuart and others. Two good examples are John Sanderson's nine-volume work, *Biographies of the Signers of the Declaration of Independence* (1820-27), and Longacre and Herring's *The National Portrait Gallery of Distinguished Americans* (1834). By 1854, and the auctioning off of Peale's portrait collection, however, one suspects that it was more than nationalism that goaded the City of Philadelphia into its purchases at the sale. The whole country was in desperate need of a rallying point of some kind, some unifying purpose, some reminder of what the American Revolution was supposed to have achieved.

The questions posed at the turn of the century, now made manifest, affected everyone. America had nurtured its own holocaust. It was in the 1860s, in the aftermath of war, more than at any other time perhaps, that the commemorative portrait fulfilled its purpose as a symbol. Its multifold presence in the Assembly Room of Independence Hall, where the body of Abraham Lincoln lay in state, could not have gone unnoticed by many of the thousands who queued for twenty-four hours dumbfounded, incensed, at a loss to explain how such a senseless thing could have happened.

The Centennial celebrations of 1876 helped a great deal in bringing Americans together again in a common cause of achievement and resulted in an intense interest in our heritage, and everything related to it. Again the portraits were paraded out with all the patriotic oratory the occasion seemed to require. On April 11, 1872, the Select and Common Councils of Philadelphia decreed that "Independence Hall is hereby set apart forever, and appropriated exclusively to receive such furniture and equipments of the room as it originally contained in July, 1776, together with the portraits of such men of the revolution as by their presence or action served to give the building its historic renown, and forever endear it to the hearts of patriots."[27]

The decree was a license to collect for a good purpose if there ever was one. And collect they did—everything from a lock of Washington's hair to newly manufactured glass Liberty Bells. They did even better than that, and across the land Washington beds vied with Hancock chairs for preeminence in numbers. The accomplishments of the Centennial celebration, however, were considerable. One was the acquisition of forty-five of the portraits from the original collection of James Sharples. The collection had miraculously survived virtually intact, and, when offered for sale in Baltimore, a selection of them was made for Independence Hall.

The Councils' ordinance of 1872 had its negative effect, however, since it gave to city officials a carte blanche to acquire things of questionable historic value for the Hall. From the Centennial into the first quarter of the twentieth century this practice resulted in the admission of copies of portraits, and some of subjects with the most tenuous of historical associations with either the city or the Revolution. What matter if a painting was a life portrait or not? After all, it was the subject that counted most, and, as long as the figure was recognizable, what more could be wanted?

Our thinking on that score has been very much turned around, thanks to the coordinated contributions of scholars of several disciplines. Countless writers from antiquity to the present have attested to the efficacy of a life portrait, the truthfulness of which is sapped dry in copy work. One could not gain much by way of insight into the character of "Old Hickory" from David Rent Etter's copied likeness. Andrew Jackson was a fire-spitting, headstrong, argumentative, stubborn and crafty individual—one capable of be-heading that "Hydra of corruption," the Second Bank of the United States. If he looked as we see him here, however, we would have to conclude that he was a timid soul and quite the opposite in character. How insipid this portrait becomes when contrasted with that of Timothy Matlack, the last portrait that Peale painted in his lifetime and a tour de force in character study. Matlack, once a firebrand of a man, is now wracked by old age, but his tenaciousness is revealed in the features and the way Peale has so understand-ingly preserved them for us.

In his essay on the "Uses of Great Men," Ralph Waldo Emerson wrote:

> The world is upheld by the veracity of good men; they make the earth wholesome—We call our children and our lands by their names. Their

147. Andrew Jackson (1767-1845), by David Rent Etter, c. 1829-37.

148. Timothy Matlack (1736-1829), by Charles Willson Peale, 1826. This is the last portrait painted by Peale.

> names are wrought into the words of language, their works and effigies are in our houses, and every circumstance of the day recalls an anecdote of them . . . But he must be related to us, and our life receive from him some promise of explanation . . . Certain men affect us as rich possibilities, but helpless to themselves and to their times,—the sport, perhaps, of some instinct that rules the air; they do not speak to our want. But the great are near; we know them at sight.[28]

And so it is that the images, the character, the work of sacrifice and reward in behalf of human liberties of persons like Washington, Jefferson, Adams, and others—given whatever faults of character each and every one may have had—have become graven in our minds through symbols of them in the form of portraiture. In the introduction to a catalogue of an exhibition of portraits, Mitchell Wilder writes about these same persons: "The years have added to their reputation as revolutionaries, yet it is most unlikely that our heroic patriots saw themselves in any greater role than that of outraged citizens."[29] If such was the case it brings them down to our level, and while we might protest the absence of portraits of those who we might call the common man, we overlook the purposefulness that someone like Peale had in mind. And, if we choose to look at these objects, the chairs, the teapots, the portraits, as either "art" or artful, it could do no less than contribute to our rational entertainment.

Notes to the Text

Introduction

[1] The words of Washington and Adams were paraphrased as a book title by Catherine Drinker Bowen, *Miracle at Philadelphia* (Boston: Little, Brown and Company, 1966) and the source acknowledged in her introductory remarks.

[2] Bernard Bailyn, *The Ideological Origins of the American Revolution* (Cambridge: The Belknap Press of Harvard University Press, 1967), p. 19.

[3] John A. H. Sweeney, "Introduction," in *Material Culture and the Study of American Life*, ed. Ian M. G. Quimby (New York: W.W. Norton & Company, Inc., 1978), p. 1.

[4] Standard references to the methodology and philosophy of symbolism in the visual arts are Irwin Panofsky, "The History of Art as a Humanistic Discipline," in *Meaning in the Visual Arts* (Garden City, N.Y.: Doubleday & Company, Inc., 1955); and Susanne H. Langer, *Philosophy in a New Key* (Cambridge: Harvard University Press, 1951).

[5] The essays by different authors contained in Quimby, *Material Culture*, are particularly revealing in the new information about historical events that has been gleaned through the study of America's material culture. As John A.H. Sweeney summarizes the contribution of Cary Carson's article, "Doing History with Material Culture," Carson "offers the point of view of the New History in which the social sciences and the application of quantification techniques are integrated with the study of history . . . he shows that the interests of some historians are for the first time converging with those of the 'thing' people."

[6] Panofsky, pp. 36-37.

[7] Ananda K. Coomaraswamy, *Christian and Oriental Philosophy of Art* (New York: Dover Publications, Inc., 1956), p. 20.

[8] Michael Kammen, *A Season of Youth* (New York: Alfred A. Knopf, 1978), p. 16.

[9] Ibid., p. 94.

[10] Russell Lynes, *The Tastemakers* (New York: Grosset & Dunlap, 1954).

[11] Edward M. Riley, *Independence National Historical Park*, National Park Service Historical Handbook Series, No. 17 (1956), pp. 56-58.

[12] David H. Bishop, *Assent to Significance: The Evolution of the Liberty Bell As a Cultural Symbol*, TS., American Studies Senior Thesis, Temple University (1975), pp. 20 ff.

[13] Riley, p. 41.

[14] A more detailed account of this history is contained in Susanna Koethe Morikawa, *History of the Portrait Collection*, Museum Office TS., Independence National Historical Park Papers (Philadelphia, 1975).

[15] On the subject of nationalism vs. sectionalism in the United States see: George Dangerfield, *The Awakening of American Nationalism 1815-1828* (New York: Harper & Row, 1965); on the subject of Peale's efforts to nationalize his museum see: Charles Coleman Sellers, *Mr. Peale's Museum* (New York: W.W. Norton & Company, 1980); on the subject of museums in the United States see Alma S. Wittlin, *Museums: In Search of a Useable Future* (Cambridge: The M.I.T. Press, 1970).

[16] Wittlin, pp. 39-53.

[17] D. W. Belisle, *History of Independence Hall* (Philadelphia: James Challen & Son, 1859), p. 9.

[18] Lillian B. Miller, *Patrons and Patriotism* (Chicago: The University of Chicago Press, 1966), p. vii.

[19] Frank M. Etting, *An Historical Account of the Old State House of Pennsylvania* (Philadelphia: Porter and Coates, 1891), p. 180.

[20] John C. Milley, "History and Analysis of Congress Hall Furniture," app. III, in *Furnishings Plan for the Second Floor of Congress Hall*, pt. D, Museum Office TS., Independence National Historical Park Papers (Philadelphia, 1965).

[21] Cited in Morikawa, p. 18.

[22] Riley, pp. 46-49.

Chapter 1

[1] Lawrence C. Wroth, *The Colonial Printer*, 2nd ed. (1938; rpt. Charlottesville: Dominion Books, 1964), pp. 12-13, 16, 19-20, 224-26.

[2] Isaiah Thomas, *The History of Printing in America*, ed. Marcus A. McCorison (New York: Weathervane Books, 1970), pp. 42-67, 340-44, 354-55, 458.

[3] *American Printmaking: The First 150 Years* (Washington, D.C.: Smithsonian Institution Press, 1969), p. 16.

[4] Benjamin Franklin wrote about contriving needed sorts while in the employ of Samuel Keimer. See: *The Autobiography of Benjamin Franklin*, ed. Leonard W. Labaree (New Haven: Yale University Press, 1964), p. 110. The first American production of type fonts with moderate success was by Abel Buell, a Connecticut silversmith and lapidary, in 1769. Christopher Sower, Jr., a German printer in Philadelphia, began casting letters in German more successfully in 1770, but he used imported matrices whereas Buell had made his own. By early 1775 type production had increased considerably in Pennsylvania, and type was listed in the non-importation resolutions in January of that year. For more detailed information see: Lawrence C. Wroth, *The First Work with American Types* (Cambridge, 1925), and Wroth, *Colonial Printer*, pp. 98-108.

[5] Norman B. Wilkinson, *Papermaking in America* (Greenville, Delaware: The Hagley Museum, 1975), pp. 19-21.

[6] *American Printmaking*, pp. 17-20.

[7] *The American Weekly Mercury*, 5 May 1720; *American Printmaking*, p. 20.

[8] Peter Collinson, who acted as a purchasing agent for the Library Company in London, sent the print under cover to the Honourable Thomas Penn to give to the group. They recorded that "The Print of the Orrery our Proprietor, sent to the Library, where it was fram'd & hung up at our late annuall Election of Officers. . . ." *A Book of Minutes containing An Account of the Proceedings of the Directors of the Library Company of Philadelphia*, Vol. 1, pp. 25, 30.

[9] Sinclair H. Hitchings, "The Graphic Arts in Colonial New England" in *Prints in and of America to 1850*, John D. Morse, ed. (Charlottesville: The University Press of Virginia, 1970), p. 100.

[10] Franklin, *Autobiography*, pp. 119-21.

[11] Franklin's Agreements of Partnership usually stipulated that he supply the press and letters, pay one-third of the expenses, and receive one-third of the profits. After six years his associates usually bought out his share of the business. He extended this financial assistance to printers in New York, Charleston, Lancaster, and Antigua, as well as to several German printers in Philadelphia. *Autobiography*, pp. 166, 181.

[12] Franklin, *Autobiography*, p. 141.

[13] Having accepted Collinson's offer of his services free of charge, the Library Company instructed him to ". . . deal with a Bookseller that should use us well; the Directors suspecting that many of the last parcel were overcharged—and to let us have them come bound." *Minutes*, Volume 1, p. 45.

[14] Michael Kraus, *Intercolonial Aspects of American Culture on the Eve of the Revolution* (1928; rpt. New York: Octagon Books, 1964), p. 105.

[15] Franklin, *Autobiography*, p. 164.

[16] Hugh Honour, *The New Golden Land: European Images of America from the Discoveries to the Present Time* (New York: Pantheon Books, 1975), p. 109.

[17] For a more detailed discussion of Popple and the map see "Popple Map added to Cartographic Collection," *Winterthur Newsletter*, XIX (1973), No. 9, 1-3.

[18] *Pennsylvania Gazette*, 13 October 1748.

[19] *The Maryland Gazette*, 5 April 1749, in Alfred Coxe Prime, *The Arts & Crafts in Philadelphia, Maryland and South Carolina, 1721-1785* (The Walpole Society: 1929), p. 35; *The New-York Gazette Revived in the Weekly Post-Boy*, 24 August 1752, in Rita S. Gottesman, *The Arts and Crafts in New York, 1726-1776* (New York: New-York Historical Society, 1938), pp. 19-20.

[20] For an extremely thorough analysis and history of the map, including a list of its various states, see Coolie Verner, "The Fry and Jefferson map," *Imago Mundi*, XXI (1967), 70-94. The map is also discussed in Dumas Malone, ed., *The Fry & Jefferson Map of Virginia and Maryland* (Charlottesville: The University Press of Virginia, 1966).

[21] The map's original subscribers, in fact, were the pilots and shipmasters who sailed the Delaware River. For a detailed discussion of Fisher and the chart, see Lawrence C. Wroth, "Joshua Fisher's 'Chart of Delaware Bay and River,'" *The Pennsylvania Magazine of History and Biography*, LXXIV (1950), 90-109.

[22] Heap finished his rendering before the State House bell tower was completed; to assure that the image would be as up-to-date as possible, he used the scale plans for the belfry to complete his drawing. The map was *A Map of Philadelphia, and Parts Adjacent, With a Perspective View of the State-House . . . 1752*. Martin P. Snyder, *City of Independence: Views of Philadelphia before 1800* (New York: Praeger Publishers, 1975), pp. 36-37.

[23] Snyder, *City of Independence*, pp. 42-43.

[24] Peter C. Marzio, "Illustrated News in Early American Prints" in *American Printmaking before 1876: Fact, Fiction and Fantasy* (Washington, D.C.: Library of Congress, 1975), pp. 59-60; *American Printmaking*, pp. 22-23.

[25] Snyder, *City of Independence*, pp. 53-55; *Pennsylvania Staatsbote*, 6 June 1763, in Prime, *Arts & Crafts, 1721-1785*, p. 15; *American Printmaking*, p. 25.

[26] As is clear from some of these entries, all sorts of prints were referred to as "pictures" in eighteenth-century inventories. As Abbott Lowell Cummings suggests, ". . . much of what is mentioned in the inventories was more apt to be representative of the graphic arts." For further detail and elaboration see: Cummings, ed., *Rural Household Inventories Establishing the Names, Uses and Furnishings of Rooms in the Colonial New England Home, 1675-1775* (Boston: The Society for the Preservation of New England Antiquities, 1964), especially pp. xxxiv-xxxvi.

[27] The titles of Cadwalader's prints included classical, religious, and genre topics, among them "Diana & Colisto," "Elijah Raising the widow's son," and "Jocond Peasants." Kennedy was also paid for framing and glazing many of the prints. For a complete list of the titles enumerated on Kennedy's bill, and a general discussion of the purchases, see: Nicholas B. Wainwright, *Colonial Grandeur*

in Philadelphia: The House and Furniture of General John Cadwalader (Philadelphia: The Historical Society of Pennsylvania, 1964), pp. 49-50.

28   *Prints Pertaining to America* (The Walpole Society: 1963), p. 20; *Pennsylvania Chronicle,* 12 December 1768, in Prime, *Arts & Crafts, 1721-1785,* p. 33; for an especially interesting discussion of this topic see: Joan Dolmetsch, "Prints in Colonial America: Supply and Demand in the Mid-Eighteenth Century" in *Prints in and of America to 1850,* John D. Morse, ed.

29   *Pennsylvania Chronicle,* 20 July 1767, in Prime, *Arts & Crafts, 1721-1785,* p. 38; *Pennsylvania Gazette,* 24 July 1755, in Ibid., p. 300; *Pennsylvania Gazette,* 15 December 1763 and 12 December 1754.

30   City of Philadelphia, *Minutes of Common Council 1704-1776,* 5 October 1762. Scull's map, in progress when he died, included Southwark and the Northern Liberties. For additional information, see: Snyder, *City of Independence,* pp. 62-64, 73-74.

31   *Pennsylvania Archives,* Eighth Series, Vol. VII, 15 January 1767, pp. 5960.

32   Hazel Shields Garrison, "Cartography of Pennsylvania before 1800," *The Pennsylvania Magazine of History and Biography,* LIX (1935), 278-79.

33   Lillian B. Miller et al., *In the Minds and Hearts of the People* (Greenwich, Connecticut: New York Graphic Society, 1974), p. 15.

34   Occasionally satirical prints were even published at the request of the opposition party; it is known that Benjamin Wilson produced *The Repeal . . . of Miss Ame-Stamp* at Edmund Burke's request, to please Lord Rockingham. Michael Wynn Jones, *The Cartoon History of the American Revolution* (New York: G.P. Putnam's Sons, 1975), pp. 10-12.

35   Benjamin Franklin wrote to Deborah, his wife, from London on April 6, 1766. He enumerated the contents of a box which he was sending to her, concluding: "There are some Droll Prints in the Box, which were given me by the Painter; and being sent when I was not at home, were pack'd up without my Knowledge." One of these is known to have been a copy of *The Repeal. . . .* Leonard W. Labaree, ed., *The Papers of Benjamin Franklin* (New Haven: Yale University Press, 1969), Vol. 13, p. 234.

36   E.P. Richardson, "The Birth of Political Caricature" in *Philadelphia Printmaking: American Prints before 1860,* Robert F. Looney, ed. (West Chester, Pennsylvania: Tinicum Press, 1976), p. 71.

37   Clarence S. Brigham, *Paul Revere's Engravings* (Worcester, Massachusetts: American Antiquarian Society, 1954), pp. 41-45.

38   Brigham, *Engravings,* pp. 59-60, 79-80.

39   Charles Francis Adams, ed., *The Works of John Adams* (Boston: Charles C. Little and James Brown, 1850), Vol. II, p. 367.

40   *Pennsylvania Journal,* 11 August 1773, and *Pennsylvania Packet,* 21 March 1774, in Constance V. Hershey, *Historic Furnishing Plan for City Tavern,* November, 1974, pp. 213-14. Prints and maps were popular items of decoration in American taverns: the 1772 inventory for the Swan Tavern in Yorktown, Virginia, listed "12 Prints of the Seasons Glazed & framed," "1 large Map of Virginia," and 19 other prints. The complete inventory is listed in Hershey, *City Tavern,* pp. 194-96.

41   Marine insurance was not available in America until the Insurance Company of North America was founded in Philadelphia in 1792.

42   Julian P. Boyd, *The Declaration of Independence: The Evolution of the Text as Shown in Facsimiles of Various Drafts by its Author, Thomas Jefferson* (Princeton: Princeton University Press, 1945), pp. 5-38.

43   Worthington Chauncey Ford, ed., *Journals of the Continental Congress* (Washington, D.C.: Government Printing Office, 1906), Vol. V, p. 516.

44   Edmund C. Burnett, ed., *Letters of the Members of the Continental Congress* (Washington, D.C.: Carnegie Institution of Washington, 1923), Vol. II, pp. 1-2.

45   Ford, *Journals,* Vol. V, p. 431.

46   Adams's August, 1776, letter to Abigail went on to describe those maps already collected, framed and hung in the room, including Lewis Evan's 1755 *Map of the Middle British Colonies,* Nicholas Scull's 1759 *Map of the improved Part of the Province of Pensilvania* and William Scull's 1770 *Map of the Province of Pennsylvania.* He promised to send her a full list once the collection was completed. L.H. Butterfield, ed., *Adams Family Correspondence* (Cambridge, The Belknap Press, 1963), Vol. 2, pp. 90-92.

47   Norman, a recent English immigrant, called himself variously an architect, engraver, drawing master, and landscape-engraver. The maps described were advertised in the *Pennsylvania Journal,* 12 March 1777 and 16 July 1777, as recorded in Prime, *Arts & Crafts, 1721-1785,* pp. 23-24.

48   These were the well-known views *The Battle of Lexington, A View of the Town of Concord, The Engagement at the North Bridge in Concord* and *A View of the South Part of Lexington.* See: *American Printmaking,* pp. 33-35.

49   Snyder, *City of Independence,* p. 73; I.N. Phelps Stokes, *The Iconography of Manhattan Island, 1498-1909* (New York: Robert H. Dodd, 1915), Vol. I., pp. 340, 343.

50   Lieutenant Page incorrectly labeled Breeds Hill and Bunker Hill, and showed the higher elevation of Bunker Hill in the southeast rather than the northwest. The British Library, *The American War of Independence 1775-83* (London: British Museum Publications Limited, 1975), p. 53.

51   *Pennsylvania Gazette,* 20 August 1783; Donald A. Shelley, *The Fraktur-Writings or Illuminated Manuscripts of the Pennsylvania Germans* (Allentown: The Pennsylvania German Folklore Society, 1961), pp. 39-57, 90, 94; *Pennsylvania Gazette,* 14 May 1783.

52   Letter from Charles Willson Peale to Dr. David Ramsey, Charleston, S.C., as quoted in Library Company of Philadelphia, *Made in America: Printmaking, 1760-1860: An Exhibition of Original Prints from the Collections of the Library Company of Philadelphia and the Historical Society of Pennsylvania.* (April-June 1973), p. 9.

53   *American Printmaking,* pp. 43-44.

54   West told him that once he had raised the money to pay for the engraving of the first two paintings, the revenue from print sales would finance the remainder of the series. Irma B. Jaffe, *John Trumbull: Patriot-Artist of the American Revolution* (Boston: New York Graphic Society, 1975), pp. 82, 197.

55   Marzio, "Illustrated News," p. 54.

56   William Birch, introductory page to *The City of Philadelphia in the State of Pennsylvania North America; as it appeared in the Year 1800 consisting of Twenty Eight Plates. . . .*

Chapter 2

1   William Penn, *A Letter From William Penn Proprietary and*

Governor of Pennsylvania In America to the Committee of the Free Society of Traders of that Province, residing in London (1683), p. A. 2.

[2] Louise Belden, "Pennsylvania German Pottery," TS., The Henry Francis du Pont Winterthur Museum Library, Winterthur, Delaware 1960, pp. 3-4.

[3] Gary B. Nash, "The Transformation of Urban Politics, 1700-1765," *Journal of American History,* 60, No. 3 (December 1973), 607-608.

[4] Barbara Liggett, *Archaeology at Franklin's Court* (Philadelphia: Eastern National Park and Monument Association 1973), pp. 14-15.

[5] Harrold E. Gillingham, "Pottery, China and Glass Making in Philadelphia," *The Pennsylvania Magazine of History and Biography,* LIV (1930), 100-105; "Minutes of Common Council of Philadelphia" 20 May 1717, in Alfred Coxe Prime, *The Arts and Crafts in Philadelphia, Maryland and South Carolina, 1721-1785* (The Walpole Society: 1929), p. 127.

[6] Harold F. Guilland, *Early American Folk Pottery* (Philadelphia: Chilton Book Company 1971), p. 38.

[7] Ibid., p. 39.

[8] For more detailed information see: Robert L. Giannini III, "Anthony Duché, Philadelphia Potter, *c.* 1682-1762" TS. (Philadelphia: Independence National Historical Park).

[9] Gertrude MacKinney, "Votes and Proceedings of the House of Representatives of the Province of Pennsylvania, 14 October 1726-22 September 1741," *Pennsylvania Archives,* Eighth Series, III (Philadelphia, 1931), 2047-49.

[10] Anthony Duché, Sr., "Will #177" June 1762, MS (Philadelphia: City Hall Annex, Department of Wills and Administrations).

[11] For an especially interesting inventory of Duché's pottery see the inventory of his estate attached to: Duché, Sr., "Will #177" June 1762.

[12] *American Weekly Mercury* [Philadelphia], 11 & 18 July 1734, p. 4, col. 1; *Pennsylvania Gazette* [Philadelphia], 17 June 1762, p. 3, col. 3.

[13] James Duché, "Inventory of Personal Estate of James Duché Deceased, 27 March 1751," Inventory #20, MS (Philadelphia: City Hall Annex, Department of Wills and Administrations).

[14] Gillingham, pp. 104-105.

[15] Ruth Matzkin, "Inventories of Estates in Philadelphia County, 1682-1710" Thesis for MA, TS (University of Delaware 1959), p. 73.

[16] Matzkin, p. 73.

[17] Gillingham, pp. 100-102, 105.

[18] Arlene M. Palmer, *The Wistarburg Glassworks: Beginning of Jersey Glassmaking* (Alloway, New Jersey: The Alloway Township Bicentennial Committee 1976), pp. 4-6.

[19] Ibid., pp. 17-19.

[20] *Pennsylvania Gazette* [Philadelphia], 6 October 1757.

[21] Matzkin, pp. 71-81.

[22] *Pennsylvania Gazette* [Philadelphia], 20 April 1758.

[23] An advertisement in the *Maryland Gazette* for 2 September 1756 states that Thomas Baker of St. Mary's County, Maryland, has for sale earthenware of the same kind from Philadelphia and good workmen from Liverpool and Philadelphia. The association of Philadelphia earthenwares and workmen mentioned in the same breath with an English city is worth mention and lends support to the importance of the Philadelphia earthenware market (See: Prime, p. 112).

[24] Palmer, p. 32.

[25] Ibid., pp. 32-33.

[26] Ibid., pp. 33-34.

[27] Prime, pp. 140-52.

[28] Farrell and Bakeoven may have bought the Philadelphia Glass Works in Kensington which was offered for sale in 1777. For additional information see: *Pennsylvania Gazette* [Philadelphia], 27 August 1777; *The Pennsylvania Evening Post* [Philadelphia], 15 April 1777 and 20 May 1777.

[29] William MacPherson Hornor, Jr., *Blue Book of Philadelphia Furniture: William Penn to George Washington* (Philadelphia: 1935), pp. 133, 237, 275-76.

[30] Alexander Bartram, MS (In Attainder Papers, Household Furnishings, Records of the Secretary of the Commonwealth Division of Public Records, Harrisburg, Pa. 1961), pp. 1-4.

[31] "Tax lists for 1769 to 1774," on microfilm. (Philadelphia: Department of Revenue and Taxation, City Hall), in Independence National Historical Park Library.

[32] Daniel Topham, "Brick production, 1780," Arts & Crafts research note card file in the Independence National Historical Park Library.

[33] *New York Gazette and Weekly Mercury,* 15 March 1773.

[34] Graham Hood, *Bonnin and Morris of Philadelphia, The First American Porcelain Factory, 1770-1772* (Chapel Hill: The University of North Carolina Press 1972), p. 5.

[35] Ibid., pp. 11, 13-14.

[36] *Pennsylvania Gazette* [Philadelphia], 3 August 1772, as cited in Prime, p. 102.

[37] *Pennsylvania Gazette,* [Philadelphia], 13 January 1772, as cited in Gillingham, p. 117.

[38] Joseph Shippen, "Letter to Edward Shippen, 26 February 1771" MS (Shippen Papers; New Jersey Historical Society), as cited in Arts and Crafts research note card file in the Independence National Historical Park Library.

[39] Hood, p. 23.

[40] Alice Winchester, "Antiques, China Trade," *House and Garden Magazine,* March 1957, pp. 36, 37, 40.

[41] Dumas Malone and Basil Rauch, *Empire For Liberty,* I (New York: Appleton-Century-Crofts, Inc. 1960), 221-22.

[42] See: Underglaze Printing, Arts and Crafts research note card file in the Independence National Historical Park Library.

[43] Unidentified Inventory, August 1791, microfilm (Philadelphia: City Archives). The same is cited in: "House Furnishings, Arts & Crafts" research note card file, Independence National Historical Park Library.

[44] "Notes and Queries, Inventory of The Household Effects of John Penn, Jr., 1788," *The Pennsylvania Magazine of History and Biography,* XV (1891), 374.

[45] Joseph Stansbury offered one of the largest inventories of fine English china, glass and earthenware to appear in any Philadelphia newspaper throughout the eighteenth century. As a loyalist he was well aware of the situation in Philadelphia. The day before this advertisement, the Continental Congress resolved that Jefferson, Adams, Franklin, Sherman, and Livingston would prepare a declaration [of Independence]. Stansbury was surely trying to reduce his inventory of English imports. See: *Pennsylvania Gazette* [Philadelphia], 12 June 1776, p. 4, col. 2.

[46] *Minutes of The Supreme Executive Council of Pennsylvania, From Its Organization to the Termination of the Revolution,* XII (Harrisburg, Pa., 1853), 579. For further information on Joseph

Stansbury's loyalist activities and time spent in jail, as well as on his return to Philadelphia as a prosperous merchant, see: *Pennsylvania Gazette* [Philadelphia], 29 November 1780 and *The Independence Gazette or the Chronicle of Freedom* [Philadelphia], 3 December 1785.

[47] *Pennsylvania Gazette* [Philadelphia], 13 December 1786, p. 3, col. 3.

[48] Ibid., 30 April 1788, p. 3, col. 3.

[49] Gillingham, pp. 113-14.

[50] Philadelphia Common Council Minutes, 5 June 1789, microfilm (Philadelphia City Archives).

[51] *Maryland Journal or Baltimore Advertiser*, 11 February 1785; as cited in Prime, p. 134.

[52] *Pennsylvania Gazette*, 20 November 1781; as cited in Prime, p. 137.

Chapter 3

[1] Johann Conrad Döhla, *Diary of Johann Conrad Döhla, a Soldier from Beyreuth, during the North American War for Freedom, 1777-1783,* trans. Daniel J. Sharp (Beyreuth, Germany: The Archive for History & Archaeology of Upper Franconia, 1913), p. 60.

[2] Johann David Schoepf, *Travels in the Confederation [1783-1784],* trans. and ed. Alfred J. Morrison (Philadelphia: W.J. Campbell, 1911; rpt. New York: Burt Franklin, 1968), I, p. 100.

[3] Peter [Pehr] Kalm, *The America of 1750, Peter Kalm's Travels in North America: The English Version of 1770,* rev. & ed. Adolph B. Benson (New York: Wilson-Erickson, 1937), II, p. 651.

[4] R.B. Sheridan, *A Trip to Scarborough,* as quoted in C. W. & P. E. Cunnington and Charles Beard, *A Dictionary of English Costume 900-1900* (London: Adam and Charles Black, 1976), pp. 193-94.

[5] Archives Nationale Paris, MS. Cote M 1036, *"Manière de vivre des Americans,"* c. 1782, copied verbatim and trans. Paul G. Sifton, in card file of Independence National Historical Park.

[6] Ann Warder, "Extracts from the Diary of Ann Warder, 10th mo. 14th, 1788," ed. Sarah Cadbury, *Pennsylvania Magazine of History and Biography,* 18, (1894), p. 62, and "11th mo. 8th, 1786," p. 55. References to *Pennsylvania Magazine* hereafter cited as PMHB.

[7] Kalm, I, pp. 28, 30.

[8] William Fishbourne, "Narrative of Philadelphia Events," quoted in John F. Watson, *Annals of Philadelphia, In Olden Times &c.* (Philadelphia: John Pennington and Uriah Hunt, 1844), pp. 74-75.

[9] Gabriel Thomas, "Account of Philadelphia and the Province to the Year 1696," quoted in Watson, p. 71.

[10] Carl Bridenbaugh, *The Colonial Craftsman* (Chicago: University of Chicago Press, 1950), p. 171. Bridenbaugh discusses in detail a number of elements which contributed to the democratization of America and the close associations of her early artisans. He points out that there were a few formal craft organizations in Philadelphia, pp. 145-46. The discussion which follows on quality control is particularly interesting.

[11] A list of landlords in the market area might easily be mistaken for a list of members of the Meetings of the Society of Friends. Philip Syng and a few other Anglican church members were also well represented.

[12] Guildhall MS. of 1553, quoted in John Hatcher and T. C. Barker, *A History of British Pewter* (London: Longman Group Limited, 1974), p. 200. It should be noted that Hatcher and Barker feel the enforcement of this ruling was nominal, if attempted at all.

[13] Charles F. Montgomery, *A History of American Pewter* (New York: Praeger Publishers, 1973), p. 10, and Hatcher and Barker, p.. 236. In spite of these restrictions, raw metals for smiths were imported into Philadelphia on various occasions. For instance, an unidentified mid-February, 1750, *Pennsylvania Gazette (Index to American Culture,.* J 5 [1750] NM 14, cat 325) advertises:

> On Saturday the 24th inst. at publick vendue, under the Court House, will be sold by sample, 3 hogsheads of brimstone, and 4 hogsheads of ground sustick, which may in the mean time [sic] be viewed at Robert and Amos Strettell's house in Front-Street; where sundry European and East Indian goods, being the remain of various cargoes, are to be sold for ready money at the cost.
>
> All manufacturers of plate copper, ingot brass, and block tinn, may be supplied at said store, on the best terms; a neat assortment of cutarly [sic] ware. . . .

[14] Leonard W. Labaree, ed., *The Autobiography of Benjamin Franklin* (New Haven, Conn: Yale University Press, 1964), p. 145.

[15] *Pennsylvania Gazette,* 15 Mar. 1733, p. 2, col. 2.

[16] Montgomery, p. 205, n. 17. For studies of selected seventeenth- eighteenth-century Pennsylvania household inventories which show pewter objects at a variety of economic levels, see: Ruth Matzkin, "Inventories from Estates in Philadelphia County, 1682-1710," Thes. University of Delaware 1959, pp. 62-65, 100, 130-31. Lee Ellen Griffith, "A Survey of Kitchen Utensils in Berks County Inventories from 1755 to 1795," unpublished article, University of Pennsylvania, 1978, pp. 21-23, 37-38, 41. Agnes Downey Mullins, Ruth Matzkin Knapp, and Charles G. Dorman, *Furnishing Plan for the Todd House,* pt. D, United States National Park Service, Independence National Historical Park (Philadelphia: 1963), app. A, pp. 10-20, app. B, pp. 1-59).

[17] Philadelphia Museum of Art, catalogue entry by Donald L. Fennimore, *Philadelphia: Three Centuries of American Art* (Philadelphia: The Falcon Press, 1976) p. 93; hereafter cited as PMA, catalogue entry by. . . .

[18] Montgomery, p.8.

[19] *Pennsylvania Gazette,* 24 April, 1746, p. 4., col. 2.

[20] Ibid., 10 Oct. 1745, p. 5, col. 1.

[21] Ledlie Irwin Laughlin, *Pewter in America: Its Makers and Their Marks,* II (Boston: Houghton Mifflin Company, 1940), pp. 41-42. The full inventory is cited on pp. 156-57.

[22] Rodris Roth, *Tea Drinking in America: Its Etiquette and Equipage,* Smithsonian Institution, U.S. National Museum Bulletin 225 (Washington, D.C.: G.P.O., 1961), pp. 63-66. Gertrude Z. Thomas, *Richer Than Spices* (New York: Alfred A. Knopf, 1965), pp. 185, 190-91.

[23] Roth, p. 66.

[24] For a clear delineation of American preferences and general middle-class inclinations of American silver in all the colonies, see: Graham Hood, *American Silver: A History of Style, 1650-1900* (New York: Praeger Publishers, 1971), pp. 11-15.

[25] MS. sources quoted in Martha Gandy Fales, *Joseph Richardson and Family, Philadelphia Silversmiths* (Middletown, Conn.: Wesleyan University Press, 1974), pp. 225, 260.

[26] Louise C. Belden, "Sallie Morris' Silver," *Antiques,* August

1971, pp. 214-15.

27 Stephen G. C. Ensko, *American Silversmiths and Their Marks*, III (New York: n.p., 1948), p. 73.

28 Philadelphia and Burlington families are often interrelated. While, at present, the Hollingshead connection has not been entirely proved, I have inferred it from William Hollingshead's association with Daniel Offley (quoted in Alfred Coxe Prime, ed., *The Arts and Crafts in Philadelphia, Maryland and South Carolina, 1721-1785: Gleanings from Newspapers*, 1 [n.p.: The Walpole Society, 1929], p. 69) and Offley's connections with the Burlington family (R. Rundle Smith, "Brief of Title to Windmill or Smith's Island," PMHB, 22 [1898] p. 429). Offley was certainly a Friend, well known for speaking at meeting. (Ann Warder, PMHB, 18 [1894] pp. 51, 54. See also: Brooks Palmer, *The Book of American Clocks* [New York: The Macmillan Company, 1959], p. 214.)

29 Prime, p. 69.

30 Historical Society of Pennsylvania MS., "Non-Importation Agreement, October 25, 1765" (Hereafter cited as HSP MS "Non-Importation") and American Philosophical Society Printed Broadside, *From the Merchants and Traders of Philadelphia, in the Province of Pennsylvania, to the Merchants and Manufacturers of Great Britain*, (Philadelphia: n.p., 1766 or 1769), n.p. (hereafter cited as APS Printed Broadside, "Non-Importation"). *Index to American Culture* MS. "Quarter Sessions [of the County of Philadelphia]," Sept. p. 6-11 and [incomplete] p. 172-174" G 5 (1773-1775) NM 14.

31 Kalm, II, p. 652.

32 Quoted in Fales, p. 67.

33 For the most recent definitive information on Philp Syng, Jr., see biography and catalogue entry 21, PMA, catalogue entry by Beatrice Garvan, p. 30.

34 PMA, catalogue entry by Garvan, p. 30. Also helpful are Robert Kent Esplin, "Franklin's Colleagues and Their Club: The Junto in Philadelphia's Golden Age," Diss. University of Virginia 1970, pp. 58-60. George Maurice Abbot *A Short History of the Library Company of Philadelphia* (Philadelphia: n.p. 1913), pp. 1-17.

35 Lynford Lardner, MS *Account Book 1748-1751*, Collection of the Rosenbach Museum and Library of Philadelphia.

36 Syng served as director 1731-1732 and 1734-1755. Lardner served from 1746 to 1748 and again in 1760-1761. Abbot, app., Directors and Officers of the Library Company of Philadelphia, p. 27.

37 Discussed at length in Carl and Jessica Bridenbaugh, *Rebels and Gentlemen: Philadelphia in the Age of Franklin* (New York: Reynal & Hitchcock, 1942), especially chs. II, and pp. 86-99.

38 John to Abigail Adams, quoted in Salley Smith Booth, *Hung, Strung, & Potted* (New York: Clarkson N. Potter, Inc., 1971), p. 204.

39 PMA, Catalogue entries by Beatrice Garvan, pp. 30 and 71.

40 Quoted in Georgette Heyer, *The Foundling* (New York: Berkley Medallion Books, 1974), p. 82.

41 Benjamin Davies, *Some Account of the City of Philadelphia, The Capital of Pennsylvania, and Seat of the Federal Congress, of its Civil and Religious Institutions, Population, Trade, and Government; Interspersed with Occasional Observations* (Philadelphia: Richard Folwell, 1794), p. 36.

42 *Philadelphia Directories* of 1791, 1795, 1796, 1797, cited in Phoebe Phillips Prime, *The Alfred Coxe Prime Directory of Craftsmen by Name* (Philadelphia: n.p. microfilm and xerography, 1960) n.p. 45-47, p. 8.

43 Bridenbaugh, *Colonial Craftsmen*, pp. 118, 146. Bridenbaugh is one of many who believe that American workmanship tended toward degeneracy, and he cites the numerous regulatory laws and ordinances to support his contention that substandard workmanship was frequently encountered. These laws, however, are often based on precedents in English civil law or guild regulations and may have been enacted more as a matter of course than for due cause. Many objects of the period survive which exhibit extraordinary skill. One might convincingly argue that those surviving objects are *not* representative examples of their respective classes but were superior products, well-cared for because of their innate superiority. I feel, on the other hand, that an acceptable level of craftsmanship was generally recognized and required and that this level did not differ too much from that controlled by guilds in Europe.

44 *American Weekly Mercury*, 5 May 1720, No. 20, p. 4.

45 Rupert Gentle and Rachael Feild, *English Domestic Brass 1680-1810 and the History of its Origins* (New York: E.P. Dutton & Co., Inc., 1975), pp. 20, 98.

46 American-made brass andirons were, apparently, widely used, but a few advertisements for imported pairs exist. Unfortunately, many importers advertised specifics about the several varieties of English dry goods which were available, but resorted to ". . . tin, copper, pewter, stationary and saddlery ware, . . .Birmingham and Sheffield wares, . . ." (advertisement of Ottery, Cook, and Barton, *Pennsylvania Gazette*, Janury 8, 1760, No. 1672, p. 4, col. 2.) to describe other products. Fire tongs, warming pans, and candlesticks are specifically mentioned with far greater frequency than are andirons. As the following advertisement indicates, however, andirons were imported:

> Just imported in the Mercury, Capt. Hargrave, and the last vessels from London and Liverpool, and to be sold cheap, . . . by BENJAMIN KENDALL, . . . London nails . . . carpenters and joiners tools, joiners furniture, . . . copper sauce pans, coffee-pots, bellmetal kettles, . . . dog-irons, fire-shovels and tongs, brass candlesticks . . . (*Pennsylvania Gazette*, January 28, 1755. No. 1362, p.3, col. 1).

James and Drinker, another importing partnership, offered a huge list of goods in the *Gazette* of December 10, 1761 (no. 1720, p. 6, col. 1.) including, ". . . brass scales and weights, brass cocks, brass wire, . . . brass kettles, tea kettles, warming pans, boxes of tin, end irons [sic], shovel and tongs. . . ."

47 Quoted in PMA, Catalogue entry by Garvan, p. 102.

48 Nicholas B. Wainwright, *Colonial Grandeur in Philadelphia: The House and Furniture of John Cadwalader* (Philadelphia: The Historical Society of Pennsylvania, 1964), p. 37 and illus. of MS., p. 38.

49 Agnes Downey Mullins, et. al., app. B, pp. 1-59. These, of course, were used andirons and thesefore depreciated.

50 Charles F. Montgomery and Patricia E. Kane, eds., *American Art, 1750-1800: Towards Independence* (Boston: New York Graphic Society, 1976), pp. 234, 53.

51 John Adams to Charles Adams, March 30, 1777, in L. H. Butterfield, ed., *Adams Family Correspondence: II: June 1776 - March 1778* (Cambridge, Mass.: The Belknap Press of Harvard University Press, 1963), p. 190.

52 HSP MS. "Non-Importation," APS Printed Broadside, "Non-Importation," and also PMA, catalogue entries by Garvan, pp. 30, 71, 79. Fales, p. 42, 278.

53 Fales, p. 153.

54 PMA, catalogue entries by Garvan, pp. 30, 71.

55 Ibid., p. 79; entry by Fennimore, p. 92.

56 PMA, catalogue entry by Garvan, p. 79.

57 Quoted in Pauline Maier, *From Resistance to Revolution: Co-*

lonial Radicals and the Development of American Opposition to Britain, 1765-1776 (New York: Vintage Books, 1972), p. 224.

58   PMA, catalogue entry by Garvan, p. 79.

59   Henry J. Kauffman, *Early American Copper, Tin and Brass* (New York: Medill, McBride Co., 1950), pp. 34-35.

60   See: PMA, catalogue entry by Garvan, p. 79, for cited advertisement of London imports. Harbeson's support of non-importation indicates that he was able to dispense with London goods by 1765.

61   *Index to American Culture* MS "Records of the Mayor's Court of Philadelphia, January 5, 1763 and July [incomplete], 1763" NM14.

62   John Smilie quoted in Jackson Turner Main, *The Antifederalists, Critics of the Constitution, 1781-1788* (New York: W. W. Norton & Co., Inc., 1961) p. 42 n.

63   The Constitution of Pennsylvania, 1776. As found in Theodore Thayer, *Pennsylvania Politics and the Growth of Democracy, 1740-1776* (Harrisburg, Pennsylvania: Pennsylvania Historical and Museum Commission, 1953), pp. 211-27.

64   Main, p. 193.

65   Francis Hopkinson's report of the ceremonies in J. Thomas Scharf and Thompson Wescott, *History of Philadelphia: 1609-1884,* I (Philadelphia: L.H. Everts & Co., 1884) pp. 451-52. The entire account runs from p. 447-52.

66   So John Adams dubbed it in his diary: L. H. Butterfield, ed., *Diary and Autobiography of John Adams: II: Diary 1771-1781* (Cambridge, Mass.: The Belknap Press of Harvard University Press, 1961), p. 114.

67   Alfred Coxe Prime, ed., *The Arts and Crafts in Phiadelphia, Maryland, and South Carolina: 1786-1800: Gleanings from Newspapers,* II (n.p., The Walpole Society, 1932), pp. 85-87.

68   Doris Devine Fanelli, *Furnishings Plan for the Deshler-Morris House* (Philadelphia: Independence National Historical Park, 1976) pp. 15, 22n., 51, illus. 11, app. D, xix.

69   Fales, p. 162.

70   For examples of exported Philadelphia products compiled from cargo manifests of the eighteenth century, see: Harrold E. Gillingham, "The Philadelphia Windsor Chair and Its Journeyings," PMHB, 55 (1931), pp. 314-15, 318-22, and other MS. bills of lading in the collections of the Historical Society of Pennsylvania.

71   Prime, II, p. 143.

72   Charles Francis Adams, ed., *Letters of Mrs. Adams, The Wife of John Adams* (Boston: Charles C. Little and James Brown, 1840), p. 411.

73   Isaac Weld, Jr., *Travels through the States of North America and the Provinces of Upper and Lower Canada, during the years 1795, 1796, and 1797.* (London: Printed for John Stockdale, Picadilly, 1799), p. 18.

Chapter 4

1   William Penn to James Harrison, October 6, 1685. J. Francis Fisher Copies, Penn Papers, p. 14, Historical Society of Pennsylvania.

2   Cummings, Hubertis M. ed. "An Account of Goods at Pennsbury Manor, 1687." *Pennsylvania Magazine of History and Biography,* LXXVI (1962), 397-416; and "A Catalogue of Goods Left at Pennsbury, The 30th of the 10th Month, 1701," *Historical Society of Pennsylvania Memoirs,* XI [1870], 62-64.

3   William Penn, "Prayer for Philadelphia," quoted in William Wistar Comfort, *William Penn, 1644-1718: A Tercentenary Estimate* (Philadelphia: University of Pennsylvania Press, 1944), p. 45.

4   John F. Watson, *Annals of Philadelphia and Pennsylvania in the Olden Time,* I (Philadelphia: Leary Stuart Co., 1927), p. 14.

5   William Penn, "A Further Account of the Province of Pennsylvania and Its Improvements . . ." (1685), in *Narratives of Early Pennsylvania, West New Jersey and Delaware, 1630-1707,* ed. Albert Cook Meyers (New York: Charles Scribner's Sons, 1912), p. 251.

6   Frederick B. Tolles, *Meeting House & Counting House: The Quaker Merchants of Colonial Philadelphia 1682-1763* (Chapel Hill: University of North Carolina Press, 1948), p. 128.

7   William C. Brathwaite, *The Second Period of Quakerism* (Cambridge, England: Cambridge University Press, 1961), p. 507.

8   Writer's estimate using Philadelphia craftsmen entries in William MacPherson Hornor, *Blue Book of Philadelphia Furniture —William Penn to George Washington* (Philadelphia: Privately printed 1935, repr. Washington, D.C.: Highland House Publishers, 1977), pp. 304-306; Ethel Hall Bjerkoe: *The Cabinetmakers of America,* (Garden City, New York: Doubleday & Company, Inc. 1957), and cabinetmakers' biographical sketches by Beatrice B. Garvan in *Philadelphia: Three Centuries of American Art* (Philadelphia Museum of Art, 1976).

9   *Philadelphia: Three Centuries of American Art* (Philadelphia Museum of Art, 1976), p. 25.

10   Chew Papers, "Cliveden," Germantown, Pennsylvania. I am indebted to Raymond V. Shepherd for this information.

11   Library Company of Philadelphia MS., Thomas Chalkley Account Book, 1720, pp. 48-50.

12   Hornor, pp. 304-306.

13   Charles G. Dorman, "Delaware Cabinetmakers and Allied Artisans, 1755-1855." *Delaware History,* XI, No. 2 (October, 1960), 147-48.

14   Charles F. Montgomery, "Regional Preferences and Characteristics in American Decorative Arts," in *American Art: 1750-1800, Towards Independence,* ed. Charles F. Montgomery and Patricia E. Kane (Boston: New York Graphic Society, 1976), pp. 50-65.

15   ". . . I have chose rather to have a Scriptore, that is a large desk & book case atop, than a Chest of drawers, which I beg youl [sic] get made good for me of Walnut with glass Shutters, and send to Appoquinimy by Whillet. . . ." MS. letter, James Calder, (Eastern Shore of Maryland), October 10, 1734, found with letters received by James Steele, Philadelphia. Provincial Papers, Numismatic & Antiquarian Society, Collection, Historical Society of Pennsylvania.

16   At "Stenton," the James Logan house in Germantown, there were "10 Black leather bottom'd Chairs" in the "Front Parlor; An Arm Chair with 10 Red Leather Bottom Chairs in the "common Back Room;" and "A Cane Arm Chair & 10 Cane Chairs, in the back Parlor." Hornor, p. 52

17   Garvan, pp. 13-14.

18   Ibid., p. 22.

19   Hornor, pp. 2-5.

20   L.G.G. Ramsay, ed., *The Complete Encyclopedia of Antiques* (New York: Hawthorn Books, 1962), p. 227.

21   Joseph K. Kindig, III, *The Philadelphia Chair: 1685-1785* (York, Pa.: The Historical Society of York County, 1978).

[22] Charles G. Dorman, *Furnishing Plan for the Second Floor of Independence Hall* (Philadelphia: Independence National Historical Park, 1971), pt. D, p. 41.

[23] Thomas Acherly, MS. voucher, account with Province of Pennsylvania, in volume labeled Loan Office Accts., 1759-1766, Norris Papers, Historical Society of Pennsylvania.

[24] *Pennsylvania Archives,* ser. VIII, vol. XI, 5272.

[25] Hornor, p. 304.

[26] Conversations with Benno Forman, teaching associate, Henry Francis du Pont Winterthur Museum, Summer 1979.

[27] Hornor, p. 81.

[28] Ibid., p. 72.

[29] Henry Clifton (working before 1745, died 1771) is important to the student of American furniture because he made and signed a mahogany high chest upon legs in the full Philadelphia Chippendale style one year before the publication of *The Director.* . . . A chalk inscription on the back panel reads, "Henry Cliffton [sic] . . .Thomas Carteret, November 15 1754." Carteret is not known at present. He may have been an apprentice, or perhaps the original purchaser. Colonial Williamsburg collection.

[30] Savery (1721-87) would have completed his apprenticeship to Solomon Fussell about 1742. His maple rush-seat chairs of this era are pure Queen Anne in style, while the highboy used as the frontispiece by Hornor is high-style Chippendale and made of mahogany.

[31] Hornor, p. 317-26.

[32] Hornor points out that Joseph Armitt (working c. 1738-47) used a similar chamfered corner and foot on his straight-sided furniture. See: Hornor, pp. 96, 115, 116.

[33] Legend on label fragment in drawer of Pembroke table in Park collection (fig. 116).

[34] Clarence W. Brazer, "Jonathan Gostelowe . . ." in *Philadelphia Furniture and Its Makers,* ed. John J. Snyder, Jr. (New York: Universe Books, 1975), p. 49.

[35] Bjerkoe, p. 181.

[36] Garvan, pp. 112, 113. The writer has observed in the Loockerman house in Dover, Delaware, a Marlborough leg armchair in the Philadelphia Gothic Chippendale style which has on the seat frame the inscription in ink: "Benj. Randolph/Philad[a] 1765."

[37] Garvan, p. 98; Hornor, p. 176.

[38] "Thomas Affleck, Cabinet-Maker, Takes this method to acquaint the public, and particularly those who have been pleased to favor him with their custom, that he has removed his shop in Union street to Second Street, a little below the Bridge, and opposite Henry Lisle's, where he carries on the cabinet-making business in all its various branches. . . ." (*Pennsylvania Chronicle,* Dec. 12, 1768.) Alfred Coxe Prime, *The Arts and Crafts in Philadelphia, Maryland and South Carolina, 1721-1785.* (n.p.: Walpole Society, 1919), p. 158.

[39] Garvan, p. 100.

[40] John C. Milley, *Furnishing Plan For the Second Floor of Congress Hall* (Philadelphia: Independence National Historical Park, 1965), pt. D, p. 131.

[41] Hornor, p. 76.

[42] Charles G. Dorman, *Furnishing Plan For The Assembly Room-Independence Hall* (Philadelphia: Independence National Historical Park, 1970), pt. D, pp. 61-68.

[43] Max Farrand, ed., *The Records of the Federal Convention of 1787* II (New Haven: Yale University Press, 1937), pp. 648-49.

[44] Brazer, "Early American Craftsmen," in Snyder, p. 62.

[45] Ibid., p. 63.

[46] Margaret Berwind Schiffer, *Furniture and Its Makers of Chester County, Pennsylvania* (Philadelphia: University of Pennsylvania Press, n.d.), p. 97.

[47] Dorman, *Furnishing Plan, Assembly Room* . . . , pt. D., pp. 48-57.

[48] Milley, pt. C, app. J.

[49] Charles Dorman, *Furnishing Plan for the Bishop White House* (Philadelphia: Independence National Historical Park, 1961), pt. D, sec. 3.

[50] Ibid., pt. D, sec. 6.

[51] Harold Donaldson Eberlein, "190 High Street, The Home of Washington and Adams, 1790-1800" in *Transactions of the American Philosophical Society* . . . vol. 43, pt. 1 (1953), pp. 161-78.

[52] Hornor, p. 241.

[53] Prime, p. 165.

[54] Robert C. Alberts, *The Golden Voyage: The Life and Times of William Bingham* (Boston: Houghton Mifflin Company, 1979), p. 158.

[55] Bjerkoe, p. 220.

[56] Dorman, *Delaware Cabinetmakers* . . . , pp. 96-98.

[57] Bjerkoe, p. 220.

[58] Kathleen M. Catalano, "Cabinetmaking in Philadelphia 1820-1840," in *Winterthur Portfolio 13, American Furniture and Its Makers,* ed. Ian M.G. Quimby (Chicago: University of Chicago Press, 1979), p. 81.

[59] Robert C. Smith, "Furniture of Anthony G. Quervelle," pt. I; The Pier Tables, *Antiques,* May 1973, pp. 984-94; pt. II: The Pedestal Tables, *Antiques,* July 1973, pp. 90-99; pt. III; The Work Tables, *Antiques,* August 1973, pp. 260-68; pt. IV: Some Case Pieces, *Antiques,* January 1974, pp. 180-93.

Chapter 5

[1] Designed by William Strickland in 1818, and constructed between 1819 and 1824, the Second Bank of the United States, or its influence in regulating the Nation's economy, became the election issue of 1832. For a discussion of the controversial issues involved see: Bray Hammond, "The Second Bank of the United States," *Transactions of the American Philosophical Society,* NS 43, part 1, (1953). For an introduction to the architectural style of the Second Bank see: Talbot Faulkner Hamlin, *Greek Revival Architecture in America* (London: Oxford University Press, 1941).

[2] Although several institutions in the United States had impressive collections of portraits by this time, especially Yale College, which had purchased John Trumbell's collection in 1831 (the nucleus of the Yale University Art Gallery), and although numerous museums throughout Europe had their portrait collections, it is interesting to note that the National Portrait Gallery in London was not founded until 1854. Several copies of the sale catalogue, *Peale's Museum Gallery of Oil Paintings* (Philadelphia: Thomas & Sons, Auctioneers, 1854), are extant, including Rembrandt Peale's personally annotated copy in the library of the American Philosophical Society.

[3] Frank M. Etting's *An Historical Account of the Old State House of Pennsylvania* (Philadelphia: Porter & Coates, 1891), contains interesting accounts of the development of Independence

Hall as a shrine, and it is especially useful with reference to the preparations made during the Centennial to establish the building as a National Museum.

[4]   Quoted in part in John Pope-Hennessy, *The Portrait in the Renaissance,* Bollingen Series XXXV-12 (Princetin, N.J.: Princeton University Press, 1967), p. 72. For a more complete quotation see: C. Plinius Secundus, *Natural History,* compacted by Lloyd, (New York, 1957), pp. 147-48.

[5]   This distillation of the thoughts contained in Roger de Piles, *Cours de Peinture par Principes* (Paris, 1708), is indebted to the analysis of Rémy G. Saisselin, *Style, Truth and the Portrait* (Cleveland: The Cleveland Museum of Art, 1963), p. 5. The reference to Reynolds comes from my own reading of Sir Joshua Reynolds, *Discourses Delivered to the Students of the Royal Academy 1767-1780,* ed. Roger Fry, (London: Seeley & Co. Ltd., 1905) in conjunction with my study: "Jacob Eichholtz 1776-1842, Pennsylvania Portraitist," Diss. University of Delaware, 1960.

[6]   Quoted by Samuel M. Green, "The English Origin of Seventeenth-Century Painting in New England," *American Painting to 1776:A Reappraisal,* ed. Ian M. G. Quimby (Charlottesville: The University Press of Virginia, 1971), p. 31.

[7]   Saisselin, p. 1.

[8]   Quoted in Neil Harris, *The Artist in American Society: The Formative Years 1790-1860,* (1966; rpt. New York: Simon and Schuster, 1970), p. 9.

[9]   Charles Coleman Sellers, *Portraits and Miniatures of Charles Willson Peale,* 42, Part 1, *Transactions of the American Philosophical Society* (Philadelphia, 1952), p. 9.

[10]   Charles Coleman Sellers, *Charles Willson Peale,* I, (Philadelphia: The American Philosophical Society, 1947), p. 10.

[11]   It is interesting that Barbara Novak, *American Painting of the Nineteenth Century,* (New York: Praeger Publishers, 1969), concentrates upon West and Copley to the total exclusion of Peale in her prologue to the subject. By the omission she is one of the first to suggest that they not be considered as a triumvirate.

[12]   Harold Osborne, *Aesthetics and Art Theory* (New York: E.P. Dutton & Co., Inc., 1970), p. 17.

[13]   Osborne, p. 31.

[14]   Quoted in Sellers, *Charles Willson Peale,* II, pp. 392-93.

[15]   This and the following passages are paraphrased from Alma S. Wittlin, *Museums: In Search of a Useable Future* (Cambridge, Mass.: MIT Press, 1970), pp. 39-52, 60-74.

[16]   Wittlin, p. 42.

[17]   Ibid., fig. 14.

[18]   Some of the paintings have a number painted on one of the unfinished corners—e.g., "10" on that of Charles Thomson—possibly to designate the order in which they were painted for the gallery, but Peale was inconsistent in the practice. A close study of Titian Ramsay Peale's watercolor sketch of the museum in the Long Gallery of Independence Hall reveals a name plate attached to the frames. When the frames were restored in 1973, in preparation for the opening of the Portrait Gallery, two screw holes were found in the center of the bottom moldings of several frames underneath several layers of gilt, attesting to their originality.

[19]   Charles Coleman Sellers, *Charles Willson Peale with Patron and Populace: A Supplement to Portraits and Miniatures by Charles Willson Peale,* NS 59, part 3, *Transactions of the American Philosophical Society,* (Philadelphia, 1969), p. 9.

[20]   Saisselin, p. 8.

[21]   Pope-Hennessy, pp. 8, 30, 64, 72, 132.

[22]   Jules David Prown, "Style in American Art 1750-1800," in *American Art, 1750-1800: Towards Independence* (Boston: New York Graphic Society, 1976), contains some interesting observations on the differences between pre- and post-Revolutionary picture frames.

[23]   See: Katherine McCook Knox, *The Sharples: Their Portraits of George Washington and His Contemporaries* (New Haven: Yale University Press, 1930); and John C. Milley, "Thoughts on the Attribution of Sharples Pastels," in *University Hospital Antiques Show Catalogue* (Philadelphia, 1975).

[24]   Ananda K. Coomaraswamy, *Christian and Oriental Philosophy of Art* (New York: Dover Publications, Inc., 1956), pp. 64-65.

[25]   Wayne Craven, "The Grand Manner in Early Nineteenth Century American Painting: Borrowings from Antiquity, the Renaissance, and the Baroque," XI, 2, *The American Art Journal* (1979).

[26]   Peter C. Marzio, "The Forms of a Democratic Art," in *Papers on American Art,"* ed. John C. Milley (Philadelphia: The Friends of Independence National Historical Park, 1976), p. 24.

[27]   Susanna Koethe Morikawa, "History of Portrait Collection," TS. *Independence National Historical Park Papers,* (Philadelphia, 1975).

[28]   Ralph Waldo Emerson, "Uses of Great Men," in *Representative Men: Seven Lectures* (Philadelphia: David McKay, Publisher, n.d.). pp. 7, 9.

[29]   James Thomas Flexner, *The Faces of Liberty* (New York: Clarkson N. Potter, Inc., 1975), Preface.

Selected Bibliography

General

Alberts, Robert C. *The Golden Voyage: The Life and Times of William Bingham 1752-1804.* Boston: Houghton Mifflin Company, 1969.

American Philosophical Society. *Philadelphia: From the Founding until the Early Nineteenth Century.* Vol. 43, Pt. 1, of the *Transactions of the American Philosophical Society.* Philadelphia, 1953.

Axtell, James, ed., *America Perceived: A View from Abroad in the 18th Century.* West Haven, Conn.: Pendulum Press, 1974.

Bailyn, Bernard. *The Ideological Origins of the American Revolution.* Cambridge: The Belknap Press of Harvard University Press, 1967.

Beckman, Gail McKnight, comp. *The Statues at Large of Pennsylvania in the Time of William Penn.* Vol. 1, 1680-1700. New York: Vantage Press, 1976.

Belisle, D. W. *History of Independence Hall.* Philadelphia, 1859.

Bishop, David H. Assent to Significance: The Evolution of the Liberty Bell As a Cultural Symbol, TS., 1975. Independence National Historical Park, Museum Records, "Liberty Bell."

Booth, Sally Smith. *Hung, Strung, & Potted.* New York: Clarkson N. Potter, Inc., 1971.

Bowen, Catherine Drinker. *Miracle at Philadelphia: The Story of the Constitutional Convention, May to September, 1787.* Boston: Little, Brown and Company, 1966.

Boyd, Julian P. *The Declaration of Independence: The Evolution of the Text as Shown in Facsimiles of Various Drafts by Its Author, Thomas Jefferson.* Princeton: Princeton University Press, 1945.

Bradley, Rose M. *The English Housewife in the Seventeenth & Eighteenth Centuries.* London: Edward Arnold, 1912.

Bridenbaugh, Carl. *The Colonial Craftsman.* Chicago: University of Chicago Press, 1950.

_____ and Jessica. *Rebels and Gentlemen: Philadelphia in the Age of Franklin.* New York: Reynal & Hitchcock. 1942.

Briggs, Richard. *The New Art of Cookery, According to the Present Practice; Being a Complete Guide to all Housekeepers, on a Plan Entirely New; Consisting of Thirty-Eight Chapters.* Philadelphia, 1792.

Coomaraswamy, Ananda K. *Christian and Oriental Philosophy of Art,* New York: Dover Publications, Inc., 1956.

Cumming, W.P., S.E. Hillier, D.B. Quinn and G. Williams. *The Exploration of North America 1630-1776.* New York: G.P. Putnam's Sons, 1974.

Cummings, Abbott Lowell, ed. *Rural Household Inventories, Establishing the Names, Uses and Furnishings of Rooms in the Colonial New England Home, 1675-1775.* Boston: The Society for the Preservation of New England Antiquities, 1964.

Cunnington, C.W. & P.E., and Charles Beard. *A Dictionary of Engligh Costume 900-1900.* London: Adam and Charles Black, 1976.

Davies, Benjamin. *Some Account of the City of Philadelphia, The Capital of Pennsylvania, and Seat of the Federal Congress; of its Civil and Religious Institutions, Population, Trade, and Government; Interspersed with Occasional Observations.* Philadelphia, 1794.

Deetz, James J. *In Small Things Forgotten: The Archaeology of Early American Life.* Garden City, N.Y.: Anchor Press/Doubleday, 1977.

Etting, Frank M. *An Historical Account of the Old State House of Pennsylvania.* Philadelphia, 1891.

Farley, John. *The London Art of Cookery, and Housekeeper's Complete Assistant.* 4th ed. London, 1787.

Fowler, John and John Cornforth. *English Decoration in the 18th Century.* Princeton, N.J.: The Pyne Press, 1974.

Glasse, Mrs. *The Art of Cookery, Made Plain and Easy; which far exceeds any Thing of the Kind yet published.* New ed. London, 1789.

Glassie, Henry H. *Patterns in the Material Folk Culture of the East-*

ern United States. Philadelphia: University of Pennsylvania Press, 1969.

Gottesman, Rita S. *Arts and Crafts in New York, 1726-1776.* New York: New York Historical Society, 1938.

Hamlin, Talbot Faulkner. *Green Revival Architecture in America.* London and New York: Oxford University Press, 1941.

Hazelton, John H. *The Declaration of Independence: Its History.* New York: Dodd, Mead & Co., 1906.

Henretta, James A. *The Evolution of American Society, 1700-1815; An Interdisciplinary Analysis.* Lexington, Mass.: D.C. Heath and Company, 1973.

Hindle, Brooke. *The Pursuit of Science in Revolutionary America.* Chapel Hill: University of North Carolina Press, 1956.

Hume, Ivor Noël, *Artifacts of Colonial America.* Alfred A. Knopf, New York, 1970.

Kalm, Peter. *The America of 1750, Peter Kalm's Travels in North America: The English Version of 1770.* Revised & ed. Adolph B. Benson. New York: Wilson-Erickson, 1937.

Kammen, Michael. *A Season of Youth: The American Revolution and the Historical Imagination.* New York: Alfred A. Knopf, 1978.

Liggett, Barbara. *Archaeology at Franklin's Court.* Harrisburg, Pa.: The McFarland Company, 1973.

Lynes, Russell. *The Tastemakers.* New York: The Universal Library; Grosset & Dunlap, 1954.

Maier, Pauline. *From Resistance to Revolution: Colonial Radicals and the Development of American Opposition to Britain, 1765-1776.* New York: Vintage Books, 1972.

Main, Jackson Turner. *The Antifederalists: Articles of the Constitution, 1781-1788.* New York: W. W. Norton & Co., Inc., 1961.

Matzkin, Ruth. "Inventories from Estates in Philadelphia County, 1682-1710." Thesis, University of Delaware, 1959.

Miller, Lillian B., et al. *In the Minds and Hearts of the People: Prologue to the American Revolution: 1760-1774.* Greenwich, Conn.: New York Graphic Society, 1974.

Milley, John C. "Independence National Historical Park." *Antiques,* July 1971, pp. 99-103.

Montgomery, Charles F. and Patricia E. Kane, eds. *American Art: 1750-1800 Towards Independence.* Boston: New York Graphic Society, 1976.

Osborne, Harold. *Aesthetics and Art Theory.* New York: E.P. Dutton & Co., Inc., 1970.

Philadelphia: Three Centuries of American Art. Philadelphia: Philadelphia Museum of Art, 1976.

Prime, Alfred Coxe, ed. *The Arts and Crafts in Philadelphia, Maryland and South Carolina, 1721-1785: Gleanings from Newspapers, [1].* n.p.: The Walpole Society, 1929.

_____. *The Arts and Crafts in Philadelphia, Maryland and South Carolina, 1721-1785: Gleanings from Newspapers.* Series 2. n.p.: The Walpole Society, 1932.

Prime, Phoebe Phillips, comp. *The Alfred Coxe Prime Directory of Craftsmen; from the Philadelphia City Directories 1785-1800, Listed by Subject and alphabetically by name.* 4 vols. [Philadelphia?] n.p., 1960.

Quimby, Ian M.G., ed. *Arts of the Anglo-American Community in the Seventeenth Century,* Winterthur Conference Report. Charlottesville: University Press of Virginia, 1975.

_____. *Material Culture and the Study of American Life.* New York: W.W. Norton & Company, Inc., 1978.

_____, and Polly Anne Earl, eds. *Technological Innovation and the Decorative Arts,* Winterthur Conference Report, Charlottesville: The University Press of Virginia, 1974.

Riley, Edward M. *Independence National Historical Park.* National Park Service Historical Handbook Series, No. 17. Washington, D.C.: G.P.O., 1956.

Roth, Rodris. *Tea Drinking in America; Its Etiquette and Equipage.* Washington, D.C.: Smithsonian Institution, U.S. National Museum Bulletin 225.

Sachse, Julius Friedrich. *The German Pietists of Provincial Pennsylvania, 1694-1708.* Philadelphia, 1895.

Saunders, Richard Henry. "American Decorative Arts Collecting in New England 1840-1920." Diss., University of Delaware, 1973.

Scharf, J. Thomas and Thompson Westcott. *History of Philadelphia, 1609-1884.* 3 vols. Philadelphia, 1884.

Schoepf, Johann David. *Travels in the Confederation, 1783-1784.* Trans and ed. Alfred J. Morrison. Philadelphia, 1911; rpt. New York: Burt Franklin, 1968.

Sellers, Charles Coleman. *Mr. Peale's Museum.* New York: W.W. Norton & Co., Inc., 1980.

Silverman, Kenneth. *A Cultural History of the American Revolution.* New York: Thomas Y. Crowell Company, 1976.

Smith, Abbot Emerson. *Colonists in Bondage: White Servitude and Convict Labor in America, 1607-1776.* Chapel Hill: University of North Carolina Press, 1947.

Tatum, George B. *Philadelphia Georgian: The City House of Samuel Powel and Some of Its Eighteenth-Century Neighbors.* Middletown, Conn.: Wesleyan University Press, 1976.

Thomas, Gertrude Z. *Richer Than Spices.* New York: Alfred A. Knopf, 1965.

Tolles, Frederick B. *Meeting House and Counting House: The Quaker Merchants of Colonial Philadelphia, 1682-1763.* Chapel Hill: University of North Carolina Press, 1948.

U.S. Department of Congress, Bureau of Census. *Historical Statistics of the United States.* Especially "Series D 715-717: Average Daily Wage Rate of Artisans Laborers, and Agricultural Workers, in the Philadelphia Area: 1785-1830." vol. 1, p. 163. Washington, D.C.: G.P.O., 1976.

Wainwright, Nicholas B. *Colonial Grandeur in Philadelphia: The House and Furniture of General John Cadwalader.* Philadelphia: The Historical Society of Philadelphia, 1964.

Warder, Ann. "Extracts from the Diary of Ann Warder." Ed. Sarah Cadbury. *Pennsylvania Magazine of History and Biography* 17 (1893), 441-61; and 18 (1894), 51-63.

Warner, Samuel Bass, Jr. *The Private City: Philadelphia in Three Periods of Its Growth.* Philadelphia: University of Pennsylvania Press, 1968.

Watson, John F. *Annals of Philadelphia, In Olden Times: Being a Collection of Memoires, Anecdote, and Incidents of the City and Its Inhabitants . . .* 3 vols. Philadelphia, 1844.

Weld, Isaac, Jr. *Travels through the States of North America and the Provinces of Upper and Lower Canada, during the years 1795-1796, and 1797.* London, 1799.

Wolf, Edwin, II. *Philadelphia, Portrait of an American City: A Bicentennial History.* Harrisburg Pa.: Stackpole Books, 1975.

Independence National Historical Park Research Reports

Colburn, Robert J. Furnishings Plan for the Second Floor of Congress Hall, Parts A-C., TS., 1963.

Dorman, Charles G. Furnishings Plan for the Assembly Room, Independence Hall, Parts C-F., TS., 1970.

_____. Furnishings Plan for the Second Floor of Independence Hall, Parts D-F., TS., 1971.

Fanelli, Doris Devine. Furnishings Plan for the Deshler-Morris House, Parts D-F., TS., 1977.

Hershey, Constance V. Historic Furnishings Plan for City Tavern, TS., 1974.

Kimball, David A., Frederick B. Hanson and Ruth Matzkin. Furnishings Plan for the First Floor of Congress Hall, Parts A-E., TS., 1961.

Milley, John C. Furnishings Plan for the Second Floor of Congress Hall, Part D., TS., 1963.

Mullins, Agnes Downey, Ruth Matzkin Knapp, and Charles G. Dorman, Furnishings Plan for the Todd House, Parts A-F., TS., 1963.

Independence National Historical Park Archaeological Reports

Bogucki, Peter I., and Richard E. Cauffiel. Archaeological Investigations at the Thaddeus Kosciuszko National Memorial, TS., 1975.

Cotter, John L. Archaeological Report on the Investigation of a Brick Vault Catchment, "Cistern #2" Beneath the Cement Floor Basement, Old City Hall, TS., 1963.

_____, and Lee H. Nelson. Summary of Archaeological Cooperative Work at the North and South Entrances, Independence Hall, and in Front of the East Wing Building, Independence Hall, TS., 1964.

Cousans, Betty, et al. Franklin Court Report, TS., 1974.

Crozier, Daniel G. Archaeological Investigation, Area F, TS., 1977.

Moore, Jackson W., Jr. "Archaeological Data" Historic Structures Report, Dilworth-Todd-Moyland House, Part II, TS., 1960.

Parrington, Michael. Salvage Archaeology at Area F, TS., 1979.

Powell, Bruce B. Independence Archaeological Project 9, Independence Square, TS., 1957.

_____. Archaeological Excavations of Carpenters Court, TS., 1958.

_____. Archaeology at Franklin Court, TS., 1962.

Schumacher, Paul J.F. Archaeology at Franklin Court, TS., 1953.

_____. Archaeological Field Notes, Project 14 New Hall, Carpenters Court, TS., 1956.

_____. Archaeological Field Notes, Archaeological Project 15, Bishop White House Basement, 309 Walnut St., TS., 1956.

Ceramics and Glassware

Atterbury, Paul. _English Pottery and Porcelain._ New York: The Main Street Press, 1978.

Barka, Norman F. The Excavations of the Yorktown Pottery Factory: Final Report On The 1972 Excavations, TS., 1973. College of William and Mary, Williamsburg, Va.

Belden, Louise C. Pennsylvania German Pottery, TS., 1960. The Henry Francis du Pont Winterthur Museum Library, Delaware.

Brears, Peter C.D. _The English Country Pottery: Its History and Techniques._ Rutland, Vt.: Charles E. Tuttle Company, 1971.

Charleston, R.J. and Towner, Donald. _English Ceramics 1580-1830: A Commemorative Catalogue of Ceramics and Enamels to Celebrate the 50th Anniversary of the English Ceramic Circle, 1927-1977._ London: Sotheby Parke Bernet, 1977.

Cooper, Ronald G. _English Slipware Dishes, 1650-1850._ London: Alec Tiranti, 1968.

Davis, Frank. _Early 18th-Century English Glass._ Hong Kong: Hamlyn House, 1971.

Garner, Frederick Horace. _English Delftware._ London: Faber and Faber, 1948.

Gillingham, Harrold E. "Pottery, China and Glass Making in Philadelphia" _The Pennsylvania Magazine of History and Biography,_ 54 2 (1930), 97-129.

Goyle, G.A.R. "First Porcelain Making in America," _The Chronicle of the Early American Industries Association, Vol. 1-11, November, 1933 - December, 1958: A Reprint of the First Twenty-five Years._ Ambridge, Pa.: The Early American Industries Association, 1976. Vol. I, No. 8, pp. 3; No. 9, pp. 3, 7; No. 11, p. 6.

Guilland, Harold F. _Early American Folk Pottery._ Philadelphia: Chilton Book Company, 1971.

Honey, W.B. _English Pottery And Porcelain._ London: Adam & Charles Black, 1947.

Hood, Graham. _Bonnin and Morris of Philadelphia: The First American Porcelain Factory, 1770-1772._ Chapel Hill: University of North Carolina Press, 1972.

Hume, Ivor Noël. _Pottery and Porcelain in Colonial Williamsburg's Archaeological Collections._ Williamsburg, Va.: Colonial Williamsburg, 1969.

Hunter, Charles E. and Levy, Herbert W. Report on the Archaeological Salvage Excavations on the Northwest Side of Market & Front Streets; Philadelphia, Pa., Winter, 1976, TS., 1976. The Pennsylvania Historical and Museum Commission, Harrisburg, Pa.

Miller, J. Jefferson, II. _English Yellow-Glazed Earthenware._ Washington, D.C.: Smithsonian Institution Press, 1974.

Mountford, Arnold R. _The Illustrated Guide to Staffordshire Salt-Glazed Stoneware._ New York: Praeger Publishers, 1971.

Palmer, Arlene M. "Benjamin Franklin and the Wistarburg Glassworks," _Antiques,_ Jan. 1974, pp. 207-10.

_____. A Winterthur Guide to Chinese Export Porcelain. New York: Crown Publishers, Inc., 1976.

_____. The Wistarburgh Glassworks: The Beginning of Jersey Glassmaking. Alloway, New Jersey: n.p., 1976.

Quimby, Ian M.G., ed. _Ceramics in America._ Winterthur Conference Report, Henry Francis du Pont Winterthur Museum, Wilmington, Del., 1972.

Ramsay, John. _American Potters and Pottery._ New York: Tudor Publishing Co., 1947.

Ray, Anthony. _English Delftware Pottery in the Robert Hall Warren Collection Ashmolean Museum, Oxford._ Boston: Boston Book & Art Shop, 1968.

Shepard, Anna O. _Ceramics for the Archaeologist._ Washington, D.C.: Carnegie Institution of Washington, 1957.

South, Stanley A. Excavation Report; Unit S15, Lot 28, Brunswick Town, N.C.: Judge Maurice Moore's Kitchen, 1759-1776, TS. State Department of Archives and History of North Carolina.

Spargo, John. _Early American Pottery and China._ New York: Garden City Publishing Co., 1948.

Stradling, Diana and J. Garrison. _The Art of the Potter, Redware and Stoneware._ New York: The Main Street Press, 1976.

Towner, Donald. _Creamware._ London: Faber and Faber, 1978.

Watkins, Lura Woodside. _Early New England Potters and Their Wares._ Cambridge, Mass.: Harvard University Press, 1950.

Metal Wares

Avery, C. Louise. _Early American Silver._ New York and London: The Century Company, 1930.

Belden, Louise C. "Sallie Morris' Silver." *Antiques,* Aug. 1971, pp. 214-16.

Butler, Joseph T. *Candleholders in America: 1650-1900.* New York: Crown Publishers, Inc., 1967.

Cooke, Lawrence S. ed. *Lighting in America.* New York: The Main Street Press, 1976.

Cotterell, Howard Herschel. *Old Pewter: Its Makers and Marks in England, Scotland, and Ireland: An Account of the Old Pewter & His Craft.* London, 1929; rpt. Rutland, Vt. and Tokyo: Charles E. Tuttle Co., 1969.

Daumas, Maurice. *Scientific Instruments of the Seventeenth and Eighteenth Centuries.* Mary Hollbrook, trans. and ed. New York and Washington: Praeger Publishers, 1972.

Davidson, Marshall B. "Bits of Brass." *Antiques,* Jan. 1972, pp. 193-200.

Ensko, Stephen G.C. *American Silversmiths and Their Marks, III.* New York: n.p., 1948.

Evans, John L. "Love-birds & Lions: A Pewter Mystery Solved." *Antiques,* Aug. 1959, pp. 142-43.

Fales, Dean A., Jr. "Notes on Early American Brass and Copper." *Antiques,* Dec. 1958, pp. 534-38.

Fales, Martha Gandy. *Early American Silver.* New York: Dutton, 1973.

_____. *Early American Silver for the Cautious Collector.* New York: Funk & Wagnalls, 1970.

_____. *Joseph Richardson and Family, Philadelphia Silversmiths.* Middletown, Conn.: Wesleyan University Press, 1974.

Gentle, Rupert and Rachael Feild. *English Domestic Brass 1680-1810 and the History of Its Origins.* New York: E.P. Dutton & Co., Inc., 1975.

_____. "The Genesis of English Ormolo." *The Connoisseur,* 189, No. 760, June 1975, pp. 110-15.

Grimwade, Arthur C. *London Goldsmiths 1697-1837: Their Marks and Lives.* London: Faber and Faber, 1976.

Hatcher, John and T.C. Barker. *A History of British Pewter.* London: Longman Group Limited, 1974.

Hindes, Ruthanna. "Collectors Notes: That Love-bird Pewter." *Antiques,* Jan. 1956, pp. 55-56.

Hood, Graham. *American Silver: A History of Style, 1650-1900.* New York: Praeger Publishers, 1971.

Kauffman, Henry J. *The American Pewterer: His Techniques & His Products.* Camden, New Jersey: Thomas Nelson, 1970.

_____. *Early American Copper, Tin and Brass.* New York: Medill, McBride Co., 1950.

_____ and Quentin Bowers. *Early American Andirons and other Fireplace Accessories.* Nashville, Tenn.: Thomas Nelson Inc., 1974.

_____. *Early American Ironware, Cast and Wrought.* Rutland, Vt.: Charles E. Tuttle Company, 1966.

_____. *The Colonial Silversmith.* Camden, New Jersey: Thomas Nelson, Inc., 1969.

Kent, Robert. "Franklin's Colleagues and Their Club: The Junto in Philadelphia's Golden Age." Thesis, University of Virginia, 1970.

Kermodie, George H. and Thomas M. Pitkin, "The Whittinghams: Brassfounders of New York." *Antiques,* Apr. 1957, pp. 350-53.

Kolter, Jane Bentley, ed. *Early American Silver and Its Makers.* New York: Mayflower Books, Inc., 1979.

Laughin, Ledlie Irwin. *Pewter in America: Its Makers and Their Marks.* 2 vols. Boston: Houghton Mifflin Company, 1940.

Mitchell, James R., ed. *Antique Metalware.* New York: The Main Street Press, 1977.

Montgomery, Charles F. *A History of American Pewter.* New York: Praeger Publications, 1973.

Phillips, John Marshall. *American Silver.* New York: Chanticleer Press, 1949.

Schiffer, Peter, Nancy, and Herbert. *The Brass Book: American, English and European, Fifteenth Century through 1850.* Exton, Pa.: Schiffer Publishng Ltd., 1978.

Thwing, Leroy. *Flickering Flames.* Rutland, Vt.: C.E. Tuttle Company, 1958.

Wills, Geoffrey. *Candlesticks.* New York: Clarkson N. Potter, Inc., 1974.

Furniture

Bishop, Robert. *Centuries and Styles of the American Chair 1640-1970.* New York: E.P. Dutton & Co., Inc. 1972.

Comstock, Helen. *American Furniture: Seventeenth, Eighteenth, and Nineteenth-Century Styles.* New York: The Viking Press, 1962.

Dorman, Charles G. *Delaware Cabinetmakers and Allied Artisans 1655 - 1855.* Vol. IX, No. 2 (1960) of *Delaware History.*

Downs, Joseph. *American Furniture: Queen Anne and Chippendale Periods in the Henry Francis du Pont Winterthur Museum.* New York: The Macmillan Company, 1952.

Eckhardt, George H. *Pennsylvania Clocks and Clockmakers.* New York: The Devin-Adair Company, 1955.

Gillingham, Harrold E. "The Philadelphia Windsor Chair and Its Journeyings." *The Pennsylvania Magazine of History and Biography,* 55 (1931), 301-32.

Hayward, Helena. *Thomas Johnson and English Rococo.* London: Alec Tiranti, 1964.

Hornor, William Macpherson, Jr. *Blue Book of Philadelphia Furniture: William Penn to George Washington.* Philadelphia: n.p., 1935.

Hummel, Charles F. *A Winterthur Guide to American Chippendale Furniture: Middle Atlantic and Southern Colonies.* New York: Crown Publishers, Inc., 1976.

Kindig, Joseph K., III. *The Philadelphia Chair 1685-1785.* York: The Historical Society of York County, 1978.

Kirk, John T. *Early American Furniture.* New York: Alfred A. Knopf, 1970.

_____. *American Chairs: Queen Anne and Chippendale.* New York: Alfred A. Knopf, 1972.

McElroy, Cathryn J. "Furniture in Philadelphia: The First Fifty Years." In *American Furniture and Its Makers, Winterthur Portfolio 13.* Ed. Ian M. G. Quimby. Chicago: University of Chicago Press, 1979, pp. 61-80.

Montgomery, Charles F. *American Furniture: The Federal Period in the Henry Francis du Pont Winterthur Museum.* New York: The Viking Press, 1966.

Palmer, Brooks. *The Book of American Clocks.* New York: The Macmillan Company, 1959.

Ward-Jackson, Peter. *English Furniture Designs of the Eighteenth Century.* London: Her Majesty's Stationery Office, 1958.

Wills, Geoffrey. *English Furniture 1550-1760.* New York: Doubleday & Co., 1971.

Painted and Printed Materials

Altick, Richard D. *The Shows of London.* Cambridge, Mass.: Belknap Press of Harvard University Press, 1978.

American Printmaking Before 1876: Fact, Fiction, and Fantasy. Washington, D.C.: Library of Congress, 1975.

American Printmaking: The First 150 Years. Washington, D.C.: Smithsonian Institution Press, 1969.

Brigham, Clarence S. *Paul Revere's Engravings.* Worcester, Mass.: American Antiquarian Society, 1954.

The British Museum. *Catalogue of Prints and Drawings . . .Political and Personal Satires.* London: The Trustees of the British Museum, 1870-1952.

Craven, Wayne. "The Grand Manner in Early Nineteenth Century American Painting: Borrowings from Antiquity, the Renaissance, and the Baroque." *The American Art Journal.* Vol XI, No. 2 (1979), 5-43.

Cumming, William P. *British Maps of Colonial America.* Chicago: The University of Chicago Press, 1974.

Ebert, John & Katherine. *Old American Prints for Collectors.* New York: Charles Scribners' Sons, 1974.

Evans, Charles. *American Bibliography: A Chronological Dictionary of all Books, Pamphlets and Periodical Publications . . .* New York: Peter Smith, 1941-42.

Evans, Nancy Goyne. "Documenting Fraktur in the Winterthur Collection: Part I." *Antiques,* Feb. 1973, pp. 307-18.

Flexner, James Thomas. *The Faces of Liberty.* New York: Clarkson N. Potter, Inc., 1975.

Green, Samuel M. "The English Origin of Seventeenth Century Painting in New England." In *American Painting to 1776: A Reappraisal.* Ed. Ian M.G. Quimby. Charlottesville: The University Press of Virginia, 1971.

Garrison, Hazel Shields. "Cartography of Pennsylvania Before 1800." *The Pennsylvania Magazine of History and Biography,* LIX (1935), 255-83.

George, Mary Dorothy. "America in English Satirical Prints." *William and Mary Quarterly,* X (1953), 511-37.

Gillingham, Harrold E. "Old Business Cards of Philadelphia." *The Pennsylvania Magazine of History and Biography,* 53 (1929), 203-29.

Goff, Frederick R. *The John Dunlap Broadside; The First Printing of the Declaration of Independence.* Washington, D.C.: Library of Congress, 1976.

Halsey, R.T. "Impolitical Prints." *Bulletin of the New York Public Library,* XLIII (1939), 811, 823.

Harris, Neil. *The Artist in American Society: The Formative Years 1790-1860.* 1966; rpt. New York: Simon and Schuster, 1970.

Hart, Charles Henry. *Catalogue of the Engraved Portraits of Washington.* New York: The Grolier Club, 1904.

_____. "Edward Savage . . . and His Unfinished Copperplate of The Congress Voting Independence." *Proceedings, Massachusetts Historical Society,* 2nd series, XIX (1905).

Honour, Hugh. *The European Vision of America.* Cleveland: Cleveland Museum of Art, 1975.

_____. *The New Golden Land: European Images of America from the Discoveries to the Present Time.* New York: Pantheon Books, 1975.

Jones, Michael Wynn. *The Cartoon History of the American Revolution.* New York: G.P. Putnam's Sons, 1975.

Knox, Katharine McCook. *The Sharples: Their Portraits of George Washington and His Contemporaries.* New Haven: Yale University Press, 1930.

Library of Congress, Division of Maps and Charts. *A List of the Maps of America in the Library of Congress.* Washington, D.C.: G.P.O., 1901.

Library Company of Philadelphia. *Made in America. Printmaking, 1760-1860: An Exhibition of Original Prints from the Collections of the Library Company of Philadelphia and the Historical Society of Pennsylvania* (April-June 1973).

Malone, Dumas, ed. *The Fry & Jefferson Map of Virginia and Maryland.* Charlottesville: The University Press of Virginia, 1966.

Marzio, Peter C. "The Forms of a Democratic Art." In *Papers on American Art.* Ed. John C. Milley. Philadelphia: The Friends of Independence National Historical Park, 1976.

Miller, C. William. *Benjamin Franklin's Philadelphia Printing.* Philadelphia: American Philosophical Society, 1974.

Miller, Lillian B. *Patrons and Patriotism: The Encouragement of the Fine Arts n the United States 1790-1860.* Chicago: The University of Chicago Press, 1966.

Milley, John C. *Portrait Gallery Guidebook: Faces of Independence.* Philadelphia: Eastern National Park and Monument Association, 1974.

_____. "Thoughts on the Attribution of Sharples' Pastels." In *University Hospital Antiques Show Catalogue.* Philadelphia: 1975.

Morse, John D., ed. *Prints in and of America to 1850.* Charlottesville: The University Press of Virginia, 1970.

Mulcahy, James M. "Congress Voting Independence: The Trumbull and Pine-Savage Paintings." *The Pennsylvania Magazine of History and Biography,* LXXX (1956), 74-91.

Nebenzahl, Kenneth. *A Bibliography of Printed Battle Plans of the American Revolution 1775-1795.* Chicago: The University of Chicago Press, 1975.

Novak, Barbara. *American Painting of the Nineteenth Century.* New York: Praeger Publishers, 1969.

Phillips, P. Lee. *A Descriptive List of Maps and Views of Philadelphia in the Library of Congress 1683-1865.* Philadelphia: n.p., 1926.

Pope-Hennessy, John. *The Portrait in the Renaissance.* Washington, D.C.: Pantheon Books, 1963.

Powell, John H. *The Books of a New Nation: United States Government Publications, 1774-1814.* Philadelphia: University of Pennsylvania Press, 1957.

Prints Pertaining to America . . . A Checklist of Prints . . . from the Collection of the Henry Francis du Pont Winterthur Museum. The Walpole Society, 1963.

Richardson, E.P. "The Birth of Political Caricature." In *Philadelphia Printmaking: American Prints Before 1860.* Ed. Robert F. Looney. West Chester, Penn.: Tinicum Press, 1976.

_____. "Stamp Act Cartoons in the Colonies." *The Pennsylvania Magazine of History and Biography,* XCVI (1972), 275-97.

Saisselin, Rémy G. *Style, Truth and the Portrait.* Cleveland: The Cleveland Museum of Art, 1963.

Sellers, Charles Coleman. *Benjamin Franklin in Portraiture.* New Haven: Yale University Press, 1962.

_____. *Charles Willson Peale.* 2 vols. Philadelphia: The American Philosophical Society, 1947.

_____. *Charles Willson Peale with Patron and Populace: A Supplement to Portraits and Miniatures by Charles Willson Peale.* Issued as New Series, vol. 59, pt. 3 of the *Transactions of the American Philosophical Society.* Philadelphia: 1969.

_____. *Portraits and Miniatures of Charles Willson Peale.* Issued as vol. 42, pt. 1 of the *Transactions of the American Philosophical Society.* Philadelphia: 1952.

Shelley, Donald A. *The Fractur-Writings or Illuminated Manuscripts of the Pennsylvania Germans.* Allentown, Pa.: The Pennsylvania German Folklore Society, 1961.

Smith, Edgar Newbold. *American Naval Broadsides: A Collection of Early Naval Prints (1745-1815).* New York: Philadelphia Maritime Museum and Clarkson N. Potter, Inc., 1974.

Snyder, Martin P. "Birch's Philadelphia Views: New Discoveries." *The Pennsylvania Magazine of History and Biography,* LXXXVIII (1964), 164-73.

_____. *City of Independence: Views of Philadelphia Before*

1800. New York: Praeger Publishers, 1975.

_____. "William Birch: His Philadelphia Views." *The Pennsylvania Magazine of History and Biography,* LXXIII (1949), 270-315.

Stauffer, David M. *American Engravers upon Copper and Steel.* New York: The Grolier Club, 1907.

Stewart, Robert G. *Robert Edge Pine, a British Portrait Painter in America, 1784-1788.* Washington, D.C.: Smithsonian Institution Press, 1979.

Stokes, I.N. Phelps. *The Iconography of Manhattan Island, 1498-1909.* Vol. I: 1498-1811. New York: Robert H. Dodd, 1915.

Thomas, Isaiah. *The History of Printing in America.* Ed. Marcus A. McCorison. New York: Weathervane Books, 1970.

Townsend, J. Benjamin, ed. *This New Man: A Discourse in Portraits.* Washington, D.C.: Smithsonian Institution Press, 1968.

Verner, Coolie. "The Fry and Jefferson Map." *Imago Mundi,* XXI (1967), 70-94.

Wilkinson, Norman B. *Papermaking in America.* Greenville, Del.: The Hagley Museum, 1975.

Wroth, Lawrence C. *Abel Buell of Connecticut: Silversmith, Type Founder & Engraver.* Acorn Club of Connecticut, 1926.

_____. *The Colonial Printer.* 1938; rpt. Charlottesville, Va.: Dominion Books, 1964.

_____. *The First Work with American Types.* Cambridge, Mass.: 1925.

_____. "Joshua Fisher's 'Chart of Delaware Bay and River.'" *The Pennsylvania Magazine of History and Biography,* LXXIV (1950), 90-109.

_____. "The St. Mary's Press: A New Chronology of American Printing." *The Colophon,* New Series, I, No. 3.

PEALE'S MUSEUM GALLERY

OF

OIL PAINTINGS.

THOMAS & SONS, AUCTIONEERS.

CATALOGUE

OF THE

NATIONAL PORTRAIT AND HISTORICAL

GALLERY,

ILLUSTRATIVE OF AMERICAN HISTORY,

COMPRISING

269 ORIGINAL PORTRAITS AND HISTORICAL PAINTINGS,

Formerly belonging to Peale's Museum, Philada.

TO BE SOLD, WITHOUT RESERVE, AT PUBLIC SALE,

On FRIDAY, 6th October, 1854, at 10 o'clock precisely,

AT THE NEW AUCTION STORE,

Nos. 67 & 69 South Fourth Street, Philadelphia.

M. THOMAS & SONS, AUCTIONEERS.

N. B.—The entire Collection will be arranged for examination, with Catalogues, one month previous to the Sale, in the large East Room, second story, of the Auction Store.

Orders from a distance will be attended to by the Auctioneers, without extra charge.

The Sale will commence precisely at 10 o'clock, and continue without adjournment until the whole are sold.

PHILADELPHIA:

WM. Y. OWEN, PRINTER, No. 21 SOUTH THIRD STREET.

1854.

Title page, sale catalogue of the National Portrait and Historical Gallery (Peale's Museum, Philadelphia), Philadelphia, 1854.

Catalogue of Objects

Plates

I. Tower Bell ("Liberty Bell")

John Stow and John Pass (d. 1754), brass founders.

Philadelphia, 1753.

Copper, tin, lead and iron; OH. 36″ (91.5 cm.), ODiam. 47″ (119.4 cm.), OW. (yoke) 48⅝″ (123.6 cm.).

Cast, on shoulder: "PROCLAIM LIBERTY THROUGHOUT ALL THE LAND UNTO ALL THE INHABITANTS THEREOF. LEV. XXVV X."; below: "BY ORDER OF THE ASSEMBLY OF THE PROVINCE OF PENSYLVANIA [sic] FOR THE STATE HOUSE PHILAD^A"; on bell: "PASS AND STOW / PHILAD^A / MDCCLIII.

John Stow was the sole Philadelphia brass founder advertising in the city at the time. For the recasting of the bell, he took John Pass, a native of Malta, as a partner.

Boland, Charles M. *Ring in the Jubilee*. Riverside, Conn.: The Chatham Press, Inc., 1973.

Hanson, Victor F., et al. "The Liberty Bell: Composition of the Famous Failure." *American Scientists,* November-December, 1976, pp. 614-619.

The bell was owned by the State of Pennsylvania until 1818 when all its property in the Independence Square complex was sold to the City of Philadelphia. Liberty Bell Pavilion. Cat. 11862. Acc. 1.

II. *Interior View of Independence Hall*

Louis N. Rosenthal (active c. 1850-75), lithographer, after Max Rosenthal (1833-1918), Stayman and Brother, publisher.

Philadelphia, 1856.

Chromolithograph on paper; image: OH. 14½″ (36.8 cm.), OW. 18¾″ (46.9 cm.).

On stone, lower left: "On Stone by Max Rosenthal."; center: "Entered, According To Act Of Congress In The Year 1856 By Stayman & Brother, In The Clerks Office Of The Eastern District Court of Penna."; right: "Lith & Printed in Colors by L.N. Rosenthal, Cor. 5th & Chestnut, St. Phil."; center: "Interior view of INDEPENDENCE HALL, Philadelphia."; center below title: "Published by Stayman & Brother, 210 Chestnut St. Phila."

Among the principal objects depicted in this view of the Assembly Room are Henry Inman's portrait of William Penn; Thomas Sully's portrait of Lafayette; the bust portraits purchased at the sale of Charles Willson Peale's Museum in 1854; the chandelier purchased in 1824 for the reception of Lafayette; and the "Liberty Bell" surmounted by a stuffed eagle from Peale's Museum.

The Rosenthal brothers were born in Poland. Max immigrated to Philadelphia via Paris in 1849 or 1850. He was followed shortly by Louis and Simon. All were trained lithographers.

Wainwright, Nicholas B. *Philadelphia in the Romantic Age of Lithography*. Philadelphia: The Historical Society of Pennsylvania, 1958, p. 153, pl. 185.

Gift of Eastern National Park & Monument Association, 1959. Second Bank, Faces of Independence Gallery. Cat. 1396. Acc. 316.

III. *Seal of the City of Philadelphia*

John A. Woodside (1781-1852), artist.

Philadelphia, c. 1816.

Oil on canvas; OH. 108″ (274.3 cm.), OW. 64½″ (163.9 cm.).

According to Scharf and Westcott's *History of*

Philadelphia, Woodside was paid $60 for painting the city coat of arms. It was placed in the Common Council Chamber, in the building known today as Old City Hall.

Woodside was born in Philadelphia, where he became one of Philadelphia's best-known sign and ornamental painters.

Found in basement of Congress Hall, 1951. Second Bank, Pennsylvania Galleries. Cat. 11836. Acc. 1.

IV. Armchair ("Rising Sun")

John Folwell (working 1762-80 d.), cabinetmaker.

Philadelphia, 1779.

Mahogany, white oak secondary; replaced leather upholstery; OH. 61″ (154 cm.), HS. 19″ (48.2 cm.), WS. 26″ (66 cm.), DS. 19″ (48.2 cm.).

John Folwell was a master cabinetmaker in Philadelphia. His works include the pulpit of Christ Church and the case for David Rittenhouse's orrery at the University of Pennsylvania.

Max Farrand, ed. *The Records of the Federal Convention of 1787.* New Haven, 1937. Madison's Notes, vol. 2, pp. 648-49.

Hornor, William M., Jr. *Hornor's Blue Book on Philadelphia Furniture,* pp. 74-76, pl. 97.

Journal of House of Representatives of Pennsylvania 1776-1781. Phila. 1782, p. 636.

Ordered by Pennsylvania Assembly in 1779. Taken to Lancaster in 1799, and to Harrisburg in 1812, with successive changes in the state capital. In 1867 it was returned to Philadelphia and placed in the Assembly Room of Independence Hall where it still stands. Cat. 11826. Acc. 1.

V. *Bishop White's Study*

John Sartain (1808-97), artist.

Philadelphia, 1836.

Oil on canvas, original gold leaf frame; OH. 18⅛″ (46.1 cm.), OW. 24³⁄₁₆″ (61.4 cm.)

According to family tradition, Sartain's painting was commissioned by the Bishop's granddaughter, Elizabeth White Bronson, immediately after the Bishop's death in 1836.

Sartain, born and trained in London, arrived in New York in 1830. He is credited with having revived the art of mezzotint in America. Sartain was art director of the 1876 Centennial Exposition.

Courtesy of Dr. & Mrs. Vincent Vermooten and Children, 1967. Second Bank, Pennsylvania Gallery. Cat. 7817. Acc. 2254.

VI. *The Second Bank of the United States*

William Henry Bartlett (1809-54), artist.

Philadelphia, c. 1836-39.

Watercolor on paper; OH. 8⅝″ (21.9 cm.), OW. 13³⁄₁₆″ (33.5 cm.).

Inscribed in pencil, lower left of image: "United States Bank/Philadelphia."

An English landscape artist, Bartlett visited the United States between 1836 and 1852. About 1840 he published a series of prints entitled *American Scenery,* with text by Nathaniel P. Willis.

Purchased with funds donated by Eastern National Park & Monument Association, 1959. Second Bank, foyer hall. Cat. 1412. Acc. 307.

VII. *A Map of the British Empire in America . . .*

Henry Popple (d. 1743), cartographer; William H. Toms, map engraver; R.W. Seale, map engraver; Clement Lempriere, cartouche artist; Bernard Baron (c. 1700-66), cartouche engraver.

London, 1733. Index map, *American Septentrionalis,* illustrated.

Hand-colored engraving, bound in modern marbled boards with leather backstrip; Large map, consisting of 15 folded sheets, OH. 20½″ (52 cm.), OW. 28″ (71.1 cm.) and 5 single sheets, OH. 20½″ (52 cm.), OW. 14″ (35.6 cm.); Index map OH. 20¼″ (51.4 cm.), OW. 20⅜″ (51.8 cm.).

Inscribed in plate, both maps, middle right: "To the QUEEN'S Most/EXCELLENT MAJESTY/This MAP is most humbly/Inscribed by/Your MAJESTY'S/most Dutiful, most/Obedient, and most/Humble Servant/Henry Popple."; large map, lower left: "A MAP/of the BRITISH EMPIRE in/AMERICA/with the FRENCH and SPANISH/SETTLEMENTS adjacent thereto./by Henry Popple."; large map, lower left: "C. Lempriere inv. & del."; "B. Baron Sculp."; large map, lower right: "London Engrav'd by Willm Henry Toms & R.W. Seale, 1733."

The map, composed of twenty sheets, is the largest map of North America printed during the colonial period.

Henry Popple's cartographic work was apparently secondary to other employment. Clement Lempriere, an experienced cartographer and surveyor, is thought to have helped Popple with the map and to have executed the ornamental landscapes. Bernard Baron, a French-born engraver, is thought to have done the non-scenic decorations, including the figures.

Cumming, William P. *British Maps of Colonial America.* Chicago, 1974, pp. 12, 34, 36.

INHP purchase, 1965, with funds donated by the American Federation of Womens' Clubs. Independence Hall, Assembly Room. Cat. 5834. Acc. 1698.

VIII. *Left:* celestial globe

Leonard Cushee, globe maker.

London, c. 1750.

Hand-colored engraving (map), over pasteboard and wood globe frame, mahogany stand; OH. 16½″ (41.9 cm.), OW. 17½″ (44.5 cm.).

Inscribed on plate, within a laurel sprig cartouche: "A New Celestial/GLOBE/By L. Cushee."

Wynter, Harriet. "The Terrestrial Globe." *The Antique Dealer and Collectors Guide,* February, 1973, pp. 55-58.

INHP purchase, 1972, with funds donated by the National Society, Daughters of the American Revolution. Independence Hall, Governor's Council Chamber. Cat. 8744. Acc. 2653.

Right: terrestrial globe

Hand-colored engraving (map), over pasteboard and wood globe frame, mahogany stand; OH. 16½″ (41.9 cm.), OW. 17½″ (44.5 cm.).

Inscribed in plate, inside cartouche: "A NEW/GLOBE/OF THE EARTH/Laid down according to the latest/Observations/By/Leonard/Cushee."; in rectangle below cartouche: "Sold by Cushee near/St. Dunstan's Church Fleet Street LONDON."

Cat. 8743. Acc. 2653.

IX. *The Right Honourable William Pitt, Esq.*

Richard Houston (1721-75), engraver.

London, 1766.

Hand-colored mezzotint; plate: OH. 24⅛″ (61.3 cm.), OW. 16¾″ (42.7 cm.).

Inscribed in plate, beneath image: "Done from an Original Picture in the Possession of EARL TEMPLE;—by Richd Houston./The Right Honourable William Pitt, Esq./One of His Majesty's Most Honble Privy Council/London: Printed for Robert Sayer . . . 1766."

Richard Houston, an esteemed mezzotint engraver, executed a great many portraits and miscellaneous subjects.

INHP purchase, 1975. City Tavern, hall. Cat. 10993. Acc. 3030.

X. *A Youth Rescued from a Shark . . .*
Valentine Green (1739-1813), engraver.

London, 1779.

Hand-colored mezzotint; plate: OH. 19½″ (49.5 cm.), OW. 23⁹⁄₁₆″ (59.8 cm.).

Inscribed in plate, left, below image: "Painted by John Singleton Copley, R.A. Elect."; right, below image: "Engrav'd by V. Green, Mezzotinto Engraver to his Majesty . . ."; center left, below image: "A YOUTH RESCUED FROM A SHARK . . ." followed by explanatory text in English; center right, below image: title and text in French; below text: "Engraved from the Original Picture in the Possession of Brook Watson. . . ."

Valentine Green, an unsuccessful line engraver, taught himself the mezzotint process and became one of its most accomplished practitioners. He completed nearly 400 plates, from both contemporary and historical sources, and was elected one of six Associate Engravers of the British Royal Academy in 1775.

Museum of Fine Arts, Boston. *Catalogue of Paintings.* 1921, p. 184, #586.

INHP purchase, 1975. City Tavern, bar. Cat. 10994. Acc. 3030.

XI. *The Country Club.*

Henry William Bunbury (1750-1811), artist; William Dickinson (1746-1823), engraver and publisher.

London, 1788.

Hand-colored engraving; plate: OH. 15¼″ (38.8 cm.), OW. 19¹¹/₁₆″ (50 cm.).

Inscribed in plate, lower left corner: "H. Bunbury Esqʳ Delinᵗ"; lower right corner: "W. Dickinson Excudit."; beneath image: "THE COUNTRY CLUB./Eamus/Quo ducit Gula./LONDON, Publish'd June 26th, 1788, by W. DICKINSON Engraver Nº 158 Bond Street."

Henry William Bunbury, a member of London's high society, designed humorous subjects and caricatures. He exhibited occasionally at the Royal Academy and was a contributor to Boydell's *Shakespeare Gallery.* William Dickinson, an English engraver, obtained a premium for his work from the Society of Arts in 1767. In his later years he moved to France, where he continued to work as an engraver.

The British Museum. *Catalogue of Prints and Drawings . . . Political and Personal Satires.* London, 1935, Vol. 6, pp. 563-64.

INHP purchase, 1974, with funds donated by Eastern National Park & Monument Association. City Tavern, bar. Cat. 10339. Acc. 2812.

XII. Untitled cartoon *(Toestand der Engelsche Natie)*

Maker unknown.

Unknown; probably European, copied from Dutch print, c. 1780.

Hand-colored engraving and etching; plate: OH. 8⅜″ (21.5 cm.), OW. 11″ (28 cm.).

Inscribed in plate, right corner, above city skyline: "PHILADELPHIA."; stern of ship: "EAGLE."; bucket: "B. FRANK. . . ."

This print originally appeared in the *Westminster Magazine,* March 1, 1778, with an explanation of the figures and their significance. The print was frequently reissued in England, Holland, France, and America, and the design later appeared on Staffordshire pottery. This version appears to be a variant of the print numbered 5726 (or 5726a) in the British Museum *Catalogue.*

The British Museum. *Catalogue of Prints and Drawings . . . Political and Personal Satires.* London, 1935, Vol. 5, pp. 285-86, 449-50.

Keyes, Willard E. "The Cow and the Sleeping Lion." *Antiques,* XXXIX (1941), 25-27.

Gift of Eastern National Park & Monument Association, 1965. Second Bank, Documents Room. Cat. 6115. Acc. 1759.

XIII. Fraktur: Equestrian Washington

Attributed to the "Sussel-Washington" Master.

Pennsylvania, c. 1780-90.

Watercolor and ink on paper; OH. 7⅞″ (19.7 cm.), OW. 6¼″ (15.8 cm.).

Inscribed in ink, upper left: "ein Mahlen laden zum salat/ein Schwaben da man strauble hat,/ ein Schweizer zu ein Zregenkas/ein baier zu der aderlas/ein sachsen zum spec und zum schuncken darf . . ." [Last line missing—paper torn]; bottom center: "excelenc Georg General Waschingdon."

The artist is unidentified; he is so named because there are several renderings of George and Martha Washington in his hand, one of which was in the collection of Arthur J. Sussel.

Evans, Nancy Goyne. "Documented Fraktur in the Winterthur Collection: Part I." *Antiques,* February, 1973, pp. 307-18.

Found tipped between the pages of a bound volume of Pennsylvania-German almanacs, INHP catalog number 374. Second Bank, Washington Room. Cat. 2768. Acc. 1.

XIV. *Second Street, North from Market Sᵗ . . .*

William R. Birch (1755-1834), artist and engraver; Thomas Birch (1779-1851), artist and engraver.

Philadelphia, 1799.

Hand-colored engraving; plate: OH. 11⅛″ (28.3 cm), OW. 13¼″ (33.6 cm.).

Inscribed in plate, lower left, below image: "Drawn & Engraved by W. Birch & Son."; lower right, below image: "Published by R. Campbell & Cº Nº 30 Chestnut Street Philadᵃ 1799."; center, below image: "SECOND STREET North from Market Sᵗ wᵗʰ CHRIST CHURCH./PHILADELPHIA."

William Birch conceived of his *Views of Philadelphia* as a way to pay homage to his new residence. He reissued the series several times during the first quarter of the nineteenth century, deleting some views and adding others.

Birch was born in England where he worked as a landscape painter. He emigrated to America, arriving in Philadelphia in 1794, and by 1798 he had completed all of the preliminary work for his book of views, *The City of Philadelphia,* first published in 1800. Thomas Birch emigrated from England with his father and assisted him

with the *Views.* He soon established himself as a prominent artist in his own right and was particularly well known for his marine views.

Snyder, Martin P. "Birch's Philadelphia Views: New Discoveries." *The Pennsylvania Magazine of History and Biography,* LXXXVIII (1964), 164-73.

_____. "William Birch: His Philadelphia Views." *The Pennsylvania Magazine of History and Biography,* LXXIII (1949), 270-315.

Gift of Eastern National Park & Monument Association, 1957. Second Bank, Birch Room. Cat. 1186. Acc. 211.

XV. Dinner plates, set of seven

Maker unknown.

Bristol, c. 1750.

Earthenware, tin glazed, underglaze decoration; ODiam. ranges from 8⅞″ (28.5 cm.) to 9″ (23.9 cm.).

INHP purchase, 1973. Independence Hall, Governor's Council Chamber. Cat. 10233-34, 10236-10240. Acc. 2760.

XVI. *Left to right, foreground:*

Sugar bowl with lid

Maker unknown.

Derby or Stoke-on-Trent, England, c. 1815.

Porcelain, underglaze decoration, overglaze enamels and gilt; OH. 5½″ (14 cm.), OW. 4¼″ (10.8 cm.), OD. 6½″ (16.5 cm.).

Overglaze gilt, on bottom: "136."

The bowl and the following set of eight pieces are the gift of Mrs. Evan Randolph, Sr., 1976. Bishop White House, dining room. Cat. 11467. Acc. 3185.

Waste bowl

OH. 2¹³/₁₆″ (7.2 cm.). ODiam. 6½″ (16.5 cm.).

Overglaze gilt, on bottom: "N. 136."

Cat. 11468. Acc. 3185.

Cup

OH. 2¼″ (5.8 cm.), OW. 3⅞″ (9.8 cm.), ODiam. 3⅛″ (8 cm.)

Cat. 11472. Acc. 3185.

Saucer

ODiam. 5½″ (14 cm.).

Cat. 11480 Acc. 3185.

Cream jug

OH. 4¾″ (12.1 cm.), OW. 3¼″ (8.25 cm.), OD. 6″ (15.3 cm.).

Overglaze gilt, on bottom: "N 130."

Cat. 11466. Acc. 3185.

Stand

OH. 1″ (2.5 cm.), OW. 5¹¹⁄₁₆″ (14.5 cm.), OL. 7⁵⁄₁₆″ (18.6 cm.).

Overglaze gilt, on bottom: "N 136."

Cat. 11469. Acc. 3185

Left to right, background:

Teapot with lid

OH. 7″ (17.8 cm.), OW. 5″ (12.6 cm.), OL. 10¼″ (26.2 cm.).

Cat. 11465. Acc. 3185.

Cake plate

ODiam. 8⅞″ (22.6 cm.).

Overglaze red enamel, on bottom: "N.⁰ 136".

Cat. 11470. Acc. 3185.

Cake plate

ODiam. 8⅞″ (22.6 cm.).

Cat. 11471. Acc. 3185.

XVII. *Left to right:*

Dinner plate

Maker unknown.

China, early 19th century.

Porcelain, Fitzhugh pattern, underglaze decoration; ODiam. 10″ (25.4 cm.).

INHP purchase, 1974. Visitor Center. Cat. 10383. Acc. 2849.

Dinner plate

Maker unknown, attributed to factory of Josiah Wedgwood.

Staffordshire, England, c. 1770-80.

Cream-colored earthenware, green glaze; ODiam. 9⁷⁄₁₆″ (24 cm.).

INHP purchase, 1975. Visitor Center. Cat. 10593. Acc. 2891.

Dinner plate

Maker unknown.

Probably Liverpool, England, c. 1790-1800.

Pearl ware, underglaze and overglaze decoration; ODiam. 9⅝″ (24.5 cm.).

Noël-Hume, Ivor. "Pearlware: Forgotten Milestone of English Ceramic History." *Antiques.* March, 1969, pp. 390-97, figs. 1, 3.

INHP purchase, 1973. Visitor Center. Cat. 10289. Acc. 2763.

XVIII. *Left to right:*

Jug

Maker unknown.

American, possibly Pennsylvania, 19th century.

Red earthenware, brown manganese glaze, applied handle, incised dot beading at shoulder; OH. 7½″ (19.0 cm.), OW. 6½″ (16.5 cm.),

ODiam. 6″ (15.2 cm.).

INHP purchase, 1961. Bishop White House, kitchen. Cat. 3155. Acc. 651.

Dish

Maker unknown.

American, probably Pennsylvania, early 19th century.

Red earthenware, applied slip decoration; OH. 2⅜″ (6.1 cm.), ODiam. 13⅞″ (35.3 cm.).

INHP purchase, 1966. Todd House, kitchen. Cat. 6715. Acc. 1912.

Mold

Maker unknown.

American, c. 1850.

Red earthenware, lead glaze, sponge applied manganese decoration; OH 3½″ (8.9 cm.), ODiam. 9″ (22.9 cm.).

Impressed, inside hollow core near bottom: "9."

INHP purchase, 1968. Todd House, kitchen. Cat. 8271. Acc. 2381.

Dish

Maker unknown.

Southeastern Pennsylvania, 1750-1875.

Red earthenware, applied slip, impressed decoration; OH. 1½″ (3.9 cm.), ODiam. 9⅝″ (24.5 cm.).

Gift of William Spawn, 1971. Todd House, kitchen. Cat. 8569. Acc. 2568.

Pie plate

Maker unknown.

Pennsylvania, early 19th century.

Red earthenware, applied slip, impressed decoration; OH. 1¾″ (4.5 cm.), ODiam. 11¹⁄₁₆″ (28.1 cm.).

INHP purchase, 1961. Todd House, kitchen. Cat. 3093. Acc. 622.

Jar

Maker unknown.

Possibly Pennsylvania, early 19th century.

Red earthenware, manganese glaze, incised decoration; OH. 12″ (30.5 cm.), ODiam. 9¼″ (23.5 cm.).

INHP purchase, 1964. Todd House, kitchen. Cat. 5170. Acc. 1315.

Jar

Maker unknown.

American, possibly New Jersey, c. 1800-25.

Red earthenware, lead glaze, manganese decoration, applied handles, overall incised decoration; OH. 10″ (25.4 cm.), ODiam. 8½″ (21.6 cm.).

INHP purchase, 1963. Todd House, kitchen. Cat. 5062. Acc. 1159.

XIX. *"Four Continents"*

Maker unknown.

Derby, England, c. 1780.

Porcelain, underglaze polychrome, overglaze gilt, molded and applied relief decoration; *Africa:* OH. 9⅛″ (23.2 cm.), OW. 4⅝ (11.8 cm.), OD. 4⅛″ (10.5 cm.); *America:* OH. 9½″ (25.2 cm.), OW. 4⅝ (11.8 cm.), OD. 4¾″ (12.1 cm.); *Europe:* OH. 9¹³⁄₁₆″ (24.9 cm.), OW 4⅜″ (11.1 cm.), OD. 4⅛″ (10.5 cm.); *Asia:* OH. 9¹⁄₁₆″ (23.0 cm.), OW. 5½″ (13.9 cm.), OD. 4¹⁄₁₆″ (10.2 cm.).

These Derby figures, like other English versions, are based on Meissen groups of the "Four Continents," first produced as early as 1746. British potteries began producing sets around 1759. A Chelsea ensemble of "classical children," made in 1759, may have served as the model for this group.

Dixon, J. L. *English Porcelain of the Eighteenth Century.* New York, Pitman Publishing Corp: n.d.

Lane, Arthur. *English Porcelain Figures of the Eighteenth Century.* London: Faber & Faber, 1961.

Purchased with funds donated by Eastern National Park & Monument Association, 1976. Deshler-Morris House, parlor. Cat. 11210-13. Acc. 3085.

XX. *Left to right::*

"Elijah"

Maker unknown.

England, 1800-20.

Pearl ware, translucent underglaze and overglaze enamel polychrome decoration; OH. 9½″ (24.2 cm.), OW. 4½″ (11.4 cm.), OD. 4⅜″ (11. 1 cm.).

INHP purchase, 1967. Bishop White House, parlor. Cat. 7483. Acc. 2167.

"St. Philip"

Maker unknown.

Pearl ware, translucent underglaze and overglaze enamel, molded and applied relief decoration; OH. 14¹⁄₁₆″ (35.8 cm.), OW. 4¾″ (12.1 cm.), OD. 3⅝″ (9.2 cm.).

Painted, front of plinth: "S! Phillip" [sic]; impressed, back of plinth: "121."

INHP purchase, 1967. Bishop White House, parlor. Cat. 7481. Acc. 2167.

"The Widow and Her Children"

Maker unknown.

England, c. 1810.

Pearl ware, translucent underglaze and

overglaze enamel decoration; OH. 7⅜″ (18.8 cm.), OW. 3⅝″ (9.2 cm.), OD. 2⅞″ (7.3 cm.).

Conventional representation of "Charity."

INHP purchase, 1960. Bishop White House, bedroom. Cat. 5196. Acc. 440.

"Nicodemus"

Maker unknown.

England, 1786-1820.

Cream-colored earthenware, underglaze and overglaze polychrome enamel, molded and applied relief decoration; OH. 10¹³⁄₁₆″ (27.5 cm.), OW. 6¼″ (15.9 cm.), OD. 5⅝″ (14.3 cm.).

Impressed, then overglaze enameled, on shield held by figure: "CHRIST TEACHETH/NIGODEMUS [sic, enamel only]/IOHN 3/GH 3 [sic, enamel only]."

INHP purchase, 1967. Bishop White House, parlor. Cat. 7482. Acc. 2167.

XXI. Bowl

Maker unknown.

Probably Bristol, England, c. 1730-40.

Earthenware, tin glazed; OH. 6¾″ (17.2 cm.), ODiam. 11½″ (29.2 cm.).

Liggett, Barbara. *Archaeology at Franklin's Court.* Philadelphia: Eastern National Park and Monument Association, 1973.

Excavated in Franklin Court, 1972, Feature 22, Context III. Franklin Court, Archaeology Exhibit. Cat. V-327. Acc. 2668.

XXII. "The Vicar and Moses"

Probably Ralph Wood, Jr. (1748-95), maker.

Staffordshire, England, second half of 18th century.

Pearl ware, underglaze translucent polychrome, molded and applied relief decoration; OH. 9¹³⁄₁₆″ (25 cm.), OW. 4⁵⁄₁₆″ (11.0 cm.), OD. 5⁹⁄₁₆″ (14.1 cm.).

Impressed, front of pulpit: "THE VICAR/AND MOSES."

Ralph Wood, Jr., was the son of a Burslem potter. Both specialized in figural work. Wood, Sr., first produced the "Vicar and Moses" group.

Towner, Donald. *Creamware.* London: Faber and Faber, 1978.

Gift of Mrs. Samuel B. Oster, 1976. Bishop White House, parlor. Cat. 11449. Acc. 3176.

XXIII. Coffeepot

Maker unknown.

England, c. 1760.

Red earthenware, lead glaze, engine-turned decoration; OH. 10½″ (26.7 cm.), OL. 9¼″ (23.5 cm.), ODiam. 5½″ (14 cm.).

INHP purchase, 1963. Bishop White House, kitchen. Cat. 3159. Acc. 1021.

XXIV. Candlesticks, pair

Maker unknown.

England, c. 1760.

Brass; OH. 8⅛″ (20.6 cm.), ODiam. 4¼″ (10.8 cm.).

INHP purchase, 1965. Bishop White House, dining room. Cat. 6295-96. Acc. 1822.

Candlesticks, pair

Maker unknown.

England, c. 1760.

Brass; OH. 9⅜″ (23.8 cm.), ODiam. 4⅝″ (11.8 cm.).

INHP purchase, 1968. Bishop White House, dining room. Cat. 4838-39. Acc. 1565.

XXV. Slat-back side chair

Maker unknown.

Delaware Valley, second half of 18th century.

Maple and hickory, early iron oxide paint, replaced rush seat; OH. 43³⁄₁₆″ (109.4 cm.), OW. 19½″ (49.4 cm.), HS. 15″ (38.1 cm.), DS. 14⁹⁄₁₆″ (37.0 cm.).

INHP purchase, 1965. Todd House, kitchen. Cat. 4939. Acc. 1610.

Table

Maker unknown.

Probably Pennsylvania, early 19th century.

Pine and walnut [?], painted red; OH. 27¾″ (70.5 cm.), OW. 33⅜″ (104.1 cm.), OD. 41½″ (105.5 cm.).

INHP purchase, 1964. Todd House, kitchen. Cat. 4614. Acc. 1515.

Dish

Probably Andrew Abbott (active c. 1780-1810, d. 1819), maker.

Staffordshire, England, last quarter of the 18th century.

Red earthenware, combed slip decoration; OH. 3″ (7.5 cm.), OW. 16⅝″ (42.5 cm.), OD. 13¾″ (35.0 cm.).

Impressed, on bottom: "ABBOTT POTTER."

Andrew Abbott worked at Lane End, Staffordshire during the last two decades of the 18th century and into the 19th century. Between 1781 and 1787 he was working with John Turner, a competitor of Wedgwood. The mark "ABBOTT POTTER" has turned up on at least one other combed ware dish (Chaffers, p. 743).

Chaffers, William. *Marks & Monograms on European and Oriental Pottery and Porcelain.* Frederick Litchfield, ed. London: William

Reeves Bookseller, 1954. 14th rev. ed.

Mankowitz, Wolf, and Reginald G. Haggar. *The Concise Encyclopedia of English Pottery and Porcelain.* New York: Hawthorn Books, 1957.

INHP purchase, 1964. Todd House, kitchen. Cat. 4428. Acc. 1521.

Basket

Maker unknown.

Probably American, 19th century.

Hickory splint and rush; OH. 4¾″ (12 cm.), ODiam. 12⅛″ (33.0 cm.).

INHP purchase, 1963. Todd House, kitchen. Cat. 5070. Acc. 1167.

Colander

Maker unknown.

England or Europe, late 18th century.

Brass; OH. 6⅞″ (16.3 cm.), OW. 16¼″ (41.2 cm.), ODiam. 11⅝″ (29.4 cm.).

INHP purchase, 1965. Todd House, kitchen. Cat. 5734. Acc. 1659.

Coffeepot

Maker unknown.

America, probably Pennsylvania, 19th century.

Tin, brass finial; OH. 10⅞″ (7.6 cm.), OL. 11⅛″ (28.2 cm.), ODiam. 7⅜″ (18.7 cm.).

INHP purchase, 1968. Todd House, kitchen. Cat. 8160. Acc. 2352.

Canister, one of set of four

Maker unknown.

America or Europe, probably first quarter of 19th century.

Clear glass painted tin lid; OH. 9¼″ (23.5 cm.), ODiam. 4⅝″ (11.8 cm.).

One of four removed from a Salem, New Jersey drug store, in continuous operation for over 100 years, disbanded c. 1936. Gift of Charles G. Dorman, 1966. Todd House, kitchen. Cat. 6735. Acc. 1982.

Windsor side chair

John Lambert (active c. 1791-93, d. 1793), chairmaker.

Philadelphia, c. 1790.

Seat: tulip poplar; bowed back and spindles: hickory; legs and stretchers: maple; OH. 36¹³⁄₁₆″ (93.5 cm.), OW. 21⅞″ (55.6 cm.), HS. 16⁹⁄₁₆″ (42.0 cm.), DS. 16⅛″ (41.0 cm.).

Branded, once on underside of chair seat: "LAMBERT."

John Lambert, chairmaker, appeared in the Philadelphia *Directories,* 1791-93. His obituary notice and estate advertisement appear in the *Federal Gazette* (Philadelphia) November 29, 1793.

INHP purchase, 1965. Todd House, kitchen. Cat. 5623. Acc. 1630.

XXVI. Chest of drawers

Maker unknown.

Probably Philadelphia, last quarter 18th century.

Mahogany, pine drawer bottoms, poplar sides, brass drawer pulls and escutcheons (may be original), replaced brass and steel locks; OH. $33\frac{5}{8}$" (85.4 cm.), OW. $37\frac{5}{8}$" (97.6 cm.), OD. $21\frac{1}{2}$" (54.6 cm.).

INHP purchase, 1977. Todd House, kitchen bedchamber. Cat. 11572. Acc. 3025.

Low-post bedstead

Maker unknown.

America, probably Delaware Valley, late 18th or early 19th century.

Pine, wrought-iron bolts, iron oxide paint over Prussian blue (probably original); OH. $24\frac{13}{16}$" (63 cm.), OW $43\frac{5}{8}$" (110.8 cm.), OL. $70\frac{1}{8}$" (178.2 cm.).

INHP purchase, 1964. Todd House, kitchen bedchamber. Cat. 4842. Acc. 1565.

Stand

Maker unknown.

Probably Pennsylvania, c. 1790-1810.

Poplar, red paint; OH. $29\frac{3}{4}$" (75.5 cm.), OW. $20\frac{1}{4}$" (51.3 cm.), OD. $16\frac{3}{8}$" (41.7 cm.).

INHP purchase, 1961. Todd House, kitchen bedchamber. Cat. 2990. Acc. 559.

XXVII. Coffeepot

William Hollingshead (active c. 1754-85), silversmith.

Philadelphia, c. 1780-85.

Silver, fruitwood handle; OH. $13\frac{13}{16}$" (35.0 cm.), OW. $9\frac{1}{4}$" (23.5 cm.).

Stamped, bottom of pot, four times: "WH" (in script) in conforming rectangle reserve; engraved, body, midway between handle and spout: "MC" (in script) enclosed in oval foliated wreath.

William Hollingshead worked in Philadelphia from 1754 to 1785. Little documentary evidence of his career has been uncovered to date.

Gift of Mr. and Mrs. Newcomb T. Montgomery, 1977. Coffeepot was inherited through Mary H. White, granddaughter of Bishop William White. Bishop White House, dining room. Cat. 1659. Acc. 3245.

Candlestick, one of pair

Maker unknown.

England, probably Sheffield, c. 1780-1810.

Sheffield plate (silver and copper); OH. $10\frac{3}{4}$" (27.3 cm.), OW. $4\frac{5}{8}$" (11.8 cm.).

INHP purchase, 1976. Deshler-Morris House, parlor. Cat. 11015. Acc. 3038.

Tray

Maker unknown.

Probably England, c. 1770.

Mahogany; OH. $\frac{3}{4}$" (2.0 cm.), OW. $7\frac{3}{4}$" (19.7 cm.), OL. $11\frac{3}{4}$" (29.8 cm.).

INHP purchase, 1967. Bishop White House, dining room. Cat. 7576. Acc. 2190.

XXVIII. Inkstand

John White (c. 1697-1789), silversmith.

London, 1730/31.

Silver; tray: OH. $1\frac{9}{16}$" (4.0 cm.), OL. $8\frac{11}{16}$" (22.0 cm.), OW. $6\frac{3}{8}$" (16.2 cm.); quill pot: OH. $2\frac{3}{16}$" (5.6 cm.), ODiam. $2\frac{1}{8}$" (5.3 cm.); ink pot: OH. $2\frac{3}{4}$" (7.0 cm.), ODiam. $2\frac{1}{8}$" (5.3 cm.).

Tray marks: stamped, underside, "IW" in pillowed rectangle reserve, lion passant gardant, leopard's head crowned, and P (datemark for 1730/31); inscribed, underside of tray, once, "25, 18"; engraved, center top, arms of Sharpe (Sharp) family and unidentified crest, apparently a demi-wolf in asymmetrical cartouche with rococo surround. Quill pot: stamped, underside, twice (off register), "IW" in pillowed rectangle reserve; one time, lion passant gardant; engraved, shoulder, demi-wolf [?] crest. Ink pot: engraved shoulder, demi-wolf [?] crest.

John White, from the County of Dorset, was apprenticed to Robert Cooper in 1711, and was a journeyman by 1719. White entered the mark struck on this piece in 1725 and used it until 1739, when all London goldsmiths were required to produce new touchmarks.

Grimwade, Arthur C. *London Goldsmiths 1697-1837: Their Marks and Lives.* London: Faber & Faber, 1976, pp. 698-99. Mark 1735, p. 128.

INHP purchase, 1969, with funds donated by the National Society, Daughters of the American Revolution. Independence Hall, Governor's Council Chamber. Cat. 8390. Acc. 2459.

Taperjack

Attributed to John Langford, II, and John Sebille, silversmiths (working as partners c. 1763-73).

London, 1765/66.

Silver, steel spring bar; OH. $6\frac{5}{8}$" (16.7 cm.), OL. $4\frac{15}{16}$" (12.5 cm.), ODiam. $3\frac{3}{4}$" (9.5 cm.).

Stand: stamped, underside, "IL·IS" arranged on arms of cross-shaped reserve; pellet, centered; lion rampant gardant, leopard's head crown, and "k" (mark for 1765/66). Wax arm: stamped, underside of drip pan, lion passant gardant; inscribed, underside of drip pan, "056" "1", 950 "; stamped, terminal, proper left handle. "IL·IS" arranged on arms of cross-shaped reserve; pellet centered.

No records of the apprenticeship or freedom for either partner can be found. In 1770, *The Gentleman's Magazine* recorded their bankruptcy. However, a Parlimentary Report listed the goldsmiths working in London (1773). No mark is registered for them, but it may have been entered in a register covering 1758 and 1763 which is missing from the records of the Worshipful Company of Goldsmiths.

Grimwade, Arthur C. *London Goldsmiths 1697-1837: Their Marks and Lives.* London: Faber & Faber, 1976, pp. 575, 654. Marks 3656-57, p. 260.

INHP purchase, 1973, with funds donated by the National Society, Daughters of the American Revolution. Independence Hall, Governor's Council Chamber. Cat. 9964, Acc. 2702.

XXIX. Trunk

James Anderson, (fl. 1793-98), saddler, harness maker, and trunk maker.

Philadelphia, c. 1795.

Cedar or pine, covered with cowhide, lined with printed laid paper; iron lock, hasp, and hinges; woven tape braces; ornamental brass tacks; OH. $10\frac{5}{8}$" (27.0 cm.), OW. $25\frac{5}{16}$" (61.8 cm.), OD. $12\frac{1}{4}$" (31.2 cm.).

Picked out in tacks, center outside lid: "J • W." Laid paper label, applied, center, inside lid: "JAMES ANDERSON,/Sadler, Harness-Maker, and Trunk-Maker,/Respectfully informs the Public, that he has removed to No. 208,/Market Street, between Sixth and Seventh Streets (southside);/—WHERE he makes and sells, by wholesale and retail, . . . a com-/plete assortment of TRUNKS, of different sizes: . . . /Orders from any part of the United States will be gratefully receiv-/ed, and duly executed, on the shortest notice./ . . . Philadelphia, April, 24, 1795/ . . ."

James Anderson, saddler, is listed in Philadelphia directories from 1794, at 90 North Second Street; through 1798, at 208 High (Market) Street.

INHP purchase, 1975. The Thaddeus Kosciuszko National Memorial, bedchamber. Cat. 11106. Acc. 3048.

XXX. Andirons, pair

Maker unknown.

Philadelphia or New York, c. 1785; or English, c. 1765.

Brass and iron; OH. $27\frac{15}{16}$" (71.0 cm.), OW. $14\frac{1}{4}$" (36.2 cm.), OD. $23\frac{5}{8}$" (60.0 cm.).

INHP purchase, 1972, with funds donated by the National Society, Daughters of the

American Revolution. Independence Hall, Governor's Council Chamber. Cat. 8693-94. Acc. 2636.

XXXI. Casket

Maker unknown.

Imported from England or possibly France, c. 1810, and sold in Philadelphia, 1811-14.

Wood with painted and stenciled decoration; OH. 5¼″ (13.3 cm.), OW. 7½″ (19.0 cm.), OD. 8¾″ (22.2 cm.).

Labeled, engraved laid paper, inside lid: "Joseph Anthony & Son/Jewellery [illegible]/ and Fancy Store/94 High Street./Philad." in shield.

Joseph Anthony, Jr., (1762-1814), silversmith, son of Joseph and Elizabeth Anthony of Newport, Rhode Island, moved with his family to Philadelphia in 1782. He advertised and sold not only his own silver but also wares imported from England. Anthony advertised at 94 High Street from 1811 until his death, but with "Sons," and not "Son," as in this label.

Gillingham, Harrold E. "Old Business Cards of Philadelphia." *The Pennsylvania Magazine of History and Biography,* 53 (1939), pp. 203-29.

Philadelphia: Three Centuries of American Art. Philadelphia: Philadelphia Museum of Art, 1976. pp. 79-80.

INHP purchase, 1966. Deshler-Morris House, northeast bedroom. Cat. 6367. Acc. 1864.

XXXII. Bellows

John Eckstein and Ross Richardson (in partnership, 1819-23).

Philadelphia, 1819-23.

Wood, leather and brass, painted with stencil and free-hand decoration; OL. 19⁵⁄₁₆″ (49 cm.), OW. 7¼″ (18.3 cm.), OD. 4¹⁄₁₆″ (10.3 cm.).

Label, printed on orange paper: "ECKSTEIN AND RICHARDSON,/PHILADELPHIA" (printed around interior of circle composed of printed asterisks) "PATENT/No. 36,/North third/Street" (centered line by line, inside circle).

John Eckstein and Ross Richardson established the Philadelphia Bellows Manufactory in 1819. The site "in Callowhill, Near Eighth Street . . ." apparently belonged to Richardson, who had advertised from 1814 at that address or at addresses near that site. Eckstein seems to be associated with the stores which the partners operated at "36, N. Third St and 138, Market St.," but he was also listed as a brushmaker at various addresses from 1814 through 1819. He continued at 36 N. 3d from 1825 through 1839.

INHP purchase, 1967. Bishop White House, bedroom. Cat. 7723. Acc. 2228.

XXXIII. Sectional dining table with drop and loose leaves

Maker unknown.

London, c. 1745.

Mahogany, oak secondary, brass casters (probably replaced); OH. 29″ (73.7 cm.), OW. 58½″ (1 m. 48.7 cm.), OL. 13′ (3 m. 96.6 cm.).

INHP purchase, 1978, with funds donated by the National Society, Daughters of the American Revolution. Independence Hall, Governor's Council Chamber. Cat. 11704. Acc. 3279.

See also XXXVI.

XXXIV. Desk and bookcase.

Maker unknown.

Philadelphia, c. 1740.

Mahogany, poplar, pine, white cedar. Secondary; original brass hardware; mirrors (probably replaced); OH. 8′ 4¾″ (2 m. 56 cm.), OW. 42½″ (1 m. 8 cm.), OD. 23⅝″ (60 cm.).

This desk and bookcase was originally owned by Phebe Guest Morris (Mrs. Anthony Morris, III) who was born in Philadelphia "28th of 7th month 1685" and died "18th of 3rd month 1769." It descended in the family to her great-great grandson, Mifflin Wister, M.D. and was left by his widow to her husband's cousin Elliston P. Morris, Sr., in 1900.

Gift of Mr. and Mrs. Elliston P. Morris, 1974. Independence Hall, Governor's Council Chamber. Cat. 10359. Acc. 2843.

XXXV. Tall Case Clock

Works with musical movement: Peter Stretch (1670-1746), clockmaker. Case: maker unknown.

Case: Philadelphia, c. 1725-40.
Works: Philadelphia, c. 1740.

Case: Mahogany, tulip, poplar; works: brass; OH. 8′ 11¼″ (2 m. 73 cm.), OW. 22¼″ (56.5 cm.), OD. 10⅞″ (27.5 cm.).

Clock works and case located separately, but believed to have been a unit originally, until their separation about 1875.

Born in Leek, Staffordshire County, England, Peter Stretch was apprenticed to his uncle, Samuel Stretch, clockmaker. Peter immigrated to Philadelphia in 1702. There he succeeded in the clockmaking business, and undoubtedly trained his son Thomas (1695-1765) in the same craft. In 1753 Thomas was called upon to make the clock for the Pennsylvania State House.

Stretch, Carolyn W. "Early Colonial Clockmakers in Philadelphia." *The Pennsylvania Magazine of History and Biography,* LVI (1932), 225-35.

INHP purchase, 1978, with funds donated by the National Society, Daughters of the Ameri-

can Revolution. Independence Hall, Governor's Council Chamber. Cat. 10385. Acc. 2842.

XXXVI. Upholstered armchairs, pair

Thomas Affleck (1740-95), cabinetmaker.

Philadelphia, c. 1768.

Mahogany, American oak secondary, replaced upholstery; *left:* OH. 41″ (1 m. 4 cm.), OW 27¾″ (70.5 cm.), HS. 18″ (45.8 cm.); *right:* OH. 40¾″ (1 m. 3.5 cm.), OW. 28½″ (72.4 cm.), HS. 17¾″ (45 cm.).

Thomas Affleck was born in Aberdeen, Scotland, and received his training as a cabinetmaker in Edinburgh, and possibly London as well. In 1763 he immigrated to Philadelphia, where he prospered under the patronage of wealthy Quaker families.

Hornor, William MacPherson, Jr. *Blue Book of Philadelphia Furniture: William Penn to George Washington.* Philadelphia: n.p., 1935. pl. 285.

Philadelphia: Three Centuries of American Art. Philadelphia: Philadelphia Museum of Art, 1976. pp. 98-101, Pl. 79.

Two of a set of twelve chairs made for John Penn. At the public sale of Penn items in 1788, these two chairs were purchased by Samuel W. Fisher, who presented them to Friends Hospital in April 1817. Gift of Friends of Independence National Historical Park, 1977. Independence Hall, Governor's Council Chamber. Cat. 11591-92. Acc. 3214.

XXXVII. Desk

Maker unknown, attributed to Thomas Affleck (1740-95), cabinetmaker.

Philadelphia, 1790.

Mahogany, holly inlay, poplar, pine secondary; OH. 30″ (76 cm.), OW. 60½″ (1 m. 53.6 cm.), OD. 27″ (68.6 cm.).

The desk was part of the original furnishings for Congress Hall, perhaps made by Affleck in 1790.

See note to pl. XXXVI.

Milley, John C. "History and Analysis of Congress Hall Furniture," Furnishing Plan for the Second Floor of Congress Hall, Appendix III, pt. D., TS., 1963.

Gift from the Commonwealth of Pennsylvania to the City of Philadelphia, 1873. Congress Hall, Senate Chamber. Cat. 11827. Acc. 1.

XXXVIII. Cellarette-on-stand

Maker unknown.

Philadelphia, c. 1770.

Tiger-stripe maple, yellow pine secondary; OH. 32⅞″ (83.5 cm.), OW 19½″ (49.6 cm.), OD. 14⅝″ (37 cm.).

INHP purchase, 1974, with funds donated by

the National Society, Daughters of the American Revolution. Independence Hall, Governor's Council Chamber. Cat. 10082. Acc. 2718.

XXXIX. Lyre-base center table

Maker unknown.

Philadelphia or Baltimore, c. 1815.

Mahogany, poplar, oak secondary; original stamped brass pulls and casters; OH. 28″ (71.1 cm.), OW. 57¾″ (1 m. 46.7 cm.), OD. 26″ (66 cm.).

A matching pair of card tables were acquired by the Park together with the center table.

INHP purchase, 1974. Second Bank, Foreign Dignitaries' Gallery. Cat. 10373. Acc. 2840.

XL. Armchair

Maker unknown.

Philadelphia, c. 1745.

Walnut, yellow pine secondary; modern needlepoint seat cover; OH. 44¼″ (1 m. 12.3 cm.), OW. 39⁹⁄₁₆″ (80.2 cm.), OD. 18¹⁵⁄₁₆″ (48.1 cm.).

Inscribed in ink, under slip seat: "Chair given to Joshua Humph/reys, who designed the Consti/tution and her sister frigates/about 1793. The chair was given/him by his Mother in Law./It was bequeathed to me by my/aunt Mrs. Jean Murray McCrabb/The chair is now probably/175 years old/Sam[l] H. Yonge/August 11, 1930."

Owned by Joshua Humphreys, Southwark shipbuilder; descended through family to Allene B. Archer. Gift of Miss Allene B. Archer and her sister, Mrs. F. R. Swanson, 1977. Independence Hall, Governor's Council Chamber. Cat. 11622. Acc. 3225.

XLI. Windsor armchair, one of set of five

Robert Taylor (active 1799-d. 1817), chairmaker.

Philadelphia, c. 1806.

Mahogany, maple, painted yellow ochre, glazed, with decoration; OH. 33¾″ (85.6 cm.), WS. 19″ (48.3 cm.), DS. 16½″ (42.0 cm.).

Thought to have been purchased for the Board of Directors Room in the First Bank of the United States. Known to have been used in the bank when it was occupied by the Girard National Bank.

Robert Taylor was living in Philadelphia by 1792 and listed himself at the address of 99 South Front Street between 1802 and 1806. He was probably trained as a turner, as his early work was in this craft.

Hornor, William Macpherson, Jr. *Blue Book of Philadelphia Furniture: William Penn to George Washington.* Philadelphia: n.p., 1935. pp. 298, 302, Pls. 501, 502.

Gift of Mrs. Evan Randolph, Sr. 1972. First Bank. Cat. 9725. Acc. 2675.

XLII. Chest-on-chest

Maker unknown.

Philadelphia, c. 1770.

Mahogany, white cedar and poplar secondary; original brass pulls, replaced cartouche; OH. 7′ 5″ (2 m. 26 cm.), OW. 44½″ (1 m. 13 cm.), OD. 21½″ (54.6 cm.).

Label on back of lower case: "P[ ]/Inherit[ed] by E.M.J. [ ] from/Pearl,/Mother, Aunt Lou[isa]/Kisselman, her parents F[ ] /Kisselman & his wife [/] von Kisselman wh[ ]/ 25 [August] 1774."

Hornor, William Macpherson, Jr. *Blue Book of Philadelphia Furniture: William Penn to George Washington.* Philadelphia: n.p., 1935, pl. 138.

Probably made for Miss Louisa Augusta von Kisselman. Descended in her family until purchased by Joseph Sprain, partial gift from Sprain, 1977. Bishop White House, bedroom. Cat. 11563. Acc. 3206.

XLIII. *Left to right:*

Thomas Jefferson (1743-1826)

Charles Willson Peale (1741-1827), artist.

Philadelphia, 1791.

Oil on canvas, OH. 23¼″ (59 cm.), OW. 19″ (48.2 cm.).

In 1944, Fiske Kimball attributed the painting to Rembrandt Peale, but restoration and research have confirmed the C.W. Peale attribution, as recorded by Bush in *The Life Portraits of Thomas Jefferson.* The 1791 dating is documented by letters from the artist to Jefferson, as recorded in Sellers, *Supplement.*

Bush, Alfred L. *Life Portraits of Thomas Jefferson.* Catalogue. Charlottesville: Virginia Museum of Fine Arts, 1962. pp. 30-33.

Sellers, Charles Coleman. *Charles Willson Peale with Patron and Populace: A Supplement to Portraits and Miniatures by Charles Willson Peale.* Issued as New Series, Vol. 59, Part 3 of the *Transactions of the American Philosophical Society.* Philadelphia: 1969. No. 68.

Peale Museum Sale, 1854 (82). Second Bank, Signers' Gallery. Cat. 11883. Acc. 1.

Richard Henry Lee (1732-94)

Charles Willson Peale (1741-1827), artist.

Philadelphia, 1784.

Oil on canvas; OH. 23½″ (59.7 cm.), OW. 19¼″ (48.9 cm.).

Sellers dates this portrait to late 1784, after the issuance of the first published catalogue of Peale's Museum, October 13, 1784. Lee was elected President of the Continental Congress on November 30, 1784, a fact which Sellers believed caused Peale to add Lee's portrait to his museum.

Lee was a delegate from Virginia to the First Continental Congress in 1774 and a signer of the Declaration of Independence. In 1784 he was elected President of Congress. He was one of the first Senators from Virginia under the Federal Constitution.

Sellers, Charles Coleman. *Portraits and Miniatures by Charles Willson Peale.* Issued as Vol. 42, Part I of the *Transactions of the American Philosophical Society.* Philadelphia: 1952. No. 79, No. 472.

Peale Museum Sale, 1854 (49). Second Bank, Signers' Gallery. Cat. 11882. Acc. 1.

John Adams (1735-1826)

Charles Willson Peale (1741-1827), artist.

Philadelphia, c. 1791-94.

Oil on canvas; OH. 23″ (58.4 cm.), OW. 19″ (48.2 cm.).

The portrait of Adams is first listed in the 1795 catalogue of Peale's Museum. Sellers dates the painting between 1791 and 1794, when Adams was residing in Philadelphia as vice president.

Peale, Charles Willson. *An Historical Catalogue of Peale's Collection of Paintings.* Philadelphia: Privately Printed, 1795. No. 53.

Sellers, *Portraits and Miniatures.* No. 3.

Peale Museum Sale, 1854 (48). Second Bank, Signers' Gallery. Cat. 11881. Acc. 1.

XLIV. *Left to right:*

John Hanson (1721-83)

Charles Willson Peale (1741-1827), artist.

Philadelphia, c. 1781-82.

Oil on canvas; OH. 23″ (58.5 cm.), OW. 19″ (48.2 cm.).

The portrait of Hanson is listed in the 1784 catalogue of Peale's Museum (No. 6), which caused Sellers to date the painting to the time of Hanson's presidency.

A wealthy Marylander of Swedish descent, Hanson gained years of legislative experience in his state's Assembly. A member of the Continental Congress beginning in 1779, he was elected the first "President of the United States in Congress Assembled," under the Articles of Confederation.

Sellers, *Portraits and Miniatures.* No. 357.

Peale Museum Sale, 1854 (166). Second Bank, Faces of Independence Gallery. Cat. 11888. Acc. 1.

William Bartram (1739-1823)

Charles Willson Peale (1741-1827), artist.

Philadelphia, 1808.

Oil on paper mounted on canvas; OH. 23″ (58.4 cm.), OW. 19″ (48.2 cm.).

As recorded by Sellers, this portrait is documented by a letter of June 20, 1808, from the artist to his son Rembrandt Peale.

Like his father John Bartram, William was a Philadelphia botanist of international acclaim. His best known work of natural history was his *Travels Through North and South Carolina, Georgia,* published in 1791.

Sellers, *Portraits and Miniatures.* No. 26.

Peale Museum Sale, 1854 (175). Second Bank, Arts and Sciences Gallery. Cat. 11889. Acc. 1.

Charles Thomson (1729-1824)

Charles Willson Peale (1741-1827), artist.

Philadelphia, c. 1781-82.

Oil on canvas; OH. 23″ (58.4 cm.), OW. 19″ (48.2 cm.).

Number "10" painted on lower right unfinished corner of front side of canvas.

The number 10 painted on the canvas possibly refers to the portrait's place in the sequence of paintings executed for Peale's Museum. The portrait is listed in the 1784 catalogue of that museum.

Born in Ireland, Thomson was called "the Sam Adams of Philadelphia." Chosen secretary of the Continental Congress in 1774, he occupied that position until the formation of a new government in 1789.

Sellers, *Portraits and Miniatures.* No. 862.

Peale Museum Sale, 1854 (52). Second Bank, Faces of Independence Gallery. Cat. 11887. Acc. 1.

XLV. *Left to right:*

John Paul Jones (1747-92)

Charles Willson Peale (1741-1827), artist.

Philadelphia, c. 1781.

Oil on canvas; OH. 22¼″ (56.5 cm.), OW. 20″ (50.8 cm.).

Although this portrait is not listed in the 1784 catalogue to Peale's Museum, Sellers dates it to Jones's longest Philadelphia stay: February-August 1781. Jones wears the French Cross of Military Merit that was presented to him by Louis XVI in 1780.

Sellers, *Portraits and Miniatures.* No. 427.

Peale Museum Sale, 1854 (42). Second Bank, Officers of the American Revolution Gallery. Cat. 11886. Acc. 1.

Samuel Smith (1752-1839)

Charles Willson Peale (1741-1827), artist.

Baltimore or Philadelphia, c. 1788-93.

Oil on canvas; OH. 23⅜″ (59.4 cm.), OW. 19¼″ (48.9 cm.).

Sellers suggests that the portrait was painted during either C.W. Peale's trip to Baltimore in 1788, or in Philadelphia in 1793, marking Smith's beginning as a Congressman. Sellers further suggests that the background and uniform are the work of James Peale, Charles's brother.

Best remembered for his valiant stand under bombardment at Fort Mifflin in 1777 and his command of Baltimore's defenses during the War of 1812, Major-General Smith also represented Maryland in the United States Congress for forty years (1793-1833).

Sellers, *Portraits and Miniatures.* No. 885.

Peale Museum Sale, 1854 (46). Second Bank, War of 1812 Gallery. Cat. 11885. Acc. 1.

Daniel Morgan (1736-1802)

Charles Willson Peale, (1741-1827), artist.

Philadelphia, 1794.

Oil on canvas; OH. 23″ (58.4 cm.), OW. 19″ (48.2 cm.).

Sellers dates the portrait to c. 1794 when Morgan was in Philadelphia on business relating to the Whiskey Rebellion. Morgan's uniform supports this date.

An unschooled Virginia backwoodsman, Morgan rose from the rank of private in the French and Indian War to that of brigadier-general in the American Revolution. He was instrumental in suppressing the Whiskey Rebellion in 1794, and two years later was elected a member of Congress.

Sellers, *Portraits and Miniatures.* No. 568.

Peale Museum Sale, 1854 (9). Second Bank, Officers of the American Revolution Gallery. Cat. 11884. Acc. 1.

XLVI. *Thayendanegea, Christened "Joseph Brant"* (1742-1807)

Charles Willson Peale (1741-1827), aritst.

Philadelphia, 1797.

Oil on canvas; OH. 25⁷⁄₁₆″ (65.6 cm.), OW. 21¼″ (54 cm.).

Sellers dates this work post-1795 because it does not appear in the 1795 catalogue of Peale's Museum. The date 1797 is based on Brant's last visit to Philadelphia, which occurred in the summer of that year.

Adopted by Sir William Johnson and educated in Connecticut, Brant understood both his native Mohican and that of the white man. Chief of the Iroquois Nation during the Revolution, he remained on the side of the British in the vain hope that a victory would check westward settlement. He later removed his people to Canada.

Sellers, *Portraits and Miniatures.* No. 79.

Peale Museum Sale, 1854 (129). Second Bank, American Statesman Gallery. Cat. 11880. Acc. 1.

XLVII. *Marie Joseph Paul Yves Roch Gilbert du Motier* (Marquis de Lafayette) (1754-1834)

Thomas Sully (1783-1872), artist.

Philadelphia, 1825-26.

Oil on canvas, OH. 7′ 10⅜″ (2 m. 37.2 cm.), OW. 59¼″ (1 m. 50.5 cm.).

A life study for this monumental painting was made by the artist in Washington, D.C.

Born in England, Thomas Sully came to the United States with his parents in 1792. After some training in Charleston, South Carolina, he began his career in Norfolk and Richmond, Virginia, in 1801. From 1805 to 1808, when he established permanent residence in Philadelphia, he worked in New York, Hartford, and Boston. After a year of study under Benjamin West in England, 1809-10, Sully quickly became the leading portraitist in Philadelphia.

The nobleman Lafayette, a professional and fearless soldier, volunteered his services to the Continental Army and was commissioned major-general. He was lionized by the American people in a triumphal return tour of the United States in 1824-25.

Biddle, Edward and Mantle Fielding. *The Life and Works of Thomas Sully.* Philadelphia: Wickersham Press, 1921. No. 1017.

Hart, Charles Henry. *A Register of Portraits by Thomas Sully.* Philadelphia: Privately Printed, 1909. No. 982.

Commissioned by a group of Philadelphia citizens in 1824, and purchased by City of Philadelphia from artist in 1827. Second Bank, Foreign Dignitaries Gallery. Cat. 11873. Acc. 1.

XLVIII. *Rebecca Doz* (1759-75)

James Claypoole, Jr. (c. 1743-c. 1800), artist.

Philadelphia, c. 1767.

Oil on canvas, OH. 39½″ (100.6 cm.), OW. 30³⁄₁₆″ (76.7 cm.).

Attributed to Claypoole by family tradition, and by E.P. Richardson.

The son of an artisan, James Claypoole, Jr., was probably born in Philadelphia. He left the city for London sometime between 1769 and 1771, but a storm forced his ship into the West Indies. Claypoole may have stayed in Jamaica until his death.

The daughter of Andrew Doz, a Philadelphia merchant, and Rebecca Cash, Rebecca Doz died at sixteen years of age. A portrait of her sister, Martha Doz (1752-1808), forms a pair in the Park's collection.

Richardson, E.P. "James Claypoole, Junior, Rediscovered," *Art Quarterly.* (Summer 1970), 171.

Gift of Miss Margaret G. Cowell, 1928. Second Bank, Pennsylvania Galleries. Cat. 11878. Acc. 1.

XLIX. *James Madison* (1751-1836)

Attributed to James Sharples, Sr. (1751-1811), artist.

Philadelphia, c. 1796-97.

Pastel on paper; OH. 9″ (22.8 cm.), OW. 7″ (17.8 cm.).

A portrait of Madison by Sharples appears on a transcription that was made of a lost catalogue of paintings which the artist printed in Bath, England, about 1802. The initials "MC" appear opposite Madison's name, meaning a Member of Congress, which Madison was at the time of Sharples' residence in Philadelphia, 1796-97. The portrait is attributed by Milley to the senior James Sharples on the grounds of style.

Knox, Katherine McCook. *The Sharples: Their Portraits of George Washington and his Contemporaries.* New Haven: Yale University Press, 1930. No. 99.

Milley, John C. "Thoughts on the Attribution of Sharples' Pastels." In *University Hospital Antiques Show Catalogue.* Philadelphia: 1975.

Ex. Coll. Mrs. James (Ellen) Sharples; Bristol Fine Arts Academy; City Art Gallery, Bristol, England. Gift of Friends of INHP, 1972. Second Bank, American Statesmen Gallery. Cat. 10051. Acc. 2716.

L. William Floyd (1734-1821)

Ralph Earl (1751-1801), artist.

Probably Long Island, New York, c. 1793.

Oil on canvas; OH. 48¼″ (122.7. cm.), OW. 36¼″ (92 cm.).

Signed and dated in paint, lower left corner "R. Earl/pinxt 17[?]"

This portrait of Floyd was probably painted at his estate, Brookhaven, in Mastic, Long Island, which is depicted in the background of the painting. The painting remained at Brookhaven from the time of its execution until the time of its donation to the Park by a descendant of Floyd.

Born in Worcester County, Massachusetts, Ralph Earl practiced in New Haven before going to England in 1778 as a loyalist sympathizer. He spent seven years in England and exhibited at the Royal Academy. From his return to America in 1785 until his death his practice was principally in Connecticut and neighboring states.

Signer of the Declaration of Independence and one of New York's first United States Congressmen (1789-91), William Floyd was a wealthy landholder, but a staunch supporter of Jeffersonian democracy.

Yearbook of the Society of the Sons of the American Revolution. State of New York: 1893.

Gift of Mrs. David Weld, (descendant), 1973. Second Bank, Signers' Gallery. Cat. 10167. Acc. 2740.

Figures

1. *Coat of Arms of Pennsylvania*

George Rutter (active c. 1780-98), artist.

Philadelphia, c. 1785.

Oil on canvas; OH. 48″ (1 m. 22 cm.), OW. 49¼″ (1 m. 25.2 cm.).

Painted on upper banner: "VIRTUE/LIBERTY &/INDEPENDENCE."; painted on lower banner: "G. RUTTER/PHILADA/PINXIT."

Minutes of the General Assembly of Pennsylvania record from 1786 petitions from George Rutter and Martin Jugiez for payment for "carving painting and gilding the arms of the State now placed over the seat of Justice in the State House, in this City." They had been commissioned to execute the painting and frame by the Supreme Executive Council.

George Rutter advertised in Philadelphia newspapers as a painter of "Landscapes, Carriages, Signs, Show-Boards and Fire-Buckets. . . ."

Sharp, Daniel J. Furnishing Plan for the Pennsylvania Supreme Court Chamber. Independence Hall, Appendix E, TS., 1980.

INHP purchase, 1961. Independence Hall, Supreme Court Chamber. Cat. 2108. Acc. 653.

2. Mounted American bald eagle

Charles Willson Peale (1741-1827), taxidermist.

Philadelphia, after 1805.

Natural history specimen, papier-mâché base; OH. 26⅜″ (67 cm.), OW. 25½″ (64.8 cm.), OD. 23″ (58.6 cm.).

From c. 1795-1805 this eagle was caged as a specimen in Charles Willson Peale's museum in Philadelphia. Drawings of the eagle were supplied by Peale to Benjamin Henry Latrobe in 1806 to serve as a model for carvings in the new United States Capitol in Washington, D.C.

Sellers, Charles Coleman. *Charles Willson Peale.* Philadelphia: 1947. Published as *Memoirs of the American Philosophical Society,* Vol. 23, Parts 1-2.

Descendants of C.W. Peale to 1873, when donated to the City of Philadelphia by Miss Mary Peale. Visitor Center. Cat. 11861. Acc. 1.

3. Inkstand and tray

Philip Syng, Jr. (1703-89), silversmith.

Philadelphia, 1752.

Silver; tray: OH. 1¼″ (3.2 cm.), OL. 10⁵⁄₁₆″ (26.2 cm.), OW. 7½″ (19.0 cm.); quill pot: 6¹⁄₁₆″ (15.4 cm.), ODiam. 2⁹⁄₁₆″ (6.5 cm.); ink pot: OH. 2⅜″ (6.1 cm.), ODiam. 1¹³⁄₁₆″ (4.6 cm.); sander: OH. 2⁷⁄₁₆″ (6.2 cm.), ODiam. 1¾″ (4.5 cm.).

Tray: stamped near center top, "PS" in conforming rectangle reserve; stamped center bottom, three times, "PS" in shield-shaped reserve with intermediate stamped scrolled leaves; inscribed, top, inside retaining lip for sander, "D" and "W. Todd"; inscribed, center bottom, "oz dwt/36 17" and, at left of maker's marks, "1800". Quill pot, ink pot, and sander: stamped, center bottom, twice, "PS" in shield-shaped reserve with intermediate stamped scrolled leaf. Sander: inscribed, below maker's marks, "HA."

Made in 1752 for the Speaker's table of the Pennsylvania Assembly, this inkstand was probably the instrument used for the signing of both the Declaration of Independence, and the Constitution of the United States.

Philip Syng, Jr., was born in Ireland. He immigrated with his family to Philadelphia in 1714. After completing his apprenticeship under his father, he went to London where he became friendly with Benjamin Franklin. He returned to Philadelphia in 1726. Syng was an active participant in the Philadelphia community.

Dorman, Charles. Furnishng Plan for the Assembly Room, Independence Hall, Part D., TS., 1970, pp. 37-39.

Gift of Commonwealth of Pennsylvania to the City of Philadelphia, 1875. Independence Hall, Assembly Room. Cat. 11860. Acc. 1.

4. *George Washington* (1732-99)

William Rush (1756-1833), sculptor.

Philadelphia, c. 1814.

Pine, painted; OH. 73″ (185.5 cm.).

According to Henri Marceau, Rush's initial intention was to reproduce casts from his figure of Washington, but the plan had to be abandoned when only two subscribers expressed interest. Rush first exhibited the statue of Washington at the Pennsylvania Academy of the Fine Arts in 1815, after which it was placed in Peale's Museum in Independence Hall.

Rush was born in Philadelphia, the son of a ship's carpenter. He was apprenticed to Edward Cutbush from London. About 1773 Rush set himself up as an independent carver.

Marceau, Henri. *William Rush: The First Native American Sculptor.* Philadelphia: The Philadelphia Museum of Art, 1937, pp. 42-46.

Purchase of City of Philadelphia from artist, 1831. Second Bank, Officers of the American

5. *The Religion of Nature Delineated*

William Wollaston (1660-1724), author; Samuel Palmer (d. 1732), printer.

London, 1725. Third edition.

Paper, leather binding; OH. 9¹³⁄₁₆″ (24.9 cm.), OW. 7⅞″ (20 cm.), OD. ⅞″ (2.2 cm.).

Printed on title page, top: "THE/RELIGION/OF/NATURE/DELINEATED."; title page, bottom: "LONDON:/Printed by S. Palmer, and sold by B. LINTOTT, W. and J. INNYS,/J. OSBORN, J. BATLEY, and T. LONGMAN. 1725."; facing title page, bottom: "Mr. Wollaston/Vertu Sculpsit." (beneath engraving of author).

Benjamin Franklin was employed as a compositor on this book in 1725. William Wollaston, an English cleric, spent many years as a recluse. This volume, his one successful and well-known work, was published in many editions. Samuel Palmer, the owner of a large printing establishment in 1725, later wrote a poor history of printing. He died bankrupt.

Franklin, Benjamin. *Autobiography.* Ed. Leonard W. Labaree. New Haven: Yale University Press, 1964.

Gift of Freeman Tilden, 1970. Franklin Court. Cat. 8515. Acc. 2508.

6. *The History of the Rise, Increase, and Progress of the Christian People called Quakers . . .*

William Sewel (1650-1725), author; Samuel Keimer (1688-1739), printer; Benjamin Franklin (1706-90), printer; Hugh Meredith (1697-1749), printer.

Philadelphia, 1728. Third edition, corrected.

Paper, calf binding; OH. 11⁷⁄₁₆″ (29 cm.), OW. 7½″ (19 cm.), OD. 2″ (5.2 cm.).

Printed on title page: "THE/HISTORY/OF THE/RISE, INCREASE, and PROGRESS,/Of the CHRISTIAN PEOPLE called/QUAKERS:/Intermixed with Several/Remarkable Occurrences./Written Originally in LOW-DUTCH, and also Tran-/slated into ENGLISH,/By WILLIAM SEWEL./The THIRD EDITION, Corrected./PHILADELPHIA:/Printed and Sold by SAMUEL KEIMER in Second Street./M DCC XXVIII." Inscribed in ink, title page, top: "Anthᵒ Morris has this book of Saml Keimer/ having Subscribed for two of them/Samuel Jackson (2) 1836."

This volume was reprinted from the first London edition of Sewel's *History* (1722) under a contract from the Philadelphia Yearly Meeting. Keimer began the work in 1725; three years later Franklin and Meredith were given a contract to print the remaining 44½ sheets. Pages 533-694, the 16-page index, and the title page came from their press.

William Sewel, an eminent Quaker historian, was Dutch. He spent twenty-five years on this, his principal work, publishing it in Amsterdam in 1717 and translating it for English publication in 1722. Samuel Keimer, one of only two printers in Philadelphia at the time, was an unsuccessful printer in England, Philadelphia, and Barbados. Franklin and Hugh Meredith, partners from 1728 until 1730, opened Philadelphia's third printing establishment. Meredith's decision to return to farming prompted the dissolution of the partnership.

Franklin, Benjamin. *Autobiography.* Ed. Leonard W. Labaree. New Haven: Yale University Press, 1964. pp. 118-19.

Miller, C. William. *Benjamin Franklin's Philadelphia Printing.* Philadelphia: American Philosophical Society, 1974, pp. 1-2.

Gift of Mr. Charles Kurz II, 1975. Franklin Court. Cat. 11110. Acc. 3051.

7. *A Map of the most Inhabited part of Virginia . . .*

Joshua Fry (1700-54), surveyor; Peter Jefferson (1707-57), surveyor; Thomas Jefferys (d. 1771), engraver and publisher; Robert Sayer (1725-94), publisher.

London, 1768. Fifth state.

Hand-colored engraving; sight: OH. 31¹⁄₁₆″ (79 cm.), OW. 48⁵⁄₁₆″ (1 m. 22.7 cm.).

Inscribed in plate, in cartouche, lower right: "A MAP of/the most INHABITED part of/VIRGINIA/containing the whole PROVINCE of/MARYLAND/with Part of/PENNSYLVANIA, NEW JERSEY and NORTH CAROLINA/Drawn by/Joshua Fry & Peter Jefferson/in 1751."; bottom center: "Printed for Robᵗ Sayer at № 53 in Fleet Street, & Thoˢ Jefferys at the Corner of Sᵗ Martins Lane, Charing Cross, London."

The fifth state of the map was published in 1768 for inclusion in Thomas Jefferys's *A General Topography of North America and the West Indies. . . .* The geographical content is identical to the comprehensive 1755 edition, and the only changes are in its inscriptions.

Joshua Fry, professor of natural philosophy and mathematics at the College of William and Mary in 1731, was made county surveyor when Albemarle County was formed in 1745. He was one of its two representatives to the House of Burgesses, and commander of the Virginia forces in the French and Indian Wars. Peter Jefferson, the father of Thomas, was official surveyor for Goochland County and deputy surveyor of Albemarle County. He became county lieutenant following Fry's death. Thomas Jefferys was one of London's most prominent and prolific map publishers and engravers during the mid-eighteenth century, and the official geographer to the Prince of Wales. Jefferys and Sayer were in partnership during the late 1760s.

Malone, Dumas, ed. *The Fry and Jefferson Map of Virginia and Maryland.* Charlottesville, Va.: The University Press of Virginia, 1966.

Verner, Coolie. "The Fry and Jefferson Map." *Imago Mundi,* XXI (1967), 70-94.

INHP purchase, 1972. Independence Hall, Long Gallery. Cat. 8779. Acc. 2641.

8. *An Accurate Map of His Majesty's Province of New Hampshire in New England . . .*

Colonel Joseph Blanchard (1704-58), cartographer; Reverend Samuel Langdon (1723-97), cartographer; Thomas Jefferys (d. 1771), engraver.

London, 1761.

Hand-colored engraving; plate: OH. 30³⁄₁₆″ (76.7 cm.), OW. 27⁹⁄₁₆″ (70 cm.).

Inscribed in plate, above map: "AN ACCURATE MAP of His MAJESTY'S PROVINCE OF NEW-HAMPSHIRE IN NEW ENGLAND, taken from ACTUAL SURVEYS/of all the inhabited Part, and from the best information of what is uninhabited . . . by COL. BLANCHARD, and the REVᴰ Mᴿ LANGDON."; inset, upper right: "A General MAP of the RIVER. Sᵀ LAWRENCE . . ."

Langdon's 1756 map, "An Accurate Map of his majesty's province of New Hampshire in New England. . . ," is believed to be the basis for this later revised version.

Joseph Blanchard was a prominent judicial figure. Samuel Langdon, a graduate and later President of Harvard, served as pastor of North Church, Portsmouth, for nearly 20 years.

Cumming, William P. *British Maps of Colonial America.* Chicago: The University of Chicago Press, 1974.

Gift of the Friends of Independence National Historical Park, 1978. Independence Hall, Long Gallery. Cat. 11966. Acc. 3310.

9. *A Chart of Delaware Bay and River*

Joshua Fisher (1707-83), cartographer; William Faden (1750-1836), engraver and publisher.

London, 1776.

Hand-colored engraving; plate: OH. 19¼″ (49 cm.), OW. 27¹¹⁄₁₆″ (70.4 cm.).

Inscribed in plate, middle right: "A CHART of/DELAWARE BAY and RIVER/ . . . Taken from the Original Chart Published at Philadelphia/by JOSHUA FISHER./Engraved by WILLIAM FADEN, Charing Cross."; upper left: "We the Subscribers having perused the annexed Draught of/DELAWARE BAY . . ." followed by a list of pilots and masters of vessels.

The first edition of Fisher's map was published in 1756, but received minimal circulation. An improved second edition was probably issued by Fisher in the early 1770s and reissued in this 1776 edition by Faden, and in another by Sayer and Bennett in 1777.

Joshua Fisher, a Quaker merchant, was born

near Lewes, Delaware, and moved to Philadelphia in 1746. The chart is his only published work. William Faden, an engraver and publisher, was Geographer to the King after the death of Thomas Jefferys in 1771.

Philadelphia: Three Centuries of American Art. Philadelphia: Philadelphia Museum of Art, 1976, #99, pp. 125-7.
Wroth, Lawrence C. "Joshua Fisher's 'Chart of Delaware Bay and River.'" *The Pennsylvania Magazine of History and Biography,* 74 (1950), 90-109.

INHP purchase, 1975. City Tavern, hall. Cat. 6509. Acc. 1854.

10. *Votes and Proceedings of the House of Representatives of the Province of Pennsylvania . . . Volume the Third.*

Benjamin Franklin (1706-90), printer; David Hall (1714-72), printer.

Philadelphia, 1754.

Paper, calf binding; leaves: OH. $14\frac{5}{8}$″ (37.2 cm.), OW. $9\frac{1}{8}$″ (23.2 cm.).

Printed on title page, top: "VOTES/AND/PRODEEDINGS/OF THE/House of Representatives/OF THE/PROVINCE of PENNSYLVANIA./Beginning the Fourteenth Day of October, 1726./VOLUME The THIRD."; title page, bottom: "PHILADELPHIA:/Printed and Sold by B. FRANKLIN, and D. HALL, at the/New-Printing-Office, near the Market. MDCCLIV."; stamped on front cover, in gilt: "ASSEMBLY OF PENNSYLVANIA".

Possibly part of the original Assembly of Pennsylvania library. The volume was rebound in 1974, but the gilt inscription on the cover was retained.

David Hall, a native of Edinburgh, came to Philadelphia in 1743 to work for Franklin. They became partners in 1748. The partnership ended at the conclusion of their 17-year agreement.

Miller, C. William. *Benjamin Franklin's Philadelphia Printing.* Philadelphia: American Philosophical Society, 1974, pp. 324-5.
Pennsylvania Archives, Eighth Series, Vol. VII, 15 January 1767, pp. 5960-61.

INHP purchase, 1963, with funds donated by the General Federation of Women's Clubs. Independence Hall, Committee of the Assembly Room. Cat. 3372. Acc. 1243.

11. *The Charters and Acts of Assembly of the Province of Pennsylvania . . . Volume 1*

Peter Miller (working 1760-62), printer.

Philadelphia, 1762.

Paper, calf binding; OH. $7\frac{7}{16}$″ (18.9 cm.), OW. 5″ (12.5 cm.), OD. $2\frac{3}{16}$″ (5.6 cm.).

Printed on title page: "THE/CHARTERS/AND/ACTS OF ASSEMBLY/OF THE/PROVINCE/OF/PENNSYLVANIA,/IN TWO VOLUMES./VOL. I./ . . . Compared with the PUBLIC RECORDS./PHILADELPHIA,/Printed by PETER MILLER AND Comp. M DCC LXII." Inscribed in ink on title page, top: "John Penn"; front fly leaf, top: "John Penn 1765/For the Use of The Council Board."

This book is thought to have been one of the reference books in the Provincial Council's library.

Peter Miller printed books in both English and German in Philadelphia during the early 1760s.

Gift of Eastern National Park and Monument Association, 1962. Independence Hall, Governor's Council Chamber. Cat. 3206. Acc. 721.

12. *Map of the Province of Pennsylvania*

William Scull, cartographer; James Nevil, printer.

Philadelphia, 1770.

Hand-colored engraving; plate: OH. $22\frac{1}{4}$″ (56.5 cm.), OW. $32\frac{1}{4}$″ (81.9 cm.).

Inscribed in plate, inside cartouche: "To the Honorable/Thomas Penn and Richard Penn Esquires/True and Absolute Proprietaries and Governors of the/Province of Pennsylvania . . . John Penn Esquire . . . THIS MAP./of the Province of/PENNSYLVANIA./Is humbly dedicated by their/Most Obedient humble serv^{t}/W. Scull."; bottom right: "Philadelphia, Printed by James Nevil for the Author April 4:st 1770." Inscribed in ink, above map: "Mr Penn's private Map."; beneath map: "★ Fry and Jefferson, make the *Western* Limits of Pennsylvania to *end* at this Star. ★ [or the Mouth of Kiskamanetas River]./Colonel Fry was sent by the Government of Virginia in the year 1752, to ascertain the Longitude of what is now called Fort/Pitt and the Western Limits of Penn's Grant."

This copy is thought to be John Penn's personal reference copy.

William Scull based this map, in part, on the 1759 map of Pennsylvania executed by his grandfather, Nicholas Scull. The map is the only record of James Nevil working as a printer in America.

Garrison, Hazel S. "Cartography of Pennsylvania Before 1800." *The Pennsylvania Magazine of History and Biography,* 59 (1935), 255-83.

INHP purchase, 1974, with funds donated by the National Society, Daughters of the American Revolution. Cat. 10351. Acc. 2803.

13. *The Repeal. Or the Funeral Procession, of Miss Americ-Stamp.*

Maker unknown; after Benjamin Wilson, (1721-88), engraver.

City of publication unknown; probably England, c. 1766.

Engraving; plate: OH. $9\frac{7}{8}$″ (25.2 cm.), OW. $13\frac{15}{16}$″ (35.4 cm.).

Inscribed in plate, beneath illustration: "THE REPEAL. Or the Funeral Procession, of MISS AMERIC-STAMP." followed by detailed explanatory text.

This version compares very closely with the British Museum *Catalogue,* number 4140 version III, with the following exceptions: the catalogue includes the inscription but no title beneath the image, and the measurements in the catalogue appear to be those for the image, rather then the plate.

Wilson was born in Leeds, later settled in London, and became a successful portraitist.

The British Museum. *Catalogue of Prints and Drawings . . .Political and Personal Satires.* London, 1883, Volume 4, pp. 368-73.
Richardson, E.P. "Stamp Act Cartoons in the Colonies." *The Pennsylvania Magazine of History and Biography,* 96 (1972), 275-97.

Gift of Eastern National Park and Monument Association, 1965. Second Bank, Documents Room. Cat. 6094. Acc. 1759.

14. *The Golden Age.*

Valentine Green (1739-1813), engraver; John Boydell (1719-1804), publisher.

London, 1777.

Hand-colored aquatint; plate: OH. $18\frac{3}{8}$″ (47 cm.), OW $22\frac{1}{8}$″ (56.5 cm.).

Inscribed in plate, below oval: "THE GOLDEN AGE."; along oval at left: "Painted by B. West, Historical Painter to his Majesty. Published by J. Boydell Engraver."; along oval, at right: "in Cheapside June 4th 1777. Engraved by V. Green, Engraver to his Majesty & to the Elector Palatine."

Valentine Green was an accomplished practitioner of the art of mezzotint. He completed nearly 400 plates, from both contemporary and historical sources, and was elected one of six Associate Engravers of the British Royal Academy in 1775.

"Small Work by Benjamin West." *Antiques,* XCIII (1968), p. 318.

INHP purchase, 1974, with funds donated by Eastern National Park and Monument Association. City Tavern, Cincinnati Room. Cat. 10345. Acc. 2812.

15. *A Chart of the Straits of Magellan*

Don Juan de la Cruz Cano y Olmedilla, cartographer; Robert Sayer (1725-94), publisher; J. Bennett, publisher.

London, 1775.

Hand-colored engraving; plate: OH. 21½″ (54.7 cm.), OW. 28$\frac{1}{16}$″ (71.3 cm.).

Inscribed in plate, middle left: "A CHART/OF THE/STRAITS OF MAGELLAN./INLARGED FROM THE CHART PUBLISHED AT MADRID in 1769./by Don Juan de la Cruz Cano y Olmedilla/of the Royal Academy of St Fernando./ and Improved . . ."; insert at top: "A CHART/ OF/MAGELLANIA/with/FALKLAND'S ISLANDS."

Robert Sayer and J. Bennett were publishers and map, book, and print sellers, in partnership in London in the 1770s.

INHP purchase, 1973, with funds donated by Eastern National Park and Monument Association. City Tavern, Subscription Room. Cat. 10187. Acc. 2742.

16. *Chart of the N W Coast of America* . . .

James Cook (d. 1779), navigator; T. Harmar, engraver.

London, 1784.

Hand-colored engraving; plate: OH. 16⅝″ (42.2 cm.), OW. 27⅛″ (68.8 cm.).

Inscribed in plate, center top: "CHART/of the/ NW COAST of AMERICA and NE COAST of ASIA/explored in the Years/1778 & 1779./The unshaded parts of the Coast of ASIA are taken from a MS Chart received from the Russians."; upper right corner: "36."

Cumming, W.P., S.E. Hillier, D.B. Quinn and G. Williams. *The Exploration of North America 1630-1776.* New York: G.P. Putnam's Sons, 1974, pp. 230-35.

INHP purchase, 1973, with funds donated by Eastern National Park and Monument Association. City Tavern, Subscription Room. Cat. 10188. Acc. 2742.

17. Untitled print (*Congress Voting Independence*)

Edward Savage (1761-1817), engraver.

Philadelphia, plate, late 18th century; print, after 1859.

Unfinished stipple engraving; plate: OH. 21⅝″ (54.9 cm.), OW. 27⅜″ (69.6 cm.).

Opinion is divided concerning the authorship of the original, incomplete oil painting: some feel that it was begun by Robert Edge Pine, who died in 1788, and completed by Edward Savage, while others feel that the painting was executed entirely by Savage. Although unsigned, Savage's work on the incomplete engraving is not disputed. Its unfinished plate was given to the Massachusetts Historical Society in 1859, at which time impressions were pulled from it.

Edward Savage was born in Massachusetts and probably trained as goldsmith. In 1795 he moved to Philadelphia, executing most of his prints there.

Mulcahy, James H. "Congress Voting Independence: The Trumbull and Pine-Savage Paintings." *The Pennsylvania Magazine of History and Biography,* 80 (1956), 74-91.
Stewart, Robert G. *Robert Edge Pine, a British Portrait Painter in America, 1784-1788.* Washington, D.C.: Smithsonian Institution Press, 1979.

INHP purchase, 1965. First Bank. Cat. 5835. Acc. 1698.

18. Declaration of Independence broadside

John Dunlap (1747-1812), printer.

Philadelphia, July 4-5, 1776.

Laid paper: OH. 17½″ (44.4 cm.), OW. 12$\frac{15}{16}$″ (32.2 cm.).

Watermarks on paper: "D & C BLAUW" at top, "B" in middle, and crown and post horn within a shield subscribed "D & C BLAUW" at bottom. Printed title: "IN . . . CONGRESS, JULY 4, 1776./A DECLARATION/BY THE REPRESENTATIVES OF THE/UNITED STATES OF AMERICA,/IN GENERAL CONGRESS ASSEMBLED."

This is one of twenty-one known copies of Dunlap's first broadside edition.

John Dunlap, a printer and newspaperman, published the *Pennsylvania Packet or General Advertiser,* which became the first daily newspaper in the country in 1784. He was printer to Congress from 1778 until 1789.

Goff, Frederick R. *The John Dunlap Broadside: The First Printing of the Declaration of Independence.* Washington, D.C.: Library of Congress, 1976.

Originally owned by John Nixon (1733-1808) who was appointed by Philadelphia's Sheriff to read the Declaration of Independence to the citizens of the city for the first time on July 8, 1776. The broadside remained in his family and was given to the Park by a descendant. Gift of Harry W. Harrison, 1951. Second Bank, Documents Room. Cat. 1071. Acc. 14.

19. *Articles of Confederation and Perpetual Union* . . .

Printer unknown.

Philadelphia, 1776. Second draft.

Laid paper; OH. 13$\frac{9}{16}$″ (34.4 cm.), OW. 8$\frac{11}{16}$″ (22.1 cm.).

Printed on first sheet: "ARTICLES/OF/CONFEDERATION AND PERPETUAL UNION,/BETWEEN THE STATES OF . . ."; inscribed in ink, last sheet, reverse: "E. Gerry"; text annotated throughout.

This is one of eighty copies of the second draft of the Articles of Confederation ordered printed secretly by the Second Continental Congress to use during debate on the final text. It was owned and annotated by Elbridge Gerry (1744-1814), a delegate from Massachusetts.

Ford, Worthington Chauncey, ed. *Journals of the Continental Congress 1774-1789,* Vol. V. Washington, D.C., 1906, pp. 555, 689.

The copy remained in the Gerry family until the 20th century. Gift of the Trustees of the Robert L. McNeil, Jr., Trust, 1963. Second Bank, Documents Room. Cat. 3111. Acc. 1118.

20. *A Plan of the City of Philadelphia* . . .

Joshua Fisher (1707-83), cartographer; Nicholas Scull (1700-62), surveyor; Andrew Dury (active 1742-78), publisher.

London, 1776.

Engraving; plate: OH. 20⅛″ (51.2 cm.), OW. 26$\frac{15}{16}$″ (68.1 cm.).

Inscribed in plate, upper right: "A PLAN/OF THE/CITY/OF/PHILADELPHIA,/the CAPITAL of/PENNSYLVANIA,/from an ACTUAL SURVEY/BY/BENJAMIN EASTBURN,/SURVEYOR GENERAL;/1776./LONDON . . ."; upper left: "A CHART OF/DELAWARE BAY/ AND RIVER,/from the Original/By Mr FISHER OF/PHILADELPHIA./1776."

Nicholas Scull, Surveyor General of Pennsylvania from 1748 until 1761, was a respected cartographer and one of the original members of Franklin's *Junto*. Andrew Dury was a publisher, engraver, map seller, and surveyor.

Snyder, Martin P. *City of Independence: Views of Philadelphia Before 1800.* New York: Praeger Publishers, 1975, pp. 62-4, 67, 73-4, 96-7.

Gift of the Friends of Independence National Historical Park, 1975. City Tavern, hall. Cat. 10604. Acc. 2889.

21. *A Plan of the City of New York & its Environs* . . .

Captain John Montresor (1736-99), surveyor; Andrew Dury (active 1742-78), publisher.

London, 1775.

Engraving; plate: OH. 25$\frac{7}{16}$″ (64.6 cm.), OW. 20$\frac{11}{16}$″ (52.6 cm.).

Inscribed in left cartouche: "A PLAN of the CITY of/NEW-YORK & its ENVIRONS/to Greenwich, on the North . . . */Survey'd in the Winter, 1775/Sold by A. Dury . . ."; in right cartouche: "To the Honble Thos Gage, Esqr Major/General and Commander in Chief of his MAJESTY'S Forces in North America. . . ."

Montresor executed the plan in the winter of 1765-66. It was reduced to half-scale for publication and printed in May, 1767. This second state is identical to the 1767 edition except for the date and publisher's information.

John Montresor, a respected British military engineer, served in America from 1754 until 1779.

Stokes, I.N. Phelps. *The Iconography of Manhattan Island, 1498-1909.* Volume I: 1498-1811. New York: 1915, Pl. 40 and pp. 339-40, 343.

Gift of Friends of Independence National Historical Park, 1975. City Tavern, hall. Cat. 10603. Acc. 2889.

22. *A Plan of the Action at Bunkers Hill.*

Captain John Montresor (1736-99), surveyor; Lieutenant Page, engineer.

London, 1775.

Hand-colored engraving; sight: OH. 19¼″ (48.8 cm.), OW. 16¾″ (42.6 cm.).

Inscribed in plate, upper right corner: "A PLAN/ OF THE/ACTION AT BUNKERS HILL./on the 17th of June 1775./Between HIS MAJESTY'S TROOPS,/Under the Command of MAJOR GENERAL HOWE,/AND THE REBEL FORCES./By LIEUT PAGE of the Engineers,/ . . . N.B. The Ground Plan is from an Actual/Survey by Captn Montresor." Inscribed in ink, lower left corner: "Number of British regular Troops was 3000. Their loss as stated by Genl Gage was 1054./19 Commissioned officers killed & 70 wounded./Number of Patriotick Americans (not regular murders) was only 1500. of/whom 139 were killed and 314 wounded and missing."

Both Montresor and Page were at the battle.

Nebenzahl, Kenneth. *A Bibliography of Printed Battle Plans of the American Revolution 1775-1795.* Chicago: The University of Chicago Press, 1975, #29.

INHP purchase, 1966. City Tavern, Cincinnati Room. Cat. 6506. Acc. 1854.

23. *The Course of Delaware River from Philadelphia to Chester . . .*

William Faden (1750-1836), engraver.

London, 1778.

Hand-colored engraving; plate: OH. 18³⁄₁₆″ (46.2 cm.), OW. 27½″ (69.8 cm.).

Inscribed in plate, center top: "THE COURSE OF/DELAWARE RIVER/from PHILADLEPHIA to CHESTER,/Exhibiting the Several WORKS erected by the REBELS to defend its Passage,/ with the ATTACKS made upon them by HIS MAJESTY'S Land & Sea Forces . . ."; lower right corner: "Profile/and/Plan/of the Sunk Frames or/Chevaux de Frize which/formed the Stackadoes/in the River," with diagram; middle left: "A SKETCH OF FORT ISLAND" with a key to the buildings.

Snyder, Martin C. *City of Independence: Views of Philadelphia Before 1800.* New York: Praeger Publishers, 1975, pp. 108-115.

Gift of the Manufacturers Life Insurance Company, 1976. City Tavern, Hall. Cat. 11333. Acc. 3129.

24. *L'Amerique Independante*

Antoine Borel (1743 - after 1810), artist; J.C. le Vasseur (1734-1816), engraver.

France, 1778.

Engraving; plate: OH. 19⅛″ (48.6 cm.), OW. 13¹³⁄₁₆″ (35.1 cm.).

Inscribed in plate, center, below image: "L'AMERIQUE INDEPENDANTE"; right, below image: "J.C. le Vasseur Sculptor . . ."; left, below image: "Borel invenct et delineavit 1778."

The *Journal de Paris* published a full description identifying the symbolism of the proposed print on May 31, 1778, seeking subscribers. Franklin refused to have the print dedicated to him. Had he accepted the honor, he would have been expected to pay the artist.

Borel was an able designer and enthusiast for American liberty, but his wider reputation was made as the creator of *sujets galants.*

Sellers, Charles C. *Benjamin Franklin in Portraiture.* New Haven: Yale University Press, 1962, pp. 120-21, 195-7, Pl. 32.

Transfer from Morristown National Historical Park, 1973. City Tavern, Cincinnati Room. Cat. 10209. Acc. 2752.

25. *The Birth of American Liberty*

Sylvester Harding (1745-1809), painter; John Ogborn(e) (c. 1725-95), engraver; Thomas Macklin (active late 18th century), publisher.

London, 1784.

Colored mezzotint; plate: OH. 15⅛″ (38.4 cm.), OW. 13⅜″ (34 cm.).

Inscribed in plate, beneath circle: "THE BIRTH OF AMERICAN LIBERTY"; right of circle: "Ogborn Sculpt"; left of circle: "S. Harding delint" Poem, 20 lines long, at bottom beneath title.

Sylvester Harding was best known as a miniaturist, and also published several larger works. John Ogborn(e), a designer and engraver, engraved many paintings by his contemporaries as well as some prints of his own design. Thomas Macklin was an engraver and publisher.

Gift of Eastern National Park and Monument Association, 1960. Deshler-Morris House, parlor. Cat. 696. Acc. 432.

26. *Display of the United States of America*

Amos Doolittle (1754-1832), engraver and publisher.

New Haven, Connecticut, c. 1790.

Stipple and line engraving; paper: OH. 20½″ (52.1 cm.), OW. 17″ (43.2 cm.).

Inscribed in plate, bottom of print: "DISPLAY of the UNITED STATES of AMERICA/To the Patrons of Arts and Sciences, in all parts of the World, this Plate/is most respectfully Dedicated by their most obedient humble Servants/Amos Doolittle & Ebn Po [ ]/Printed & Sold by A. Doolittle New Haven where Engraving & Roling Press Printing is performed." Inscribed in ink, lower right: "1790."

The print was first published in 1788 with Washington in civilian dress, but after 1790 he was depicted in military attire. This unusual state comes between the "regularly" recognized first and second states and may well be the first issued with Washington in military attire.

Amos Doolittle was born in Cheshire, Connecticut, and trained as a silversmith. Among the works he engraved and published were four scenes of the battles at Lexington and Concord by Ralph Earl, and Peter Lacour's drawing of the inauguration of George Washington at Federal Hall, New York.

American Printmaking: The First 150 Years. Washington, D.C.: Smithsonian Institution Press, 1969, p. 43, #79.
Hart, Charles Henry. *Catalogue of the Engraved Portraits of Washington.* New York: 1904, pp. 354-7, #840, 840a and 840b.

INHP purchase, 1965. Congress Hall, East Committee Room. Cat. 6077. Acc. 1798.

27. *The Death of General Montgomery . . .*

John Trumbull (1756-1843), artist; Johan Frederik Clemens (1749-1831), engraver; A.C. de Poggi, publisher.

London, 1798.

Engraving; sight: OH. 22¹⁵⁄₁₆″ (58.3 cm.), OW. 31½″ (80 cm.).

Inscribed in plate, lower center: "The Death of General Montgomery/In the Attack of Quebec Decr 1775"; lower left: "Painted by John Trumbull Esqr"; lower right: "Engravd by J F Clemens."

John Trumbull, an artist known for his historical paintings, portraits, and miniatures, also served abroad as an American diplomat. Johan F. Clemens, a Danish line engraver, studied in Denmark and France and later visited Berlin and London. This print is considered to be one of his best plates.

INHP purchase, 1961. Congress Hall, House of Representatives Chamber. Cat. 455. Acc. 558.

28. *Congressional Pugilists*

Maker unknown.

Philadelphia, after 1798.

Engraving; plate: OH. 6⅜″ (16 cm.), OW. 8⁹⁄₁₆″ (21.7 cm.).

Inscribed in plate, above image: "Congressional Pugilists."; beneath image, left: "He in a trice struck Lyon thrice/Upon his head, enrag'd Sir,"; beneath image, center: "Who seiz'd the tongs to ease his wrongs,/And Griswold thus engag'd, Sir."; beneath image, right: "Congress Hall,/in Philadª Feb. 15, 1798."

Snyder, Martin P. *City of Independence: Views of Philadelphia Before 1800.* New York: Praeger Publishers, 1975, pp. 211-12, fig. 129.

29. *A View of the Bombardment of Fort McHenry, near Baltimore*

John Bower (active 1809-19), engraver.

Philadelphia, c. 1814-19.

Aquatint; plate: OH. 14¹⁄₁₆″ (35.7 cm.), OW. 18⅞″ (48 cm.).

Inscribed in plate, below image: "A VIEW of the BOMBARDMENT of Fort McHenry, near Baltimore, by the British fleet, taken from the/observatory, under the Command of Admirals Cochrane & Cockburn, on the morning of the 13ᵗʰ of Sepʳ 1814 which lasted 24 hours, &/thrown from 1500, to 1800 shells. in the Night attempted to land by forcing a passage up the ferry branch but were repulsed with great loss."

John Bower engraved portraits and maps and illustrated books.

American Printmaking: The First 150 Years. Washington, D.C.: Smithsonian Institution Press, 1969, p. 51 #101.

Courtesy of the Friends of INHP, through the Military Order of Foreign Wars of the United States, Pennsylvania Commandery. Second Bank, War of 1812 Room. Cat. 11385. Acc. 3120.

30. *Back of the State House, Philadelphia*

William R. Birch (1755-1834), artist and engraver; Thomas Birch (1779-1851), artist and engraver.

Philadelphia, 1799.

Hand-colored engraving; plate: OH. 11³⁄₁₆″ (28.4 cm.), OW. 13⅛″ (33.4 cm.).

Inscribed in plate, lower left, below image: "Drawn Engraved & Published by W. Birch & Son"; lower right, below image: "Sold by R. Campbell & Cº Nº 30 Chestnut Street Philadª 1799."; center, below image: "BACK of the STATE HOUSE, PHILADELPHIA."

Gift of Eastern National Park and Monument Association, 1957. Second Bank, Birch Room. Cat. 1193. Acc. 211.

31. Chamber pot

Maker unknown.

England, c. 1710.

Red earthenware, slip decoration; OH. 5½″ (14 cm.), OW. 7¾″ (19.7 cm.), OD. 7″ (17.8 cm.).

Cosans, Betty, et al. Franklin Court Report, TS., 1974.

Excavated in 1972 from Franklin Court, Feature 22, Context III. 318 Market Street, Archaeological Exhibit. Cat. 11995. Acc. 2668.

32. Pie plate

Maker unknown.

Probably Philadelphia, c. 1730-60.

Red earthenware, slip decoration; ODiam. 11″ (28 cm.).

Cosans, Betty, et al. Franklin Court Report, TS., 1974.

Excavated in 1972 from Franklin Court, Feature 22, Context II & III. 318 Market Street, Archaeological Exhibit. Cat. 12204. Acc. 2668.

33. *Left:* Chamber pot

Maker unknown.

England, c. 1740-60.

White salt-glaze stoneware; OH. 4¹⁵⁄₁₆″ (12.5 cm.), ODiam. 7⅛″ (18.2 cm.).

Excavated in 1977 from privy near Front and Norris Streets. 322 Market Street, Archaeological Storage. Cat. 11997. Acc. 3220.

Right: Chamber pot.

Anthony Duché, Sr. (c. 1682-1762), potter.

Philadelphia, c. 1730-62.

Gray salt-glaze stoneware; OH. 5³⁄₁₆″ (13.1 cm.), Diam. base 5¼″ (13.3 cm.).

Impressed "AD" in rectangle on underside of handle.

Excavated in 1977 from a privy near Front and Norris Streets. 322 Market Street, Archaeological Storage. Cat. 11996. Acc. 3220.

34. Detail of touchmark on chamber pot, fig. 33.

35. Pipe bowl

Attributed to Richard Warder, maker.

Philadelphia, c. 1716.

Unglazed white pipe clay; OH. 1½″ (3.8 cm.), OW. ¾″ (1.9 cm.), OL. 1½″ (3.8 cm.).

Impressed on heel of pipe bowl: "R W", in reverse tear-drop, crowned with two asterisks, surmounting a fleur-de-lys.

Hume, Ivor Noël. *A Guide to Artifacts in Colonial America.* New York: Alfred A. Knopf, 1970. No. 14.
Powell, Bruce B. Independence National Historical Park Archeological Project 9, Independence Square, TS., 1957.

Excavated in 1957 from Independence Square, grassy plot 17, Feature 3. 320 Market Street, Archaeological Storage. Cat. 12202. Acc. 208.

36. Puzzle jug

Maker unknown.

Probably Philadelphia, c. 1740-60.

Red earthenware, brown manganese glaze; OH. 8¾″ (22.3 cm.), ODiam. 7¾″ (19.7 cm.).

"W x A" impressed on belly.

Brears, Peter C.D. *The English Country Pottery: Its History and Techniques.* Rutland, Vermont: Charles E. Tuttle Company, 1971, pp. 66-67, 108-109.

Archaeological Salvage, Area A. 320 Market Street, Archaeological Storage. Cat. 12201. Acc. 3220.

37. *Left to right:* Large dish

Maker unknown.

England, c. 1760.

Salt-glazed stoneware; ODiam. 14⅝″ (37.2 cm.).

INHP purchase, 1963. Todd House, dining parlor. Cat. 3328. Acc. 508.

Platter

Maker unknown.

England, c. 1760.

Salt-glazed stoneware; ODiam. 14¹⁵⁄₁₆″ (38 cm.).

INHP purchase, 1961. Todd House, dining parlor. Cat. 3327. Acc. 508.

Covered jug

Maker unknown.

England, mid-18th century.

Salt-glazed stoneware; OH. 5⅛″ (13 cm.).

INHP purchase, 1964. Todd House, dining parlor. Cat. 4857. Acc. 1550.

Mug

Maker unknown.

England, mid-18th century.

Salt-glazed stoneware; OH. 2⅝″ (6.8 cm.).

INHP purchase, 1967. Todd House, dining parlor. Cat. 7606. Acc. 2185.

Plate

Maker unknown.

England, mid-18th century.

Salt-glazed stoneware; ODiam. 9⅜″ (23.8 cm.).

INHP purchase, 1964. Visitor Center. Cat. 4089. Acc. 1435.

Creamer
Maker unknown.

England, mid-18th century.

Salt-glazed stoneware; OH. 3⅛″ (7.9 cm.).

INHP purchase, 1964. Todd House, dining parlor. Cat. 4263. Acc. 1486.

38. Knife box

Maker unknown.

Sheffield, England, c. 1760-80.

Sharkskin ("shagreen") covered wood case, with brass mounts; OH. 10$\frac{3}{16}$" (26 cm.), OW. 7" (17.8 cm.), OD. 4$\frac{5}{8}$" (11.9 cm.).

Pistol-handled table knife (one of a set of twelve).

Maker unknown.

Sheffield, England, c. 1760.

Steel, and salt-glazed stoneware; OL. 9" (22.9 cm.).

Stamped on knife blade: "TURIN."

"TURIN" is the mark used by the cutlery shop of William and Thomas Trickett, Sheffield, England.

Pistol-handled table forks (two of set of twelve).

Maker unknown.

Sheffield, England, c. 1760.

Steel, and salt-glazed stoneware; OL. 6¾" (17.2 cm.).

The forks were acquired together with the knives and knife box and probably were originally a set.

A Directory of Sheffield. 1787; rpt., Vol. 30, *Architecture and Decorative Arts Series,* New York: Da Capo Press, 1969. p. 46.

INHP purchase, 1973, with funds donated by the National Society, Daughters of the American Revolution. Independence Hall, Governor's Council Chamber. Cat. 10276, 10252, 10264 and 10265. Acc. 2770.

39. "Four Seasons"

Maker unknown.

Probably Derby, England, c. 1770.

Porcelain, underglaze polychrome, overglaze gilt, molded and applied relief decoration; *Left to right:* "Summer": OH. 8$\frac{5}{8}$" (22.0 cm.), OW. 6¼" (15.9 cm.), OD. 5" (12.7 cm.); "Winter": OH. 9½" (24.2 cm.), OW. 4½" (11.4 cm.), OD. 4¼" (10.8 cm.); "Spring": OH. 9¾" (24.8 cm.), OW. 4¼" (10.8 cm.), OD. 5" (12.7 cm.); "Autumn": OH. 9¾" (24.8 cm.), OW. 4½" (11.4 cm.), OD. 4¼" (10.8 cm.).

INHP purchase, 1978. Graff House, bedchamber. Cat. 11957-11960. Acc. 3306.

40. Mug (reconstructed)

Probably the factory of Caspar or Richard Wistar.

South Jersey "Wistarburg," c. 1740-60.

Glass; OH. 3$\frac{5}{8}$" (9.2 cm.), ODiam. 2¼" (5.7 cm.).

Cosans, Betty. Franklin Court 4 Archaeological Report. Philadelphia, 1974.
Palmer, Arlene M. *The Wistarburgh Glassworks: The Beginning of Jersey Glassmaking.* Alloway, N.J., 1976.

Excavated from a well in Franklin Court in 1973. 318 Market Street, Archaeological Exhibit. Cat. 12066. Acc. 2668.

Free-blown glass ball (reconstructed)

Maker unknown.

America, c. 1740-60.

Glass; ODiam. 2$\frac{3}{8}$" (6.1 cm.).

The purpose of the object is unknown.

Cosans, Betty. Franklin Court 4 Archaeological Report. Philadelphia, 1974.

Excavated from a well in Franklin Court in 1973. 318 Market Street, Archaeological Exhibit. Cat. 12067. Acc. 2668.

Bottle (reconstructed)

Probably the factory of Caspar or Richard Wistar, 1730-60.

South Jersey "Wistarburg," c. 1730-60 by context.

Glass; OH. 7¾" (19.7 cm.), ODiam. 4$\frac{1}{8}$" (10.5 cm.).

Cosans, Betty. Franklin Court 4 Archaeological Report. Philadelphia, 1974.

Excavated from a privy in Franklin Court, 1973. 322 Market Street, Archaeological Storage. Cat. 12065. Acc. 2668.

41. Bird feeder

Maker unknown.

England or America, second half of 18th century.

Glass; OH. 5$\frac{3}{8}$" (13.7 cm.), Diam. 2$\frac{3}{16}$" (5.6 cm.).

INHP purchase, 1966. Todd House, dining parlor. Cat. 7163. Acc. 2110.

42. *Left to right:* Dinner plate

Maker unknown.

England, c. 1765-95.

Cream-colored earthenware (creamware); ODiam 9$\frac{7}{8}$" (25 cm.).

INHP purchase, 1969. Visitor Center. Cat. 8331. Acc. 2423.

Saucer

Maker unknown.

England, c. 1775-1815.

Cream-colored earthenware (creamware); ODiam. 5$\frac{3}{16}$" (13.2 cm.).

INHP purchase, 1964. Todd House, dining parlor. Cat. 4272. Acc. 1486.

Chocolate cup

Maker unknown.

England, c. 1775-1815.

Cream-colored earthenware (creamware); OH. 2¾" (7.0 cm.), ODiam. 2$\frac{7}{16}$" (6.2 cm.).

INHP purchase, 1964. Todd House, dining parlor. Cat. 4273. Acc. 1486.

Teapot

Maker unknown.

England, c. 1770-1820.

Cream-colored earthenware (creamware); OH. 4½" (11.6 cm.), Diam. at base 2$\frac{5}{8}$" (6.7 cm.).

INHP purchase, 1964. Todd House, dining parlor. Cat. 3686. Acc. 1364.

Sugar bowl

Maker unknown.

England, c. 1775-85.

Cream-colored earthenware (creamware); OH. 3¾" (9.5 cm.), ODiam. 4½" (11.4 cm.).

INHP purchase, 1964. Todd House, dining parlor. Cat. 6203. Acc. 1804.

Tureen

Maker unknown.

England, c. 1790.

Cream-colored earthenware (creamware); OH. 5¼" (13.3 cm.), OW. 4$\frac{1}{8}$" (10.4 cm.), OL. 8¼" (21 cm.).

INHP purchase, 1969. Todd House, dining parlor. Cat. 8361. Acc. 2447.

Tureen stand

Maker unknown.

England, c. 1770.

Cream-colored earthenware (creamware); OL. 8½" (21.6 cm.), OW. 7" (17.8 cm.).

INHP purchase, 1969. Todd House, dining parlor. Cat. 8362. Acc. 2447.

Ladle

Maker unknown.

England, late 18th or early 19th century.

Cream-colored earthenware (creamware); OL. 6½" (16.5 cm.).

INHP purchase, 1964. Todd House, dining parlor. Cat. 4267. Acc. 1486.

Coffee pot

Maker unknown.

England, c. 1775-1815.

Cream-colored earthenware (creamware); OH. 10¾" (27.3 cm.), Diam. at base 4½" (11.4 cm.).

INHP purchase, 1965. Todd House, dining parlor. Cat. 6273. Acc. 1821.

43. Dessert molds

Maker unknown.

England, late 18th or early 19th century.

Cream-colored earthenware (creamware); *left to right:* OW. 3⅜″ (8.6 cm.); OL. 8¼″ (21 cm.); OL. 7¼″ (18.5 cm.).

INHP purchases, 1964. Todd House, dining parlor. *Left to right:* Cat. 3681. Acc. 1364. Cat. 4096. Acc. 1435. Cat. 4095. Acc. 1435.

44. Tureen

Maker unknown.

Probably France, c. 1770.

Cream-colored earthenware (creamware); OH. 8½″ (21.6 cm.), OW. 9½″ (24.2 cm.), OL. 12″ (30.5 cm.).

INHP purchase, 1969. Todd House, dining parlor. Cat. 8379. Acc. 2455.

45. *Left to right:* Miniature flat-iron

Maker unknown.

Staffordshire, England (possibly Whieldon), c. 1800-20.

Cream-colored earthenware, green glaze; OH. 1⅞″ (4.8 cm.), OW. 1¾″ (4.5 cm.), OL. 2⅞″ (7.3 cm.).

INHP purchase, 1976. Study Collection. Cat. 11574. Acc. 3186.

Miniature chair (shard)

Maker unknown.

Staffordshire, England (possibly Whieldon), c. 1800-20.

Cream-colored earthenware, green glaze; OH. 1¾″ (4.5 cm.), OW. 1⅞″ (4.8 cm.), OD. 1½″ (3.8 cm.).

Schumacker, Paul J.F. Archaeological Field Notes, Archaeological Project 15, Bishop White House basement, 309 Walnut Street, TS., 1956.

Excavated in 1955 from Bishop White House sewer outlet. 322 Market Street, Archaeological Storage. Cat. 5738. Acc. 132.

Miniature chair

Maker unknown.

Staffordshire, England (possibly Whieldon), c. 1770-1800.

Cream-colored earthenware, green glaze; OH. 3½″ (8.9 cm.), OW. 2¼″ (5.7 cm.).

INHP purchase, 1965. Study collection. Cat. 4873. Acc. 1579.

Miniature cradle

Maker unknown.

Staffordshire, England (possibly Whieldon), c. 1800-20.

Cream-colored earthenware, green glaze; OH. 3⅛″ (8.0 cm.), OW. 2″ (5.1 cm.), OL. 4½″ (11.5 cm.).

INHP purchase, 1961. Study Collection. Cat. 7897. Acc. 508.

46. Beaker

Maker unknown.

England, c. 1790-1810.

Cream-colored earthenware (creamware), transfer printed decoration; OH. 3⁵⁄₁₆″ (8.4 cm.), ODiam. 3¹⁄₁₆″ (7.8 cm.).

Transfer print, either side of cup: "SUCCESS TO TRADE/AND BILLS WELL PAID" surrounded by wreath.

INHP purchase, 1964. Todd House, Law Office. Cat. 3842. Acc. 1366.

47. Monteith

Josiah Wedgwood (c. 1730-95), potter.

Staffordshire, England, c. 1780-85.

Cream-colored earthenware (creamware), transfer printed decoration; OH. 5¾″ (14.6 cm.), OL. 12¾″ (32.4 cm.), OW. 8½″ (21.6 cm.).

Impressed, bottom: "WEDGWOOD," "F"; transfer print, exterior, side: floral motifs and arms of Continental Navy; interior, bottom: arms, surrounded by chain ring with names of the thirteen states.

The bowl is believed to have been ordered as part of a dinner service made for Robert Morris, financier of the Revolution and Agent of Marine for the Continental Navy (1781-85).

Gorely, Jean. "Monteith with Arms of the Continental Navy. . . ." *Antiques.* February, 1950, pp. 130-133.

Gift of Catherine G. Oster and Eugenia G. Kaledin. Second Bank, Pennsylvania Gallery. Cat. 8843. Acc. 2664.

48. Detail of interior of fig. 47.

49. Bowl

Maker unknown.

England, possibly Leeds, c. 1780-1820.

Cream-colored earthenware (creamware); OH. 5⅜″ (13.3 cm.), ODiam. 10⅛″ (25.7 cm.).

INHP purchase, 1969. Todd House, dining parlor. Cat. 8315. Acc. 2435.

50. *Left to right:* Cream pot

Maker unknown.

China, 19th century.

Porcelain, Nanking underglaze decoration; OH. 5½″ (14.0 cm.), OL. 5″ (12.7 cm.), ODiam. 3½″ (8.9 cm.).

INHP purchase, 1967. Bishop White House, parlor. Cat. 7431. Acc. 2160.

Cups

Maker unknown.

China, late 18th or early 19th century.

Porcelain, Nanking underglaze decoration; OH. 2″ (5.1 cm.), ODiam. 3½″ (9.0 cm.).

Shards of a similar cup and saucer were excavated from Bishop White House (Cat. 5875-76).

INHP purchase, 1964. Bishop White House, parlor. Cat. 7437 and 3724. Acc. 2160 and 1349.

Saucers

Maker unknown.

China, 19th century.

Porcelain, Nanking underglaze decoration; ODiam. *Left:* 5⅜″ (13.7 cm.), *right*: 5¼″ (13.4 cm.).

INHP purchase, 1967. Bishop White House, parlor. Cat. 7452, 7447. Acc. 2160.

Bowl

Maker unknown.

China, late 18th or early 19th century.

Porcelain, Nanking underglaze decoration; OH. 2¾″ (7.0 cm.), ODiam. 5½″ (14.0 cm.).

INHP purchase, 1961. Bishop White House, parlor. Cat. 5890. Acc. 508.

Dish

Maker unknown.

China, 19th century.

Porcelain, Nanking underglaze decoration; OH. 1⅝″ (4.15 cm.), ODiam. 8″ (20.3 cm.).

INHP purchase, 1967. Bishop White House, parlor. Cat. 7430. Acc. 2160.

Dish

Maker unknown.

England, late 18th or early 19th century.

Soft-paste porcelain, underglaze decoration imitating Nanking export porcelain; OH. ¹³⁄₁₆″ (2.5 cm.), OL. 6⅝″ (16.9 cm.), OW. 3¾″ (9.6 cm.).

INHP purchase, 1977. Bishop White House, parlor. Cat. 11594. Acc. 3216.

Sugar tongs

Robert and William Wilson (working 1825-46), silversmiths.

Philadelphia, c. 1825.

Silver; OH. 1″ (2.55 cm.), OW. 2″ (5.15 cm.), OL. 6¾″ (17.15 cm.).

Stamped, inside arm, once: "R. & W. WILSON"; engraved, outside top of bow: "A" in script, in lozenge.

Robert Wilson was working in Philadelphia by 1814. His brother William joined him in 1825.

The partners specialized in flatware, operating a "silver spoon manuf." together until Robert left the firm or died in 1846.

Philadelphia: Three Centuries of American Art. Philadelphia: Philadelphia Museum of Art, 1976, pp. 336-37, 355.

INHP purchase, 1974, with funds donated by Eastern National Park and Monument Association. Bishop White House, parlor. Cat. 10327. Acc. 2804.

Sugar bowl

Maker unknown.

China, late 18th or early 19th century.

Porcelain, Nanking underglaze decoration; OH. 4″ (10.15 cm.), ODiam. 3¹⁵⁄₁₆″ (10.0 cm.).

INHP purchase, 1967. Bishop White House, parlor. Cat. 7480. Acc. 2160.

Cup

Maker unknown.

China, 19th century.

Porcelain, Nanking underglaze decoration; OH. 2⅝″ (6.7 cm.), OL. 3½″ (8.9 cm.), ODiam. 2½″ (6.4 cm.).

INHP purchase, 1967. Bishop White House, parlor. Cat. 7561. Acc. 2175.

Saucer

Maker unknown.

China, 19th century.

Porcelain, Nanking underglaze decoration; OH. 1¼″ (3.2 cm.), ODiam. 5¼″ (13.35 cm.).

INHP purchase, 1967. Bishop White House, parlor. Cat. 7448. Acc. 2160.

51. Coffeepot

Maker unknown.

China, c. 1790-1810.

Porcelain, underglaze sepia and overglaze polychrome decoration, overglaze gilt; OH. 9¼″ (23.5 cm.), ODiam. 5⅛″ (13.0 cm.).

Gift of Mr. and Mrs. Elliston P. Morris, 1973. Deshler-Morris House, tea room. Cat. 10115. Acc. 2727.

52. Baskets, pair

Maker unknown.

China, c. 1800.

Porcelain, Canton underglaze decoration; *left:* OH. 3¼″ (8.3 cm.), OL. 8¹³⁄₁₆″ (22.4 cm.), OW. 7¾″ (19.1 cm.); *right:* OH. 3⅜″ (8.5 cm.), OL. 9″ (22.9 cm.), OW. 8″ (20.4 cm.).

Gift of Mr. and Mrs. Newcomb T. Montgomery, 1972. Bishop White House, dining room. Left, Cat. 8656, right, Cat. 8658. Acc. 2633.

Trays, pair

Maker unknown.

China, c. 1800.

Porcelain, Canton underglaze decoration; *left:* OH. 1³⁄₁₆″ (3.0 cm.), OL. 9⁷⁄₁₆″ (24.0 cm.), OW. 8⅜″ (21.2 cm.); *right:* OH. 1³⁄₁₆″ (3.0 cm.), OL. 9⁵⁄₁₆″ (23.7 cm.), OW. 8³⁄₁₆″ (20.8 cm.).

Gift of Mr. and Mrs. Newcomb T. Montgomery, 1972. Bishop White House, dining room. Left, Cat. 8659, right, Cat. 8657. Acc. 2633.

Plate

Maker unknown.

China, c. 1750-70.

Porcelain, overglaze polychrome enamel; OH. ⅞″ (2.2 cm.), ODiam. 8¹³⁄₁₆″ (22.4 cm.).

History of ownership in family of Bishop William White. INHP purchase, 1971, with funds donated by Eastern National Park and Monument Association. Bishop White House, dining room. Cat. 8565. Acc. 2552.

53. Wine Glass

Maker unknown.

England or Ireland, c. 1790.

Flint glass; OH. 5⅜″ (13.6 cm.), ODiam. 2¹³⁄₁₆″ (7.2 cm.).

Donated by the Misses Hand, 1920, to City of Philadelphia. Todd House, parlor. Cat. 11994. Acc. 1.

54. *Left to right:* Decanters, pair

Maker unknown.

England, c. 1775-1800.

Glass, cut and etched decoration, replaced stoppers; *left:* OH. 10¹¹⁄₁₆″ (21.7 cm.), ODiam. 4″ (10.2 cm.); *right:* OH. 11⅛″ (28.2 cm.), ODiam. 4″ (10.2 cm.).

INHP purchase, 1975, with funds donated by Eastern National Park and Monument Association. Deshler-Morris House, dining room. Left, Cat. 10621, right, Cat. 10622. Acc. 2905.

Decanters, pair

Maker unknown.

Ireland, c. 1790.

Glass, cut and etched decoration, replaced stoppers; *left:* OH. 10⅝″ (27.0 cm.), ODiam. 3¾″ (9.6 cm.); *right:* OH. 11⅝″ (29.4 cm.), ODiam. 3⅞″ (9.9 cm.).

INHP purchase, 1975, with funds donated by Eastern National Park and Monument Association. Deshler-Morris House, dining room. Left, Cat. 10620, right, Cat. 10623. Acc. 2905.

Wine glasses, two of a set of three

Maker unknown.

Probably England, c. 1800-20.

Blown flint glass; *front:* OH. 4¼″ (10.8 cm.), ODiam. 2⁵⁄₁₆″ (5.9 cm.); *back:* OH. 4⁷⁄₁₆″ (11.2 cm.), ODiam. 2⅜″ (6.0 cm.).

INHP purchase, 1965. Deshler-Morris House, dining room. Front, Cat. 10553, back, Cat. 10554. Acc. 2877.

55. *Left:* Decanter

Maker unknown.

Probably England, c. 1810.

Moulded cut glass; OH. 9¼″ (23.5 cm.), ODiam. 3⅞″ (9.8 cm.).

Gift of Mr. James F. Tulbutt, who received it 50 years ago as a gift from Mr. Upton White, a great-grandson of Bishop White, who retained a second decanter. According to Mr. White they had both been the property of Bishop White. Bishop White House, dining room. Cat. 2935. Acc. 920.

Right: Decanter

Maker unknown.

England or Ireland, c. 1780-1800.

Cut glass; OH. 9¼″ (23.5 cm.), ODiam. 5″ (12.7 cm.).

Originally owned by Bishop William White of Philadelphia. A gift by Mrs. Joseph F. Hughes, and children, descendants of Bishop White, in memory of Mrs. Hughes's parents, George Pepper Robbins and Margaret Washington Robbins, 1976. Bishop White House, dining room. Cat. 10868. Acc. 2954.

56. Bottles, set of twelve

Maker unknown.

Probably England, c. 1790.

Glass; OH. 10⅛″ (25.7 cm.), OW. 3½″ (9.0 cm.), (all vary slightly).

INHP purchase, 1965. Deshler-Morris House, first kitchen. Cat. 6209-6220. Acc. 1808.

Bottle Case

Maker unknown.

America or England, second half 18th century.

Pine, painted dark gray; OH. 12½″ (31.8 cm.), OL. 19″ (48.2 cm.), OW. 14½″ (36.9 cm.).

INHP purchase, 1965. Deshler-Morris House, first kitchen. Cat. 6208. Acc. 1808.

57. Plate

Enoch Wood & Sons, potters.

Staffordshire, England, c. 1818-46.

Cream-colored earthenware (creamware), overglaze decoration; OH. 1⁵⁄₁₆″ (4.6 cm.), ODiam. 7⁷⁄₁₆″ (19.2 cm.).

Impressed, bottom: "Enoch Wood & Sons, Burslem," surrounding an American eagle.

Towner, Donald. *Creamware.* London & Boston: Faber and Faber, 1978.

INHP purchase, 1963. Bishop White House, pantry. Cat. 3337. Acc. 1094.

58. Hand mirror

Maker unknown.

Possibly America, c. 1800-25.

Mahogany, painted black; mirror; OL. 11⅞″ (30.2 cm.), ODiam. 6¾″ (17.0 cm.).

Descended in the family of Isaac Franks, owner of the Deshler-Morris House, and later sold to Charles Y. Jenkins. Gift of Mr. Edward C. Jenkins, 1975. Deshler-Morris House, southeast bedroom. Cat. 10786, Acc. 2955.

59. Pair of shoe buckles

Joseph, Jr. (1752-1831), and Nathaniel Richardson (1754-1827), silversmiths.

Philadelphia, c. 1785-90.

Silver; OL. 2½″ (6.5 cm.), OW. 1¹⁵⁄₁₆″ (4.8 cm.).

Stamped, back, each piece: "I•NR" in rectangle reserve; inscribed, back: "XII" (10116) "XXXXX" (10117).

The Richardson brothers were trained in their father's shop. When Joseph Richardson, Sr., retired in 1777, they continued his business jointly until 1790. Nathaniel gave up silversmithing and became Isaac Paxton's partner in a hardware and ironmongery business. Joseph changed his punch to read "JR" and continued in trade until about 1801.

Fales, Martha Gandy. *Joseph Richardson and Family, Philadelphia Silversmiths.* Middletown, Conn.: Wesleyan University Press, 1974, pp. 153-183; Mark, fig. 135, p. 167; p. 260.

Descended in the Morris family, gift of Elliston P. Morris, Janet Morris Butler, and Marriott C. Morris, 1973. Deshler-Morris House, back bedroom. Cat. 10116-17. Acc. 2726.

Shoe buckle

Maker unknown.

Possibly England, late 18th century.

Silver buckle, mounted with paste brilliants and enamel rosettes; polished steel chapes and tongues; OL. 2¾″ (7.0 cm.), OW. 2⅝″ (6.7 cm.).

Descended in the family of Bishop William White. INHP purchase, 1962. Bishop White House, bedroom. Cat. 2434-35. Acc. 827.

Box for shoe buckles

Maker unknown.

Possibly England, late 18th century.

Wood, covered with black paper, lined with hair-filled silk cushions; OL. 6⅜″ (15.7 cm.), OW. 3½″ (8.9 cm.), OD. 1⁹⁄₁₆″ (4.0 cm.).

Label, in ink on paper, pasted on bottom of box: "Montgomery."

Believed to have been owned by Bishop White, descended in the family of Bishop William White. INHP purchase, 1962. Bishop White House, bedroom. Cat. 2472. Acc. 827.

60. Dish and drainer

Samuel Ellis (c. 1700-72, w. 1721-65), pewterer.

London, 1721-65.

Pewter; dish: OL. 21″ (53.3 cm.), OW. 16⅛″ (41.0 cm.), OD. 1½″ (3.9 cm.); drainer: OL. 18½″ (47 cm.), OW. 13¾″ (35.0 cm.), OD. ⅝″ (1.5 cm.).

Stamped, underside, each piece: Fleece touchmark (in oval, with "SAMUEL," above; "ELLIS," below, both conforming to oval outline).

Ellis was admitted to the Yoemanry of the Worshipful Company of Pewterers of London on 28 September 1721 and elected to the Livery in 1725. He was elected to the office of Master in 1748. Ellis retired from active business sometime before February 22, 1765.

Cotterell, Howard Herschel. *Old Pewter: Its Makers and Marks In England, Scotland and Ireland: An Account of the Old Pewterer and His Craft.* London: B.T. Batsford, Ltd., 1929; rpt. Rutland, Vt.: Charles E. Tuttle Company, 1963. Mark 1547, p. 203.

INHP purchase, 1964. Todd House, kitchen. Cat. 4582-83. Acc. 1530.

61. Coffee mill

Bruerton, manufacturer.

Probably England, 19th century

Iron, hardwood handle; mill: OH. 10⅜″ (26.4 cm.), OW. 11⅝″ (29.4 cm.), OD. 6″ (15.1 cm.); bracket: OH. 14½″ (37.0 cm.), OW. 2½″ (6.4 cm.), OD. 3¾″ (9.2 cm.).

Stamped, upper front of mill housing: "Bruerton/Warranted 6c."

INHP purchase, 1964. Bishop White House, kitchen. Cat. 4046. Acc. 1429.

Canister, one of set of four

Maker unknown.

America or Europe, probably first quarter of 19th century.

Glass, painted tin lid; OH. 9¼″ (23.5 cm.), ODiam. 4⅝″ (11.8 cm.).

One of four removed from a Salem, New Jersey, drug store, in continuous operation for over 100 years, disbanded c. 1936. Gift of Charles G. Dorman, 1966. Bishop White House, kitchen. Cat. 6737. Acc. 1982.

62. Table knife and fork, one of a set of eleven pieces

E.E. Marshes and Shepherd (w. 1821-c. 1850).

Sheffield, England, second quarter 19th century.

Steel, staghorn handle; knife: OL. 10¹¹⁄₁₆″ (27.1 cm.), OW. 1³⁄₁₆″ (3.0 cm.); fork: OL. 8⁵⁄₁₆″ (21.1 cm.), OW. ¾″ (2.0 cm.).

Stamped, knife blade: "MARSHES & SHEPHERD."

The Sheffield *Directory* of 1821 lists "Marsh and Shepherd, pen and pocket knife manufacturers, Castle Hill," and the firm grew to "Marshes and Shepherd" by 1825. Intermittently until 1837 *Directories* record the firm as merchants as well as manufacturers. This is borne out by commerce with at least two Philadelphia firms in the 1830s and '40s. An engraving in the general catalogue of Sheffield merchandise, Joseph Smith's *Key* of 1816, shows a similar knife to that illustrated here. [Part II, "Round Point" table knife with handle No. 27].

Kebabian, John S. ed. Joseph Smith. *Explanation or Key to the Various Manufactories of Sheffield with Engravings of each Article, of Merchants, Wholesale Ironmongers, and Travellers.* Sheffield: Joseph Smith, 1816; rpt., South Burlington, Vt.: The Early American Industries Association, 1975, especially pp. 20-21.

Descended from Pennock family of Philadelphia to Mrs. Newcomb T. Montgomery. Gift of Mr. and Mrs. N.T. Montgomery, 1972. Bishop White House, kitchen. Cat. 8677, 8672. Acc. 2633.

Ladle

I. Witman, metalsmith.

Probably Reading, Pennsylvania, early 19th century.

Brass bowl, wrought-iron handle, copper rivets; OL. 20⅝″ (52.4 cm.), ODiam. 5⅝″ (14.3 cm.).

Stamped, along top front of handle: "I. WITMAN" in serrated rectangle reserve.

Henry Kauffman lists a Jonathan Witman working in Reading in the early 19th cnetury.

Kauffman, Henry J. *Early American Copper, Tin and Brass.* New York: Medill McBride Company, 1950. p. 109.

INHP purchase, 1965. Bishop White House, kitchen. Cat 6202. Acc. 1789.

63. Chopper

Maker unknown.

America, c. 1796.

Steel, walnut handle; OH. 6¼″ (15.9 cm.), OW. 7⅞″ (20.0 cm.), OD. 1″ (2.5 cm.).

Engraved on one side of base: "AD," date "1796" on the other.

INHP purchase, 1975. Deshler-Morris House, back kitchen. Cat. 11069. Acc. 3035.

64. Bread toaster

Maker unknown.

America, last quarter of 18th century.

Wrought iron; OH. 7″ (17.9 cm.), OW. 13¼″ (33.7 cm.), OL. 17¼″ (43.8 cm.).

INHP purchase, 1961. Bishop White House, kitchen. Cat. 3055. Acc. 579.

65. Basket

Maker unknown.

America, 19th century.

Hickory splints; OH. 9⅝″ (24.5 cm.), OW. 22⅛″ (56.3 cm.), OD. 14½″ (36.9 cm.).

INHP purchase, 1963. Bishop White House, kitchen. Cat. 5073. Acc. 1169.

66. Wall-light, one of pair

Maker unknown.

England, c. 1705-15.

Silvered cast brass; OH. 14⅞″ (37.7 cm.), OW. 5³⁄₁₆″ (13.3 cm.), OL. (arm) 8⅛″ (21.6 cm.).

Engraved on boss: crest of demi-lion rampant grasping laurel branch.

Gentle, Rupert and Rachel Feild, "The Genesis of English Ormolou," *Connoisseur,* June, 1975, p. 111.

INHP purchase, 1975. Independence Hall, Committee of Assembly Room. Cat. 10946. Acc. 3004.

67. Ballot box

Maker unknown.

Delaware Valley, 18th century.

Walnut, hickory, brass escutcheon, steel key; OH. 7″ (17.8 cm.), OL. 12⁷⁄₁₆″ (31.8 cm.), OW. 6½″ (16.4 cm.).

INHP purchase, 1975. Independence Hall, Assembly Room. Cat. 11078. Acc. 3040.

68. Basin touchmark

Probably Hasselberg group (w. c. 1750-1800), pewterers.

Pewter; OH. 2⅝″ (6.7 cm.), ODiam. 10⅛″ (25.8 cm.).

Stamped, on bottom of basin twice: "LONDON" in serrated arc; once: lovebird touch (circle enclosing two facing birds under a crown. Legend "LO/VE" on either side of birds' heads), X crowned.

Abraham Hasselberg emigrated to Pennsylvania about 1750, settling finally in Philadelphia. He died in 1779. His widow married Adam Kehler (Koehler), another pewterer. John Andrew Brunstrom apparently took over Kehler's business about 1783, working until about 1793. Brunstroms touch has been found impressed with the "LONDON" and X-crowned marks exhibited on this basin.

INHP purchase, 1964. Bishop White House, kitchen. Cat. 4025. Acc. 1399.

69. *Left:* Chamberstick

Maker unknown.

Probably Birmingham, England, c. 1810-40.

Iron; OH. 4¾″ (12.1 cm.), OW. 6³⁄₁₆″ (15.8 cm.), ODiam. 6″ (15.2 cm.).

INHP purchase, 1964. Todd House, kitchen bedchamber. Cat. 3850. Acc. 1366.

Center: Candlestick, one of a pair

Maker unknown.

England, c. 1765-75.

Brass; OH. 10⅝″ (26.9 cm.), ODiam. 4⅞″ (12.4 cm.).

INHP purchase, 1955. Todd House, law office. Cat. 1163. Acc. 116.

Center, right: Candlestick

Maker unknown.

Probably Birmingham, England, late 18th or early 19th century.

Steel shaft, brass collar; OH. 6⅝″ (17 cm.), ODiam. 3⅝″ (9.2 cm.).

Stamped, ejector thumbpiece: "SHAW."

INHP purchase, 1968. Todd House, law office. Cat. 8169. Acc. 2343.

Right: Candlestick, one of a pair

Maker unknown.

England, c. 1730.

Brass, steel spring and ejector; OH. 7¾″ (19.8 cm.), ODiam. 4⁹⁄₁₆″ (11.6 cm.).

INHP purchase, 1968, with funds donated by the General Federation of Women's Clubs. Independence Hall, Supreme Court Chamber. Cat. 7595. Acc. 2206.

70. Nursing bottle

Maker unknown.

England or America, late 18th or early 19th century.

Pewter; OH. 6¾″ (17.2 cm.), ODiam. 3⅜″ (8.5 cm.).

INHP purchase, 1962. Todd House, bedroom. Cat. 2603. Acc. 924.

Funnel

Maker unknown.

Probably England, early 19th century.

Pewter; OH. 4⅝″ (11.7 cm.), ODiam. 3⅝″ (9.2 cm.).

INHP purchase, 1963. Bishop White House, kitchen. Cat. 5157. Acc. 1221.

Strainer

Maker unknown.

Probably England, c. 1800.

Pewter; OH. 2¼″ (5.7 cm.), ODiam. 3″ (7.5 cm.).

INHP purchase, 1963. Bishop White House, kitchen. Cat. 5149. Acc. 1213.

71. Plate

Thomas Byles (c. 1685-1771), pewterer.

Probably Philadelphia, 1738-71.

Pewter; ODiam. 9″ (22.8 cm.).

Stamped twice, underside of plate: touchmark of Thomas Byles, "T.B."

The touchmark is shown in fig. 72.

Thomas Byles was born in Winchester, England, and emigrated to Boston. Byles apparently moved to Newport, and then to Philadelphia with his wife, Elizabeth White.

Laughlin, Ledlie Irwin. *Pewter in America: Its Makers and Their Marks.* Boston: Houghton Mifflin Company, 1940, vol. 2, pp. 41-43, 156-57.

INHP purchase, 1975. City Tavern, bar. Cat. 10654. Acc. 2906.

72. Touchmark of pewter plate, fig. 71.

73. *Lower left:* Inkstand with ink bottle

Watts [given name unknown] (w. c. 1810-60+), pewterer.

London, last third of 19th century.

Pewter; blown glass ink bottle (may be original); inkstand: OH. 1¹⁵⁄₁₆″ (4.9 cm.), OL. 7¾″ (19.7 cm.), OW. 5⅛″ (13.0 cm.); bottle: OH. 1″ (2.5 cm.), OL. 2⅛″ (5.5 cm.), OW. 2¹⁄₁₆″ (5.3 cm.).

Stamped, floor of quill compartment: "V [crown] R," "WATTS EUSTON," conforming to circular shape and enclosed, outside and in, with concentric rings, "R^{D} 256," centered in inner rings.

Watts was in partnership with Harton until 1860, worked alone at Shoe Lane for some time, and then entered a partnership with his brother-in-law on Euston Road, the location indicated by this touch.

Cotterell, Howard Herschel. *Old Pewter: Its Makers and Marks in England, Scotland and Ireland: An Account of the Old Pewterer and His Craft.* London: B.T. Batsford, Ltd., 1929; rpt. Rutland, Vt.: Charles E. Tuttle Company, 1963. p. 227, #2177; p. 331, #4995.

INHP purchase, 1965. Independence Hall, Supreme Court Room. Cat. 4935. Acc. 1606.

Upper left: Inkstand

Maker unknown.

Probably England, mid-18th to mid-19th century.

Pewter, pewter sander; OH. 2⅝ʺ (6.7 cm.), OL. 9⅜ʺ (23.9 cm.), OW. 6⅛ʺ (15.6 cm.).

INHP purchase, 1962, with funds donated by the General Federation of Women's Clubs. Congress Hall, House of Representatives. Cat. 5001. Acc. 718.

Upper right: Inkstand

Maker unknown.

Probably England, mid-18th to mid-19th century.

Pewter, ceramic ink pot (not original to this piece); OH. 1¹⁵⁄₁₆ʺ (4.9 cm.), OL. 6½ʺ (16.5 cm.), OW. 4⅝ʺ (11.8 cm.).

Inscribed, bottom: "Butterworth" (in script).

INHP purchase, 1971, with funds donated by Eastern National Park and Monument Association. Congress Hall, Senate Chamber. Cat 8581. Acc. 2583.

Center right: Inkstand

Maker unknown.

Probably England, late 18th to mid-19th century.

Pewter, pewter sander; OH. 1¹¹⁄₁₆ʺ (4.3 cm.), OL. 6⁵⁄₁₆ʺ (16.0 cm.), OW. 4¹¹⁄₁₆ʺ (11.8 cm.).

Stamped, bottom of quill compartment, four times: lion passant gardant, in scrolled rectangular reserve.

INHP purchase, 1967. Congress Hall, secretary's office. Cat. 7688. Acc. 2215.

Lower right: Inkstand

Maker unknown.

Probably England, mid-18th to mid-19th century.

Pewter, pewter sander and blown glass ink bottle (probably not original); OH. 1¹⁵⁄₁₆ʺ (4.9 cm.), OL. 6⅞ʺ (17.4 cm.), OW. 4⅞ʺ (12.3 cm.).

INHP purchase, 1967. Congress Hall, Senate Chamber. Cat. 7306. Acc. 2138.

Center: Inkstand

Maker unknown.

Probably England, late 18th century.

Pewter; OH. 3⁵⁄₁₆ʺ (8.5 cm.), ODiam. 3¹⁵⁄₁₆ʺ (9.9 cm.).

Inscribed, underside of base: *"Edouard Giquere"* (in script).

Gift of Mrs. Z. L. Gibson. Independence Hall, Governor's Council Chamber. Cat. 8810. Acc. 2250.

74. Chocolate pot

Maker unknown.

Probably America, 1780-1840.

Tin, hardwood handle; OH. 10⅞ʺ (27.6 cm.),

OW. 9¹³⁄₁₆ʺ (25.0 cm.), ODiam. 5⁷⁄₁₆ʺ (13.9 cm.).

INHP purchase, 1965. Bishop White House, kitchen. Cat. 4917. Acc. 1597.

75. Teapot

Samuel Ellis (c. 1700-73, w. 1721-65), pewterer.

London, c. 1740-60.

Pewter, fruitwood handle (probably replaced); OH. 6¼ʺ (15.8 cm.), OW. 7⅝ʺ (19.4 cm.).

Stamped, bottom of pot: "S ELL[IS]" in rectangle reserve.

INHP purchase, 1976. The Thaddeus Kosciuszko National Memorial, bedchamber. Cat. 11435. Acc. 3165.

76. *Left to right:* Candlestick, one of a pair

Maker unknown.

England, c. 1750.

Brass; OH. 9ʺ (22.9 cm.), ODiam. 5⅜ʺ (13.7 cm.).

INHP purchase, 1972. Independence Hall, Committee of Assembly Room. Cat. 8632. Acc. 2620.

Candlestick, one of a pair

Maker unknown.

England, c. 1750.

Brass; OH. 8¾ʺ (22.3 cm.), ODiam. 5⅛ʺ (12.9 cm.).

Bobeche is cast separately and is removable.

INHP purchase, 1960. Todd House, parlor. Cat. 1459. Acc. 436.

Candlestick, one of a pair

Maker unknown.

England, c. 1750.

Brass; OH. 7½ʺ (19.1 cm.), ODiam. 4¾ʺ (12.1 cm.).

Gift of Mr. and Mrs. John W. Batdorf, 1975. West Wing, Independence Hall, Visitor Reception Room. Cat. 11006. Acc. 3032.

Candlestick, one of a pair

Maker unknown.

England, c. 1750-60.

Brass; OH. 9⅝ʺ (24.5 cm.), ODiam. 5⁵⁄₁₆ʺ (13.5 cm.).

Bobeche is cast separately and is removable.

INHP purchase, 1971. Independence Hall, Governor's Council Chamber. Cat. 8583. Acc. 2587.

Candlestick, one of a pair

Maker unknown.

England, c. 1750.

Brass; OH. 8¼ʺ (21.0 cm.), ODiam. 4⅞ʺ (12.4 cm.).

INHP purchase, 1965. Todd House, parlor. Cat. 5776. Acc. 1664.

Candlestick, one of a pair

Maker unknown.

England, c. 1740.

Brass; OH. 7ʺ (17.9 cm.), ODiam. 4⅝ʺ (11.7 cm.).

INHP purchase, 1970. Todd House, dining parlor. Cat. 4936. Acc. 1605.

77. Sugar tongs

Joseph Richardson, Jr. (1752-1831).

Philadelphia, c. 1790.

Silver; OL. 6ʺ (15.2 cm.), OW. ¾ʺ (2 cm.), OD. 1½ʺ (3.9 cm.).

Stamped, inside apex of bow: "JR" in conforming rectangular reserve; engraved, outside bow: "DSG" in lozenge.

Fales, Martha Gandy. *Joseph Richardson and Family, Philadelphia Silversmiths.* Middletown, Conn.: Wesleyan University Press, 1974. pp. 153-197. Marks: Fig. 163c, p. 183.

INHP purchase, 1961. Todd House, parlor. Cat. 3083. Acc. 486.

78. Cann

Philip Syng, Jr. (1703-89).

Philadelphia, 1749-61.

Silver; OH. 4½ʺ (11.4 cm.), ODiam. 3³⁄₁₆ʺ (8.0 cm.).

Stamped, underside, twice: "P S" in rectangular reserve with broken corners; stamped, once: leaf; inscribed: "10-oz"; engraved, opposite handle: Lardner-Branson arms, in oval cartouche with rococo surround.

Lardner-Branson (Branston) arms indicate ownership by Lynford Lardner and his first wife, Elizabeth Branson (married October 27, 1749).

Ensko, Stephen G.C., *American Silversmiths and Their Marks, III.* New York: n.p., 1948. pp. 127-8, 226.

Lardner, Lynford. *Account Book, 1748-1751,* MS., Philadelphia: Rosenbach Museum and Library. (see entry for November 4, 1749.)

Cann acquired through Penn-Lardner descendants. INHP purchase, 1973, with funds donated by the National Society, Daughters of the American Revolution. Independence Hall, Governor's Council Chamber. Cat. 9965. Acc. 2697.

79. Stocking stretcher

Maker unknown.

America, late 18th to mid-19th century.

Oak; OL. 16⅞ʺ (42.8 cm.), OW. 5⅛ʺ (13.0 cm.), OD. ⅝ʺ (1.5 cm.).

INHP purchase, 1960. Bishop White House, kitchen. Cat. 5197. Acc. 444.

80. Stick barometer in case

John Sadler (1720-89), printer; engraver unknown; barometer-maker unknown.

Liverpool, England, c. 1748-66.

Case: mahogany, brass urn and latch, glass panel; barometer: label printed on paper, mercury-filled glass tube, brass wire sliding indicator; OH. 37¼″ (94.6 cm.), OW. 6 3/16″ (15.8 cm.), OD. 2″ (5.1 cm.).

Label, engraved on laid paper, inside case, shows various readings and attendant weather conditions and concludes: ". . . Printed and Sold by John Sadler. Liverpool" inside a banner at bottom of cartouche. All enclosed in symmetrical cartouche, ornamented with acanthus leaves and bell flowers. Two globes with summer and winter axial tilts appear under the respective columns of weather indications.

John Sadler began his career in printing in 1740. By 1748 he had established a printing business in Liverpool. For about two years, beginning in 1757, he printed the *Liverpool Chronicle and Marine Gazette.* Sadler dropped his publishing business in 1766, apparently to devote full time to transfer printing on pottery. Sadler retired from business in 1770.

Price, E. Stanley. *John Sadler: A Liverpool Pottery Printer.* West Kirby, England: Published by the author and printed by Gould's, 1948, pp. 15-33.

INHP purchase, 1972, with funds donated by the National Society, Daughters of the American Revolution. Bishop White House, study. Cat. 8630. Acc. 2618.

81. Astronomical transit instrument

John Bird (1709-76), scientific instrument maker.

London, c. 1745-68.

Carbon steel, brass fittings, glass lenses and level tube; brass and mahogany stand (modern reproduction); OL. telescope 33 1/16″ (84.1 cm.), OL. balance arm 25″ (63.6 cm.), ODiam. objective lens 1 15/16″ (4.9 cm.), ODiam. eyepiece 13/16″ (2.9 cm.), OL. striding level 12 13/16″ (32.6 cm.).

Engraved, eyepiece: "John Bird" (in script).

This instrument was probably one of those supplied by John Penn for use in surveying the boundary line between Pennsylvania and Maryland. It may also have been the one used in 1769 to observe the transit of Venus from the State House yard (Independence Square). John Ewing's *Account of the Observations on the Transit of Venus over the Sun, on the 3rd of June, 1769, by the Committee appointed to observe at Philadelphia* described the instruments which Ewing and his cohorts used. After the transit of Venus had been recorded, the instrument was apparently mounted in the tower of the State House in a position to take the meridian passage of the sun at noon. It was used with Isaiah Lukens's astronomical timepiece to obtain Philadelphia's official time.

John Bird was born in Bishop Auckland, England, in 1709 and worked as a weaver. At some point before 1740 he worked at dividing and engraving clock plates. Bird moved to London about 1740 to work for the well-known scientific instrument maker Jonathan Sisson. Bird soon came under George Graham's patronage, and Graham helped him establish his own workshop in 1745. Bird was the instrument maker for the Greenwich observatory.

American Philosophical Society. *Transactions.* Vol. 1, Jan. 1, 1769-Jan. 1, 1771. Philadelphia: William and Thomas Bradford, 1771; rpt. New York: Kraus Reprint Corporation, 1966.
Daumas, Maurice. *Scientific Instruments of the Seventeenth and Eighteenth Centuries.* Mary Hollbrook trans. & ed. New York & Washington: Praeger Publishers, 1972, pp. 92, 173-74, 231-33.
Thomas Penn Letters, Jan. 9, 1761-Dec. 20, 1770, microfilm roll #9 XR176. The Historical Society of Pennsylvania.
Woolf, Harry. *The Transits of Venus.* Princeton: Princeton University Press, 1959.

This instrument was discovered in 1912 beneath the flooring of a platform in Independence Hall tower. Independence Hall, Governor's Council Chamber. Cat. 11891. Acc. 1.

82. Tall-post bed

Maker unknown.

America or England, c. 1770.

Mahogany, white oak secondary (tester not original); wool and linen coverlet: American, early 19th century; gauze mosquito netting: 20th century reproduction; OH. 8′ 9½″ (2 m. 37.5 cm.), OL. 6′ 5¾″ (1 m. 97.5 cm.), OD. 54¾″ (1 m. 39.1 cm.).

Inscribed, each slot along side rails, Roman numeral: "I-XII," slats numbered accordingly: "I-XII."

INHP purchase, 1961. Bishop White House, bedroom. Cat. 1509. Acc. 559.

83. Dissected Picture with box

John Wallis (active c. 1775-95), publisher.

London, 1788.

Puzzle: paper on unidentified wood; box: mahogany, engraved label; puzzle (assembled): OH. 16⅝″ (42.2 cm.), OW. 23⅜″ (59.3 cm.); box: OH. 2½″ (6.3 cm.), OL. 7 11/16″ (19.5 cm.), OW. 9¼″ (23.4 cm.).

Engraved label, top of box: "WALLIS's/ROYAL/Chronological Tables/of/ENGLISH HISTORY/on a Plan similar to that of the/Dissected Maps./*Published March 31st 1788* by/JOHN WALLIS. No 13 Warwick Squ/LONDON." Enclosed in an oval cartouche supported by recumbent lion (*left*) and unicorn (*right*) surmounted with a royal crown. Bearing the motto "DIEU ET MON DROIT."

John Wallis was in partnership with a Mr. Stonehouse in the publishing and bookselling business at Yorick's Head, Ludgate Street, London, in 1775. Wallis apparently struck out on his own, for his name only is listed on the label of a "dissected map" in the collection of the Henry Francis du Pont Winterthur Museum. Wallis seems to have specialized in maps and learning games for children.

Plomer, H.R., G.H. Bushnell, E.R. McC. Dix. *A Dictionary of the Printers and Booksellers Who Were at Work in England, Scotland and Ireland from 1726-1775.* Oxford: The Oxford University Press, 1932; rpt., Truexpress for The Bibliographical Society, 1968, p. 254.

INHP purchase, 1961. Bishop White House, parlor. Cat. 4955. Acc. 531.

84. Sugar bowl

Possibly William Will (1742-98), pewterer.

Philadelphia, 1785-98.

Pewter; OH. 2⅞″ (7.3 cm.), ODiam 4½″ (11.5 cm.).

Inscribed underside of base: "MK."

Parks Boyd (c. 1771-1819) also produced similar, unmarked sugar bowls, and his metal alloy is very close to that used by Will.

William Will was a member of a celebrated family of pewterers. Having served his apprenticeship in New York, probably under his brother Henry, he arrived in Philadelphia sometime before his 1764 marriage to Barbara Colp in that city. Will's 1789 declaration of bankruptcy may account for his listing in the 1791 Directory as an innkeeper. Upon his death in 1798, his wife, Ann Clampher Will, advertised her intent to carry on the pewtering business [*Federal Gazette,* March 27, 1798]. Will is perhaps best known for his inventive use of interchangeable parts.

Laughlin, Ledlie Irwin. *Pewter in America: Its Makers and Their Marks.* Boston: Houghton Mifflin Company, 1940. Vol. 2, pp. 51-55.
Montgomery, Charles F. *A History of American Pewter.* New York: Praeger Publishers, 1973.

Descended in Nuzum family (residents of southeast Pennsylvania from c. 1752 to 1802) to donor. Gift of Mrs. H. G. Halverson in honor of her mother, Mrs. Edna Nuzum Kimes, through the Sara De Soto Chapter, National Society, Daughters of the American Revolution. Independence Hall, Governor's Council Chamber. Cat. 9785. Acc. 2693.

85. Candle box

Maker unknown.

Probably England, c. 1767.

Brass; OH. 5⅞″ (15.0 cm.), OL. 11¼″ (28.5 cm.), OW. 4½″ (11.5 cm.).

Engraved, lid, surrounded by geometric punched decoration: "C. KELLY/1767."

INHP purchase, 1975. Graff House, parlor. Cat. 10555. Acc. 2877.

86. Andirons, pair

Maker unknown.

Probably Pennsylvania, c. 1720-30.

Brass and iron; OH. 23″ (58.4 cm.), OW. 13⅞″ (35.3 cm.), OL. 21¼″ (54.0 cm.).

INHP purchase, 1975, with funds donated by the National Society, Daughters of the American Revolution. Independence Hall, Committee of the Assembly Room. Cat. 10605-06. Acc. 2900.

87. *Left to right:* Candlestick

Maker unknown.

England, c. 1720.

Brass; OH. 6⅞″ (17.6 cm.), ODiam. 4⅛″ (10.4 cm.).

INHP purchase, 1960, with funds donated by the General Federation of Women's Clubs. Independence Hall, Assembly Room. Cat. 1450. Acc. 429.

Candlestick

Maker unknown.

England, c. 1720-40.

Brass; OH. 7$\frac{1}{16}$″ (18 cm.), ODiam. 3⅞″ (9.8 cm.).

INHP purchase, 1960. Independence Hall, second-floor hallway. Cat. 1456. Acc. 436.

Candlesticks, pair

Maker unknown.

Possibly French, c. 1700-30.

Brass; OH. 7⅛″ (18.1 cm.), ODiam. 4$\frac{3}{16}$″ (10.6 cm.).

INHP purchase, 1963, with funds donated by the General Federation of Women's Clubs. Independence Hall, Long Gallery. Cat. 1426-27. Acc. 340.

88. Andirons, pair

Maker unknown.

Probably Pennsylvania, second quarter, 18th century.

Brass and iron; OH. 26″ (66.0 cm.), OW. 17½″ (44.5 cm.), OL. 21″ (53.3 cm.).

INHP purchase, 1970, with funds donated by the General Federation of Women's Clubs. Independence Hall, Assembly Room. Cat. 8534-35. Acc. 2544.

89. Andirons, pair

Maker unknown.

Probably Philadelphia, c. 1785-1800.

Brass and iron; OH. 26⅛″ (66.2 cm.), OW. 14⅛″ (35.8 cm.), OL. 20$\frac{13}{16}$″ (52.6 cm.).

INHP purchase, 1960. Bishop White House, parlor. Cat. 1436-37. Acc. 390.

90. *Left to right:* Tea kettle

Benjamin Harbeson (1728-1809), coppersmith.

Philadelphia, c. 1775-1809.

Copper, brass finial; OH. 7″ (17.8 cm.), OW. 12¼″ (31.2 cm.), ODiam. 8″ (20.8 cm.).

Stamped, top side of handle: "B. HARBESON" in serrated arc reserve.

Harbeson advertised in Philadelphia as a tinplate worker in 1755. He also sold pewter, copper, and brassware imported from England.

INHP purchase, 1960. Todd House, parlor. Cat. 1463. Acc. 433.

Tea kettle

John Town (active 1801-1806), coppersmith.

Philadelphia, 1801-1806.

Copper, brass finial; OH. 7½″ (19.0 cm.), OW. 12⅞″ (32.6 cm.), ODiam. 9½″ (24.2 cm.).

Stamped, top side of handle: "JOHN TOWN" in rectangle reserve.

John Town, coppersmith, is listed in city *Directories* from 1801 until 1806.

INHP purchase, 1966. Bishop White House, kitchen. Cat. 7301. Acc. 2132.

Tea kettle

Maker unknown.

Possibly Netherlands or England, mid-18th century.

Brass, copper rivets; OH. 7¾″ (19.5 cm.), OW. 12$\frac{7}{16}$″ (31.6 cm.), ODiam. 8¾″ (22.4 cm.).

INHP purchase, 1966. Todd House, kitchen. Cat. 6595. Acc. 1921.

Tea kettle

S. Gorgas, coppersmith.

Probably Pennsylvania, early 19th century.

Copper, brass finial; OH. 9½″ (24.1 cm.), OW. 16″ (40.6 cm.), ODiam. 11$\frac{11}{16}$″ (29.8 cm.).

Stamped, top side of handle: "S. GORGAS" in serrated rectangle reserve, and "OI."

INHP purchase, 1961. Bishop White House, bedroom. Cat. 1471. Acc. 464.

91. Tea kettle, touchmark

Benjamin Harbeson (1728-1809), coppersmith.

Philadelphia, c. 1755-75.

Copper, brass finial; OH. 6⅝″ (16.7 cm.), OW. 13⅜″ (34.0 cm.), ODiam. 8$\frac{15}{16}$″ (22.3 cm.).

Stamped on handle: "B. HARBESON" in serrated arc reserve; stamped, above maker's mark: Royal Crown.

INHP purchase, 1977. Independence Hall, Governor's Council Chamber. Cat. 11678. Acc. 3253.

92. Writing box

N. Middleton, merchant.

London, late 18th century, before 1801.

Cherry, pine secondary, engraved laid paper label, brass bail handle; glass ink bottle, inset brass crown moulding; box: OH. 2$\frac{7}{16}$″ (6.2 cm.), OL. 15$\frac{5}{16}$″ (38.8 cm.), OW. 10″ (25.4 cm.); bottle: OH. 1¾″ (4.4 cm.), OL. 2¼″ (5.7 cm.), OW. 2¼″ (5.8 cm.).

Laid paper label, inside drawer bottom: "Bought of N. Middleton/original Black Lead Pencil &/POCKET BOOK MAKER *to the* KING *and* PRINCE *of* WALES,/at Nº 162 the corner of Strand Lane opposite the New Church in Ye Strand./N.B. Writing & Dressing Desks & Boxes of every Kind." With cartouche at left side consisting of the Arms of George III and the Prince of Wales. Surmounting the whole, Middleton added in engraved script, "ALL Kinds of Stationary;" at the bottom of the cartouche, "Portable & Counting House Letter Copying Machines."

INHP purchase, 1966. Congress Hall, Joint Committee Room. Cat. 7190. Acc. 2086.

93. Candle snuffer and tray

Maker unknown.

Sheffield, England, c. 1800-10.

Sheffield plate (silver and copper); snuffer: OH. 1$\frac{11}{16}$″ (4.3 cm.), OW. 2$\frac{9}{16}$″ (6.4 cm.), OD. 6$\frac{15}{16}$″ (17.7 cm.); tray: OH. 2⅛″ (5.4 cm.), OW. 4½″ (11.5 cm.), OD. 7$\frac{5}{16}$″ (18.5 cm.).

INHP purchase, 1973, with funds donated by Eastern National Park and Monument Association. Deshler-Morris House, dining room. Cat. 10150-51. Acc. 2727.

94. Sewing box, removable tray, and implements

Unidentified London Firm.

London, c. 1820-40.

Tin, japanned, painted and gilded, brass bail handle; implements of ivory, tortoise shell, and bristle; OH. 5⅞″ (15.0 cm.), OL. 11$\frac{13}{16}$″ (30.0 cm.), OW. 8¾″ (22.8 cm.).

Embossed on shield-shaped tin, soldered, underside of lid: "J. T. & C./LONDON."

INHP purchase, 1962. Bishop White House, parlor. Cat. 5020. Acc. 912.

95. Hot water urn

Maker unknown.

Sheffield, England, c. 1790-1800.

Sheffield plate (silver and copper); OH. 13⅛″ (33.3 cm.), OW. 8″ (20.3 cm.), OD. 7⅛″ (18.0 cm.).

INHP purchase, 1975. Deshler-Morris House, tea room. Cat. 11075. Acc. 3035.

96. Gate-leg table

Maker unknown.

Probably Pennsylvania, 1720-40.

Walnut, oak, poplar and pine secondary; OH. 29⅛″ (74 cm.), OW. 47¾″ (1 m. 21.2 cm.), OL. 56¹¹⁄₁₆″ (1 m. 44 cm.).

INHP purchase, 1961. Bishop White House, kitchen. Cat. 1500. Acc. 536.

97. Tall-case clock

Works: Joseph Wills (1700-59), clockmaker.

Works: Philadelphia, c. 1740; Case: Chester County, Pennsylvania.

Case: tiger-stripe maple; face and works: brass with 8-day drive; OH. 90″ (228.7 cm.), OW. 20¼″ (51.5 cm.), OD. 11″ (28 cm.).

Inscribed on face of clock: "Joseph Wills/Philadelphia." Inscribed on paper label pasted to inside of door: "Extract of the Will of Mathew Hall/dated 'marple' Chester Co. Pennsylvania/9 mo. 8th 1766. 'I do give and bequeath unto/my Son Mahlon Hall my eight day/Clock'—This clock has descended/from Mathew Hall/to Mahlon Hall/to John Hall/to James Hall/to William Ellis Hall/to Mahlon Hall Dickinson/to Mahlon Hall Dickinson, 2nd./April 9th 1900."

Gift of William Dickinson, 1961. Graff House, Parlor. Cat. 1506. Acc. 553.

98. Dressing table

Maker unknown.

Possibly New Jersey, c. 1750.

Walnut, pine secondary; OH. 28¾″ (73 cm.), OW. 33⅜″ (84.7 cm.), OD. 20⁷⁄₁₆″ (51.9 cm).

INHP purchase, 1971. Todd House, bedroom. Cat. 8622. Acc. 2611.

99. Pole screen

Maker unknown.

Pennsylvania, c. 1765. Needlework, possibly English.

Pole: mahogany; screen: wool; pole: OH. 55″ (1 m. 39.7 cm.), OW. 20½″ (52.1 cm.); screen: OH. 24″ (61 cm.), OW. 20½″ (52.1 cm.).

INHP purchase, 1969. Bishop White House,

parlor. Cat. 8345. Acc. 2424.

100. Gate-leg table

Maker unknown.

Chester County, Pennsylvania, c. 1740.

Walnut, oak and poplar secondary; OH. 29½″ (75 cm.), OL. 57″ (1 m. 44.8 cm.), OW. 47¾″ (1 m. 21.3 cm.).

INHP purchase, 1961. Independence Hall, Committee of the Assembly Room. Cat. 1469. Acc. 461.

101. Candlestand

Maker unknown.

Philadelphia, c. 1765.

Mahogany, wrought-iron underbrace; OH. 28″ (71.1 cm.), ODiam. 19¼″ (48.8 cm.).

INHP purchase, 1972, with funds donated by the National Society, Daughters of the American Revolution. Independence Hall, Governor's Council Chamber. Cat. 8586. Acc. 2588.

102. Windsor armchair

Maker unknown.

Delaware Valley, c. 1750.

Hickory, pine, maple, and oak; OH. 42¾″ (1 m. 8.6 cm.), OW. 28¼″ (71.8 cm.), HS. 19⅝″ (49.8 cm.), DS. 16¾″ (42.6 cm.).

INHP purchase, 1962 with funds donated by the General Federation of Women's Clubs. Independence Hall, Assembly Room. Cat. 2595. Acc. 866.

103. Desk

Maker unknown.

Philadelphia, c. 1755.

Mahogany, pine and poplar secondary, replaced hardware; OH. 41¾″ (1 m. 6 cm.), OW. 41½″ (1 m. 5.4 cm.), OD. 22″ (55.9 cm.).

Believed to have been owned by Benjamin Franklin.

Labaree, Leonard, ed. *The Papers of Benjamin Franklin,* New Haven: Yale University Press, 1963, Vol. 7, p. 206.

INHP purchase, 1963, partially with funds donated by Eastern National Park and Monument Association. Franklin Court. Cat. 2587. Acc. 878.

104. Upholstered armchair

Maker unknown.

England, c. 1765-70.

Mahogany, beech secondary; OH. 35″ (89 cm.), OW. 26″ (66 cm.), OD. 21″ (53.4 cm.).

Purchased by Benjamin Franklin in London.

INHP purchase, 1974, from a Hewson descendant. Franklin Court. Cat. 10278. Acc. 2775.

105. Tall-case clock

Works: David Rittenhouse (1732-96), clockmaker; Case: maker unknown.

Norristown, Pa., c. 1760.

Case: walnut; works: brass face, gilt spandrels, silver calendar wheel and dial; case: OH. 7′ 1″ (2 m. 5.9 cm.), OW. 24″ (61 cm.), OD. 11½″ (29.2 cm.).

Inscribed on boss above dial: "David Rittenhouse/Norriton."

David Rittenhouse was a central figure in the scientific and intellectual life of mid-century Philadelphia.

Gift of Mr. Oliver W. Robbins, descendant of original owner, Hugh Roberts, II, 1974. City Tavern, Subscription Room. Cat. 10231. Acc. 2768.

106. Tall-case clock

Works: Frederick Maus (active 1785-93), clockmaker; case: maker unknown.

Philadelphia, c. 1785.

Case: persimmon; clock face: enameled; case: OH. 8′ ½″ (2m. 47.9 cm.), OW. 22½″ (57.2 cm.), OD. 12½″ (31.8 cm.).

Painted on clock face: "Frederick Maus/Philadᵃ"

Detroit Institute of Art. *Bulletin* 23 (1944), p. 59.

Gift on behalf of Miss Louise Cany Herring, descendant of original owners John Thomas and wife Ann North Harvey, 1972. Second Bank, second floor, north hall. Cat. 9784. Acc. 2690.

107. Slat-back side chair, one of a set of five

Maker unknown.

Delaware Valley, c. 1750-1800.

Maple, hickory; OH. 43¼″ (1 m. 9.9 cm.), HS. 16½″ (41.9 cm.), WS. 13⅞″ (35.3 cm.).

Gift of Delaware County Chapter, Daughters of the American Revolution, 1972. Independence Hall, Committee of the Assembly Room. Cat. 8736. Acc. 2652.

Armchair, one of a pair

Maker unknown.

Delaware Valley, c. 1750-1800.

Hickory and maple; OH. 32″ (81.2 cm.), OW. 21½″ (54.6 cm.), OD. 16⅛″ (41 cm.).

Gift of Delaware County Chapter, Daughters of the American Revolution, 1972. Independence Hall, Committee of the Assembly Room. Cat. 8734. Acc. 2652.

108. Side chair

Maker unknown.

Philadelphia, c. 1770.

Mahogany, poplar secondary; OH. 37½″ (92.5 cm.), OW. 24¼″ (61.5 cm.), OD. 18″ (45.8 cm.).

Family provenance gives original owner as Captain Samuel Morris, Sr., 1711-82. Gift of Mrs. Thomas D. Thacher, 1976. West Wing, Independence Hall, Visitor Reception Room. Cat. 11126. Acc. 3056.

109. Looking glass

Maker unknown.

Philadelphia, c. 1765.

American pine, white paint and gilt highlights; OH. 51″ (1 m. 29.5 cm.), OW. 30″ (76.2 cm.).

Said to have belonged to a Morris family of New Jersey. Gift of Mr. Sanford D. Beecher, 1977. Bishop White House, parlor. Cat. 11613. Acc. 3232.

110. High chest of drawers

Attributed to Ziba Ferris, Sr. (1743-94), cabinetmaker.

Wilmington, Delaware, c. 1770.

Cherry, poplar and pine secondary; OH. 6′7″ (2 m. .7 cm.), OW. 43½″ (1 m. 10.5 cm.), OD. 22½″ (57.1 cm.).

Ziba Ferris, Sr., worked in Wilmington from 1762 to 1794.

Gift of Miss Margaret Conklin, 1975, who had inherited the chest of drawers from Ferris, her ancestor. Graff House, parlor. Cat. 10774. Acc. 2941.

111. Tea table

Maker unknown.

Philadelphia, c. 1765.

Mahogany; OH. 29¼″ (74.3 cm.), ODiam. 34½″ (87 cm.).

INHP purchase, 1975. Deshler-Morris House, parlor. Cat. 11076. Acc. 3041.

112. Looking glass

John Elliott, Sr. (1713-91), importer and cabinetmaker.

Philadelphia, c. 1763.

Mahogany frame; OH. 41″ (1 m. 4.2 cm.), OW. 21½″ (54.6 cm.).

Printed label: "John Elliott/At his Looking-glass Store, the Sign of the/Bell and Looking-Glass in Walnut-Street/in Philadelphia, imports and sells all Sorts of/English Looking-glasses at the lowest Rates./He also new Quick silvers and frames old/Glasses and supplies People with new Glass/to their old Frames./ /Johannes Elliott/ Wohnhafft zu Philadelphia in der Wallnuss/strasse, wo das Schild und Belle und Spie/gel aushangt,/etc."

INHP purchase, 1967. Bishop White House, bedroom. Cat. 4221. Acc. 1479.

113. Pier glass

Maker unknown, possibly John Elliott, Sr.

Philadelphia, c. 1770-80.

Mahogany, American pine secondary; OH. 58″ (1 m. 47.3 cm.), OW. 27½″ (69.8 cm.).

INHP purchase, 1978. City Tavern, Long Room. Cat. 11682. Acc. 3263

114. Side chairs, pair

Maker unknown.

Philadelphia, c. 1745.

Walnut, pine secondary; *left:* OH. 39⅞″ (1 m. 1 cm.); *right:* OH. 39¾″ (1 m. 1 cm.); *left* or *right:* OW. 21½″ (54.6 cm.), OD. $16\frac{7}{16}$″ (41.7 cm.).

INHP purchase, 1969, with funds donated by the National Society, Daughters of the American Revolution. Independence Hall, Governor's Council Chamber. *Left:* cat. 8368; *right:* Acc. 2450.

115. Document cabinet

Maker unknown.

Lancaster, Pennsylvania, c. 1770.

Walnut, poplar and pine secondary; OH. 42⅜″ (1 m. 7.6 cm.), OW. 29⅝″ (75.3 cm.), OD. $16\frac{9}{16}$″ (42 cm.).

INHP purchase, 1976, with funds donated by the National Society, Daughters of the American Revolution. From the estate of Elizabeth Steinman of Lancaster, Pennsylvania. Independence Hall, Governor's Council Chamber. Cat. 11384. Acc. 3132.

116. Breakfast table

Jonathan Gostelowe (1744-95), cabinetmaker.

Philadelphia, c. 1789.

Mahogany, oak and poplar secondary, replaced pull; OH. 28⅝″ (72.7 cm.), OW. 43⅜″ (1 m. 10.2 cm.), OD. 29⅝″ (75.3 cm.).

Fragment of printed label glued inside drawer on bottom: ". . ./B[eg]s [illegible]/[illegible]/occupation [illegible]/favours with t [illegible]/ shall be used b[y] [illegible]/him."

Philadelphia: Three Centuries of American Art. Philadelphia: Philadelphia Museum of Art, 1976, p. 152.

INHP purchase, 1961. Bishop White House, parlor. Cat. 1499. Acc. 534.

117. Upholstered armchair

Attributed to Thomas Affleck (1740-95), cabinetmaker.

Philadelphia, c. 1790.

Mahogany, pine and poplar secondary; OH. $51\frac{3}{16}$″ (1 m. 30 cm.), OW. 31½″ (80 cm.), OD. 36¼″ (92.1 cm.), DS. 26⅛″ (66.3 cm.).

Gift to the City of Philadelphia before 1873. Old City Hall, courtroom. Cat. 11832. Acc. 1.

118. Upholstered armchair

Thomas Affleck (1740-95), cabinetmaker.

Philadelphia, 1790-93.

Mahogany, red oak secondary; OH. 3′ (91.4 cm.), OW. 2′ (61 cm.), OD. 1′10″ (55.9 cm.).

This chair is one of a large surviving group that was originally made by Thomas Affleck for Congress Hall.

Given to City of Philadelphia in April, 1873, by Charles Crawford Dunn, Germantown, Philadelphia, descended from his father, James L. Dunn, Reading. Congress Hall, Senate Chamber. Cat. 3041. Acc. 1.

119. Low-post bed

Maker unknown.

Pennsylvania, late 18th- or early 19th century.

Poplar with red paint; quilt: American, early 19th century, glazed wood; OH. 34¼″ (87 cm.), OW. 49″ (124.5 cm.), OL. 6′2¼″ (1 m. 87.7 cm.).

INHP purchase, 1975. Thaddeus Kosciuszko National Memorial, bedchamber. Cat. 10784. Acc. 2937.

120. High-back Windsor armchair

Thomas Gilpin (1700-66), chairmaker.

Philadelphia, c. 1750.

Hickory, maple and poplar, replaced undercarriage; OH. $46\frac{7}{16}$″ (1 m. 12 cm.), OW. $25\frac{3}{16}$″ (64 cm.), OD. 23⅝″ (60 cm.). WS. 24″ (61 cm.), DS. $16\frac{9}{16}$″ (42 cm.).

Branded, underside of seat: "F. GILPIN."

Thomas Gilpin moved from Chester County to Philadelphia in 1727; he practiced his chairmaking skills in both locations. In 1759 he made a set of Windsor chairs for Pennsylvania Hospital.

INHP purchase, 1958, with funds donated by the General Federation of Women's Clubs. Independence Hall, Supreme Court Chamber. Cat. 1080. Acc. 98.

121. Gilpin brand from high-back Windsor armchair by Thomas Gilpin (not illustrated). Cat. 7070. Acc. 2070.

122. Low-back Windsor settee

Maker unknown.

Pennsylvania, c. 1770.

Walnut, pine and maple; OH. 30″ (76.2 cm.),

OW. 6′7″ (1 m. 99.8 cm.), OD. 22½″ (57.2 cm.).

INHP purchase, 1972. Independence Hall, second floor hall. Cat. 8354. Acc. 2440.

123. Sack-back Windsor armchair

Francis Trumble (c. 1716-98), cabinetmaker and chairmaker.

Philadelphia, c. 1775.

Hickory, oak, maple, walnut and poplar; OH. 37½″ (92.5 cm.), OW. 23 1/16″ (58.6 cm.), DS. 16⅜″ (41.7 cm.).

Branded, underside of seat: "F. TRUMBLE."

Goyne, Nancy A. "Francis Trumble of Philadelphia." *Winterthur Portfolio* I (1964), pp. 221-41.

INHP purchase, 1955, with funds donated by the General Federation of Women's Clubs. Independence Hall, Assembly Room. Cat. 1087. Acc. 98.

124. Brand from sack-back Windsor armchair, fig. 123.

125. Windsor settee, one of pair

John Letchworth (1759-1843), chairmaker.

Philadelphia, c. 1790.

Hickory, mahogany, poplar and maple; OH. 36⅜″ (92.5 cm.), OW. 43⅞″ (1 m. 11.5 cm.), OD. 17″ (43.2 cm.).

Branded on underside of seat: "LETCHWORTH."

John Letchworth began chairmaking in the mid-1770s, working in several different locations. In about 1805 he gave up chairmaking to pursue his calling as an itinerant Quaker minister.

Philadelphia: Three Centuries of American Art. Philadelphia: Philadelphia Museum of Art, 1976, p. 156.

INHP purchase, 1964. Bishop White House, front hall. Cat. 3596. Acc. 1323.

126. Bow-back Windsor armchairs, pair

John Brientnall Ackley (1763-1827), chairmaker.

Philadelphia, c. 1800.

Hickory, maple, mahogany; *left:* OH. 38½″ (97.8 cm.), WS. 19 9/16″ (49.6 cm.), DS. 16⅞″ (42.8 cm.); *right:* OH. 38¾″ (98.4 cm.), WS. 19⅝″ (49.7 cm.), DS. 17″ (43.2 cm.).

Branded on underside of seat: *left:* "[I •] B [•] ACKLEY"; *right:* "I•B•ACKLEY."

John Ackley was probably trained by his father Thomas, a turner and chairmaker. He leased a shop on Front Street from the Monthly Meeting of Friends of Philadelphia, as did a number of other Windsor chairmakers, and supplied firewood and chairs to the Meeting. By the early 19th century he had modernized his brand to read "J.B. ACKLEY."

Stockwell, David. "Windsors in Independence Hall." *Antiques,* September, 1952, pp. 214-5.

INHP purchase, 1955. Todd House, law office. *Left:* cat. 1102; *right:* 1103. Acc. 98.

127. Bow-back Windsor side chairs, from a set of seven

Maker unknown.

Philadelphia, c. 1795.

Hickory, poplar and maple; *left:* OH. 37¼″ (94.6 cm.), OW. 20¼″ (51.5 cm.), 16¼″ (41.3 cm.); *right:* DS. 37½″ (95.3 cm.), OW. 20″ (50.8 cm.), OD. 16½″ (41.9 cm.).

INHP purchase, 1967. Congress Hall, Joint Committee Room. Cat. 6327; *right,* 6332. Acc. 1846.

128. Bow-back Windsor armchair

John Letchworth (1759-1843), chairmaker.

Philadelphia, c. 1800.

White pine, hickory, maple, and mahogany. OH. 37⅜″ (95 cm.), OW. 21¾″ (52.7 cm.), OD. 20⅞″ (53.6 cm.).

Branded on underside of seat: "[I]•LETCHWORTH."

Owned by Bishop White, and descended through his family. Gift of William White, Jr., 1967. Bishop White House, study. Cat. 7766. Acc. 2239.

129. Writing desk

Attributed to Jonathan Gostelowe (1744-95).

Philadelphia, c. 1787.

Mahogany, poplar and pine secondary; OH. 33¾″ (85.7 cm.), OW. 24½″ (62.2 cm.), OD. 21½″ (54.6 cm.).

Made for Bishop White, and descended through his family. Presented to Christ Church. Gift of Christ Church, 1976. Bishop White House, bedroom and study. Cat. 7801. Acc. 2246.

130. Pianoforte

Charles Albrecht, musical instrument maker.

Philadelphia, c. 1790.

Mahogany, curly maple, with stringing, inlay and veneers, ivory and ebony keys, original works; OH. 33¾″ (85.7 cm.), OW. 66¼″ (1 m. 68.3 cm.), OD. 23½″ (59.7 cm.).

Painted, center keyboard fascia: "CHARLES ALBRECHT/*MAKER*/PHILADELPHIA." in lozenge-shaped cartouche with laural border; floral festoons, above, scrolled leaves, below.

In Philadelphia sometime prior to 1789, the date of his earliest extant instrument, Charles Albrecht was listed in Philadelphia directories at 95 Vine Street from 1793. His name is sometimes anglicized as "Albright."

Gift of Mrs. John Earle, 1967. Bishop White House, parlor. Cat. 7019. Acc. 2055.

131. Bracket Clock

Works: William Stephenson (active 1793-1824), clockmaker; enameled face: Thomas Parker (active c. 1785-1832), clockmaker.

Works: London, 1793-1809; enameled face: Philadelphia, c. 1793-1809.

Brass works, molding, side panels, feet, and bail handle, enameled decoration; mahogany case; OH. 15½″ (39.4 cm.), OW. 11½″ (29.2 cm.), OD. 7½″ (19.0 cm.).

Engraved, braces on back plate: Wm Stephenson/London" (*center*), "7478² "/ "/RJK" " (*top*), "L s/4/11 (*left*), "R" and "[3314" (*right*); engraved, back plate: "L 13611", bright-cut decoration surrounds back plate edges; stamped, lower left back plate: "894"; engraved, pendulum "9 7 76"; enamelled, face: "STRIKE./SILENT." Conforming to curve inside two concentric rings, separated by laurel branches, and "Thomas /Parker/Philada" each inside curvilinear ovoid cartouches, within clock face.

William Stephenson, London clockmaker, was listed in London directories in Lombard Street from 1793. Thomas Parker, Sr., (1761-1833) was a Philadelphia watch- and clockmaker and importer, working at 13 South 3rd Street from about 1783 to 1832. He had served his apprenticeship with David Rittenhouse and John Wood.

Distin, William H. and Robert Bishop. *The American Clock: A Comprehensive Pictorial Survey 1732-1900 With a Listing of 6153 Clockmakers.* New York: E.P. Dutton & Company, Inc., 1976, p. 91, #184.

INHP purchase, 1963. Bishop White House, bedroom. Cat. 2608. Acc. 957.

132. Sofa

Maker unknown.

Philadelphia, c. 1765-70.

Mahogany, yellow pine secondary, replaced moreen upholstery, restored center front leg; OH. 37″ (94.0 cm.), HS. 18½″ (47.0 cm.), OW. 7′ 5½″ (2 m. 26.7 cm.), DS. 23″ (58.4 cm.).

According to accession records, this sofa was purchased by Robert Morris from George Washington in 1797. It was offered for sale by the heirs of Robert Morris and purchased by Colonel Thomas Robinson of Naamans-on-the-Delaware. In turn his heirs presented it to the Philadelphia Sanitary Fair in 1864 as a lottery item. The Union League of Philadelphia was the successful bidder and in 1882 presented it to Independence Hall.

Hornor, William M. *Blue Book of Philadelphia Furniture* . . . Philadelphia: n.p., 1935, p. 152.

Deshler-Morris House, parlor. Cat. 11842. Acc. 1.

133. Card Table, one of a pair

Attributed to the Haines-Connelly school.

Philadelphia, c. 1810.

Mahogany, pine and red oak secondary; OH. $29\frac{5}{16}$" (74.5 cm.), OW. $35\frac{5}{16}$" (89.7 cm.), OD. (closed) $19\frac{1}{8}$" (48.6 cm.).

Gift of Mrs. Evan Randolph, Sr., 1976. Bishop White House, dining room. Cat. 11494. Acc. 3185.

134. *George Washington* (1732-99)

Rembrandt Peale (1778-1860), artist.

Philadelphia (?), c. 1824.

Oil on canvas; OH. 72" (182.9 cm.), OW. $54\frac{1}{2}$" (137.5 cm.).

This painting is from Peale's third group of Washington portraits, an idealized likeness composed from previous studies. It is traditionally regarded as a study for Peale's equestrian portrait of Washington before Yorktown.

Second son of Charles Willson Peale, Rembrandt studied at the Royal Academy in London in 1802 and independently in Paris. He was one of the founders of the Pennsylvania Academy of the Fine Arts and of the National Academy in New York.

Eisen, Gustav A. *Portraits of Washington.* New York: Robert Hamilton & Associates, 1932. I, 299-323.
Morgan, John Hill and Mantle Fielding. *The Life Portraits of Washington and Their Replicas.* Lancaster, Pa.: Lancaster Press, Inc., 1931. pp. 367-91.

In artist's estate until 1862 when purchased at estate auction by City of Philadelphia, through James L. Claghorn. Second Bank, Washington Gallery. Cat. 11867. Acc. 1.

135. *William Allen* (1704-80)

Attributed to Robert Feke (c. 1707-1752), artist.

Philadelphia, c. 1750.

Oil on canvas; OH. 42" (106.7 cm.), OW. $32\frac{7}{16}$" (82.5 cm.).

The attribution of this painting to Feke was first made by Robert G. Stewart, Curator of the National Portrait Gallery, in 1974.

Feke was probably born in Oyster Bay, Long Island. His earliest portrait appears to date from 1731. He visited Philadelphia twice, once in 1746 and again in 1749-50.

William Allen was a prominent Philadelphia merchant, Chief Justice of Pennsylvania (1750-74), and an early patron of artist Benjamin West. A Loyalist sympathizer, he went to England in 1774.

Gift of Mrs. Mary Thomas Livingstone, great granddaughter of Allen, to the City of Philadelphia, 1876. Second Bank, Pennsylvania Gallery. Cat. 11864. Acc. 1.

136. *Artemus Ward* (1727-1800)

Charles Willson Peale (1741-1827), artist.

Philadelphia, c. 1794-95.

Oil on canvas; OH. $23\frac{1}{4}$" (59.1 cm.), OW. $19\frac{3}{16}$" (48.8 cm.).

This portrait is first listed in the 1795 catalogue of Peale's Museum.

A graduate of Harvard, lawyer and jurist, Ward was a state legislator in Massachusetts for sixteen years. From 1791 to 1795 he was a member of Congress.

Sellers. *Portraits and Miniatures.* No. 893.

Peale Museum Sale, 1854 (170). Second Bank, American Statesman Gallery. Cat. 11874. Acc. 1.

137. *Friedrich Wilhelm Augustus Baron von Steuben* (1730-94)

Charles Willson Peale (1741-1827), artist.

Philadelphia, c. 1781-82.

Oil on canvas; OH. 23" (58.4 cm.), OW. $19\frac{9}{16}$" (49.7 cm.).

This portrait is a replica of the original painted by Peale in 1780.

Sellers. *Portraits and Miniatures.* No. 826.

Peale Museum Sale, 1854 (20). Second Bank, Officers of the American Revolution Gallery. Cat. 11876. Acc. 1.

138. *Benjamin Franklin* (1706-90)

Possibly Joseph S. Duplessis (1725-1802), artist.

France, c. 1779.

Oil on paper, mounted on canvas; OH. 21" (53.3 cm.), OW. $15\frac{3}{4}$" (40.0 cm.).

Sellers questions an attribution of this painting to Duplessis. Until further study is completed, however, it is listed as possible attribution on the basis of provenance.

The French portrait painter studied in Rome in 1745 and was admitted to the Academy in Paris in 1774.

Sellers, Charles C. *Benjamin Franklin in Portraiture.* New Haven: Yale University Press, 1962. No. 254.

Ex Coll. Marquise de Mun at Chateaux de Lumigny, France. Sold through Jean Cailleux, Paris art dealer, to Charles De Gaulle; presented to Harry S. Truman in 1945. Gift of President Truman to INHP, 1954. Second Bank, Signer's Gallery. Cat. 1334. Acc. 77.

139. *George Glentworth* (1735-92)

Charles Willson Peale (1741-1827), artist.

Philadelphia, 1794.

Oil on canvas; OH. $32\frac{1}{4}$" (83.1 cm.), OW. $25\frac{5}{8}$" (67.6 cm.).

Signed and dated lower left: "C.W. Peale/1794."

This is a posthumous portrait.

A native Philadelphian, George Glentworth studied medicine at the University of Edinburgh. A veteran surgeon of the French and Indian War, Glentworth became the senior surgeon of the Middle Division during the Revolution.

Sellers. *Portraits and Miniatures.* No. 305.

Gift of Henry R. and Marguerite L. Glentworth, descendants, 1947. Second Bank, Arts and Sciences Gallery. Cat. 11865. Acc. 1.

140. *Conrad Alexandre Gérard* (1729-90)

Charles Willson Peale (1741-1827), artist.

Philadelphia, 1779.

Oil on canvas; OH. 95" (241.3 cm.), OW. $59\frac{1}{8}$" (150.2 cm.).

The dating of this portrait is established by a resolution of Congress, on September 3, 1779, asking Gérard to sit for Peale. A letter from Peale dated September 18, 1779, thanks Gérard for sitting for the portrait. In the background is the earliest painted view of the Pennsylvania State House.

Foreign Minister of France under Louis XVI, Gérard signed the Treaty of Alliance with the United States in 1778 and became the first foreign minister assigned to this country.

Sellers. *Portraits and Miniatures.* No. 292.

Peale Museum Sale, 1854 (139). Second Bank, Foreign Dignitaries Gallery. Cat. 11866. Acc. 1.

141. *Mrs. Robert Morris* (née Mary White) (1749-1827)

Charles Willson Peale (1741-1827), artist.

Philadelphia, c. 1782.

Oil on canvas; OH. $51\frac{5}{8}$" (128.6 cm.), OW. $40\frac{9}{16}$" (103 cm.).

Commissioned by Robert Morris as a companion portrait, the painting was returned to Peale's Museum, perhaps because of Morris' financial problems, either before or after his death in 1806.

As sister of Bishop William White and wife of Robert Morris, Mrs. Morris was the *grande dame* of Philadelphia society while it was the national capital.

Sellers. *Portraits and Miniatures.* No. 578.

Peale Museum Sale, 1854 (130). Second Bank, Pennsylvania Gallery. Cat. 11868. Acc. 1.

142. *Alexander Hamilton* (1757-1804)

Charles Willson Peale (1741-1827), artist.

Philadelphia, c. 1791.

Oil on canvas; OH. 23½ " (59.7 cm.), OW. 19½ " (49.6 cm.).

Sellers dates this portrait to the time of the removal of the United States capital from New York to Philadelphia.

Sellers. *Portraits and Miniatures.* No. 346.

Peale Museum Sale, 1854 (66). Second Bank, American Stateman Gallery. Cat. 11877. Acc. 1.

143. *Albert Gallatin* (1761-1849)

Rembrandt Peale (1778-1860), artist.

Washington, D.C., 1805.

Oil on canvas; OH. 23⅜ " (59.5 cm.), OW. 19⅜ " (49.2 cm.).

Dating and attribution established by letter from C.W. Peale to son Rubens Peale, dated February 14, 1805.

Gallatin emigrated to America from Switzerland. He was Secretary of the United States Treasury (1801-11).

Sellers. *Charles Willson Peale.* Vol. 2, p. 190.

Peale Museum Sale, 1854 (No. 77). Second Bank, American Statesman Gallery. Cat. 11875. Acc. 1.

144. *Benjamin Rush* (1745-1813)

After James Sharples, Sr., (possibly, Ellen Sharples), artist.

Bath, England (?), c. 1803.

Pastel on paper: OH. 9 " (22.8 cm.), OW. 7 " (17.8 cm.).

Ellen Sharples recorded making several copies of her husband's portrait of Benjamin Rush, one in 1803. An attribution of this painting to Ellen Sharples was made by Milley in 1974 on the grounds of stylistic comparison.

Ellen Wallace Sharples was born in England and studied drawing under James Sharples in Bath.

In 1787 she became his third wife. During their visit to American (1793-1801) she became an artist in her own right.

A Signer of the Declaration of Independence, Dr. Rush served as a surgeon-general during the Revolution, but is better remembered for his humanitarian work during the yellow fever epidemics of 1793 and 1798 in Philadelphia.

Milley, John C. "Thoughts on the Attribution of Sharples' Pastels." In *University Hospital Antiques Show Catalogue*. Philadelphia: 1975.

Purchased by the City of Philadelphia in 1873 at a sale of the Winder collection of Sharples' portraits in Baltimore. Second Bank, Signers Gallery. Cat. 11871. Acc. 1.

145. *William Clark* (1770-1838)

Charles Willson Peale (1741-1827), artist.

Philadelphia, c. 1810.

Oil on paper, mounted on canvas; OH. 23½ " (59.7 cm.), OW. 19¼ " (48.7 cm.).

This portrait was entered into the accession book of Peale's Museum on February 20, 1810.

An American general and explorer, Clark was co-leader with Merriwether Lewis of the 1804-06 expedition to find an overland route from St. Louis to the mouth of the Columbia River.

Sellers. *Portraits and Miniatures.* No. 142.

Peale Museum Sale, 1854 (No. 189). Second Bank, Arts and Sciences Gallery. Cat. 11870. Acc. 1.

146. *William Rush* (1756-1833)

Rembrandt Peale (1778-1860), artist.

Philadelphia, c. 1810-13.

Oil on canvas; OH. 23⁹⁄₁₆ " (58.3 cm.), OW. 19¼ " (48.9 cm.).

The painting first appears in the 1813 catalogue of Peale's Museum. Sellers suggests that the painting shows evidence of Charles Willson Peale's hand and thinks it likely that both father and son worked on the portrait. However, Rem-

brandt Peale identified it as exclusively his work in his personally annotated copy of the 1854 sale catalogue.

Marceau, Henry. *William Rush*. Catalogue. Philadelphia Museum of Art. Philadelphia. 1937.

Purchased by Mary S. Dunton (daughter of Rush) at Peale Museum Sale, 1854; the painting was presented to the City of Philadelphia about 1875. Second Bank, Faces of Independence Gallery. Cat. 11872. Acc. 1.

147. *Andrew Jackson* (1767-1845)

David Rent Etter (1807-80), artist.

Philadelphia, c. 1829-37.

Oil on canvas; OH. 50¼ " (127.6 cm.), OW. 40⅜ " (102.7 cm.).

Signed and dated lower left "D. Etter/pinx/ 1835."

The portrait is a composite drawn from three or four different sources.

A native of Philadelphia, Etter is listed as a "Portrait copyist and ornamental painter" in the few sources of information on his life and work.

Gift to City of Philadelphia by Commissioners of the District of Southwark, 1854. Second Bank, American Statesman Gallery. Cat. 11873. Acc. 1.

148. *Timothy Matlack* (1736-1829)

Charles Willson Peale (1741-1827), artist.

Philadelphia, 1826.

Oil on canvas; OH. 24¹³⁄₁₆ " (64.4 cm.), OW. 20 " (50.9 cm.).

On reverse side of canvas: "Portrait Timothy Matlack Esq./aged 90/by C.W. Peale/at the age of 85."

A popular politician in his native Philadelphia, Matlack served as a militia officer in the Revolutionary War.

Sellers. *Portraits and Miniatures.* No. 539.

Peale Museum Sale, 1854 (No. 65). Second Bank, Pennsylvania Gallery. Cat. 11869. Acc. 1.

Index

Page numbers in italics indicate illustrations.